2001

Tourism and Society

Tourism and Society

A Guide to Problems and Issues

Robert W. Wyllie
Simon Fraser University

Venture Publishing, Inc.
State College, Pennsylvania

Production Manager: Richard Yocum
Design, Layout, and Graphics: Diane K. Bierly
Manuscript Editing: Diane K. Bierly
Additional Editing: Richard Yocum
Cover Design and Illustration: Diane K. Bierly

Library of Congress Catalogue Card Number 99-69890
ISBN 1-892132-16-8

For Keith

Contents

Contents

Preface

The scholarly literature on tourism has increased enormously during the past four decades, as tourism itself has become a global phenomenon of staggering proportions and can no longer be dismissed as a subject peripheral to social science's main concerns. Finding a useful way through this extensive body of research studies, commentaries, interpretations, and theoretical contributions can be a daunting task, especially for beginning students and others confronting it for the first time. The purpose of this book is to provide what I hope will be a helpful guide to the literature, while recognizing that any comprehensive review would require several volumes. In the first eight chapters I provide a "Cook's tour" of the subject, discussing and commenting on issues and problems that seem to me to be of greatest interest and importance. This is followed by two case studies of contrasting destinations which allow us to examine in more detail some of these issues and problems. In the final chapter I outline some new tourism directions and proposals for change. While the selection of topics necessarily involves a certain degree of arbitrariness on my part, I trust that it will not appear hopelessly idiosyncratic.

In reviewing, synthesizing, and commenting on the literature, I have tried to strike a balance between the critical and defensive viewpoints encountered therein, and to encourage readers to draw their own conclusions on the issues. Occasionally, however, I permit myself the luxury of allowing my personal biases to surface, especially when irked by the personal biases of others: I actually enjoy places like Waikiki and Las Vegas and feel strong bonds of sympathy with fellow mass tourists; and I admit to a certain testiness when confronted with assumptions of moral superiority on the part of certain travel writers and ecotourism advocates. For these and other sins that may be evident in the following pages, I crave the reader's indulgence and forgiveness.

Many people have contributed, directly or indirectly, consciously or unknowingly, to this book, and I can thank only a few of them here: Mark Adams, Francis Adu-Febiri, Evan Alderson, Victor Ametewee, Owusu Amoakohene, Bob Brown, Leanne Campbell, Joan Collinge, Jane Cowan, Dave De Leon, Noel Dyck, Harry Eagar, Ken Fukuoka, Greg Holoboff, Bob Johnson, Barbara Lange, Jon Matsuoka, Brian Miskae, Doris Oh, Edwin Ofosu-Yeboah, Wendy Plain, Lesley Rougeau, Yvonne Tabin, and Colin Yerbury. I would also like to acknowledge my intellectual debt to the authors of all works discussed in this book, and to thank all those students in my Tourism and Social Policy seminars whose lively discussions helped sustain my own enthusiasm for the subject.

Chapter 1
Points of Departure

A Multidisciplinary Field

My approach to tourism in this book is informed primarily from the perspectives of sociology and anthropology. However, tourism is a subject of interest to many other academic disciplines, as is evident in the *Annals of Tourism Research,* the major journal devoted to tourism studies. *Annals* publishes articles on anthropological, ecological, educational, geographic, historical, political, psychological, and sociological aspects of tourism. Other important multidisciplinary journals dealing exclusively with tourism include the *Journal of Travel Research, Tourism Management,* and *Tourism Recreation Research.*

Much of the pioneering social-scientific work on tourism was done by geographers who were mainly interested in land-use patterns and the effects of population pressure on both physical and sociocultural environments. Studies by tourism geographers are still among the most important and useful, and I will be referring to several of these in this book. The scope of geographic research on tourism has been well-documented by Mitchell and Murphy (1991). Along with geographers, economists also played a leading role in making tourism the subject of serious academic enquiry. Their work has dealt mainly with tourism as an industry, focusing on its costs and benefits, market characteristics and trends, and its role in economic development. A useful survey of tourism research by economists is presented by Eadington and Redman (1991).

Anthropologists and sociologists were somewhat tardy in recognizing tourism as a worthwhile area of investigation. Although temporary visitors were often present in the less developed societies studied by anthropologists, the "other cultures" orientation of anthropology usually resulted in the filtering out of nonnatives during field research. In this way, tourists suffered from anthropological neglect in much the same way as did resident expatriates, such as missionaries, colonial administrators, medical officers, and teachers. With the growth of Third World tourism after 1960, the presence and effects of tourists in these societies could no longer be ignored and the anthropological study of tourism quickly gained ground as part of a more general enquiry into processes of development and modernization. By 1980 the anthropological investigation of tourism in relation to development had reached a point where *Annals* could produce a special issue on the subject (7[1]). Some of the earlier anthropological studies of tourism were retrospective derivatives of fieldwork conducted for purposes other than the examination of tourism. From the 1980s onward, however, these kinds of studies have become rarer and have been largely replaced by accounts of host-tourist relations and of tourism's social and cultural effects in destination communities. Good statements on the significance of tourism for anthropological research are offered by Nash (1981, 1997) and Nash and Smith (1991).

The longstanding neglect of tourism by sociologists reflects a perception of leisure as something peripheral to life's main events, such as working, forming and maintaining a family, struggling for status or power, dealing with impersonal bureaucratic organizations, and so on. From such a blinkered perspective the sociological study of tourism and other forms of leisure could be regarded as a fairly unimportant task. It is also possible that popular assumptions about the nature and character of tourists as shallow, escapist pleasure seekers made studying them seem an especially trivial pursuit. The growth of sociological interest in tourism was sparked by the burgeoning of mass tourism in the decades following World War II. This led to a keener appreciation of its economic significance and of its political implications internationally. In 1979 a special issue of *Annals* (6[1/2]) dealt exclusively with the sociology of tourism; and an important review of the sociological literature on the subject was conducted by Cohen (1984). A later commentary on tourism as a sociological subject was offered by Dann and Cohen (1991).

Some Characteristics of Tourism Literature

There are some features of the social-scientific literature on tourism that are worth noting early, so that you can take them into account as your reading on the subject progresses.

International Tourism Studies Overrepresented

This weighting is at variance with the global realities of tourism. The World Tourism Organization (WTO) estimates that domestic tourist arrivals exceed international ones by a ratio of 10 to 1 and that domestic tourists' expenditures exceed those of international tourists by a ratio of 7 to 1. One leading tourism scholar and advocate of more research on domestic tourism believes international tourism has received more research attention for two main reasons: its foreign exchange–earning potential and its potential for enhancing understanding between peoples of different cultures (Jafari, 1986). Among other reasons for the imbalance we might suggest the following: (a) domestic tourism presents methodological problems that tend to discourage systematic enquiry—it is more difficult to obtain reliable statistical information on domestic tourists than on international tourists whose comings and goings are recorded at national points of entry and exit; and (b) for sociologists and anthropologists especially, domestic tourism seems to offer few of the research attractions of international tourism, such as touristic encounters between people of different ethnic or cultural backgrounds, or the influence of foreign visitors and foreign ideas on host societies or cultures. Whatever the reasons for this imbalance in the literature, its consequences for us as students of tourism are quite important. We should recognize that in the sociology and anthropology of tourism the concept of "tourist," as well as most theorizing about different types of tourists and the nature of host-tourist encounters, have been fashioned mainly through analyses of international tourism situations. In reality, the "average" tourist is more likely to resemble the Indian on holiday in Bombay than the American vacationing in Mexico. If we keep this in mind, we can adopt an appropriately cautious approach to those popular characterizations and stereotypes of tourists that are based on a loose equation between tourism and international tourism.

North-South Studies Overrepresented

In the literature on international tourism, studies of tourism in developing or Third World countries (sometimes referred to as *North-South tourism*) tend to be over-represented. In recent years an increasing number of books and articles have appeared dealing with the economic, social, and cultural significance of tourism for Third World countries. This trend reflects the expansion of tourism outward from well-established centers in Europe and North America to the Caribbean, Central America, Asia, and Africa; and it underscores the crucial role many observers see tourism playing in the processes of development and modernization. It should be noted, however, that North-South tourism as yet represents a relatively small component of worldwide tourism, accounting for only about 20% of all international arrivals. North-South tourism is certainly important and seems likely to become even more so in the future. Given its current place in the overall tourism picture, however, it seems unwise to generalize about tourism—or even about international tourism, for that matter—from this basis alone. Here again we have reason to question some of the common tourist stereotypes.

Prevalence of Qualitative Evaluations

Much of the literature offers qualitative evaluations of tourism. This is especially the case in anthropological and sociological studies of tourism, since assessments of such things as host-tourist encounters or the sociocultural consequences of tourism cannot be adequately expressed by quantitative measures alone. In general, these assessments have tended to be negative or critical, pointing out various social, cultural, or environmental costs that must be weighed against the more easily measurable economic benefits. This emphasis on the sociocultural and environmental *downside* was quite pronounced in many earlier anthropological studies of tourism in developing countries. It was an understandable reaction to a situation in which tourism had been evaluated primarily in terms of economic factors, while its broader social and cultural dimensions were being overlooked or downplayed. The negative cast of these anthropological studies may also have stemmed, in part, from the conservatism and aversion to modernization that once characterized anthropological thinking and is not entirely absent from it today. The influx of tourists into a community being studied by a fieldworking anthropologist inevitably means that it begins to lose some of its traditional anthropological credentials as a pristine, remote, and exotic place. This loss of "otherness" tends to undermine the traditional anthropological justifications for studying the particular community in the first place. It begins to resemble many other places in the modern world. The arrival of tourists in the anthropologist's territory can also pose a threat to the anthropologist's special position. As a temporary guest in the local community, the anthropologist was the stranger who tried to "belong" and who sought an intimate understanding of the people and their culture—an understanding that was conveyed through books, articles, or documentary films to the world outside. The arrival of untrained observers in the form of tourists who would also convey their impressions to others threatens the quasi-monopolistic position of the anthropologist. In a provocative essay, Crick (1995) argues that much in anthropology's hostile response to tourism stems from the fact that anthropologists cannot be unambiguously distinguished from tourists and that the "identities" of anthropologists and tourists may overlap. The kinship between anthropologists and "explorer" tourists is also noted by Smith (1989). In recent works anthropologists appear to have adopted a more balanced approach and to have recognized that establishing valid criteria for making qualitative assessments is highly problematic.

Other Sources of Information on Tourism

Apart from the academic literature on tourism, there are a number of other useful sources of information and insights. Modern travel narratives often contain pronouncements on the merits of "serious travel" for enlightenment and self-discovery and deplore "superficial" touristic travel. They can provide interesting insights into elitist anxieties and fears about the democratization of leisure travel. Mass tourists have often been the butt of ridicule in a number of popular films, which portray them in unflattering, stereotypical forms, for example, as blundering idiots (the *National Lampoon* series), as fun-loving "flakes" (*Blue Hawaii*), or as bewildered sheep (*If It's Tuesday, This Must Be Belgium*). More thoughtful in approach is *Shirley Valentine,* a film about an ordinary Liverpool housewife whose trip to Greece turns out to be a voyage of self-discovery and emancipation. Shirley's sensitive behavior contrasts sharply with the arrogant, boorish, and superficial antics of her fellow tourists, especially in the memorable dining room scene. Modern filmmakers seem more comfortable dealing with the comic aspects of tourist behavior, but tourists of a more serious type are depicted in *A Room With a View,* an excellent film based on the novel by E. M. Forster. Magazines such as *National Geographic Traveler* and *Condé Nast Traveler* provide a good sense of what appeals to wealthier tourists (the kind who prefer to think of themselves as "travelers" rather than "tourists"). Television travel shows as well as brochures that can be picked up from local travel agents are excellent sources of information on the "dream packaging" aspects of tourism.

Last, but not least, there are relatives, friends, and acquaintances who may be planning a trip or who may have recently returned from one. They can be valuable, firsthand sources of information about tourists' motivations, expectations, and experiences.

Research Perspectives

An ambitious attempt to analyze much of the English language literature on tourism was undertaken by Jafari (1989), who identified four main "platforms" or research perspectives in this literature:

- *The Advocacy Platform*—This emphasizes the economic importance and benefits of tourism and its positive role in national development. This perspective informed most of the writing on tourism during the 1950s and 1960s.
- *The Cautionary Platform*—Stressing the hidden economic costs and often unforeseen negative sociocultural consequences of tourism, this perspective gained prominence in the 1970s as researchers began to question the claims made by advocacy platform writers.
- *The Adaptancy Platform*—This perspective became popular in the 1980s and is directed toward the search for remedies and alternatives to mass tourism (for example, ecotourism, home-stay tourism, community-sensitive tourism, and the like).
- *The Knowledge-Based Platform*—This perspective aims at the establishment of a scientific, holistic body of knowledge on tourism, while maintaining links with the other three platforms. It is the most recent development in tourism studies.

While Jafari's classification is useful in suggesting the general direction taken in tourism research in the second half of the present century, it tends to exaggerate the special place of the knowledge-based platform. The other platforms cannot be regarded as unscientific or prescientific, or merely as bases from which to promote the interests of special groups. The new, knowledge-based platform has not rendered these other platforms obsolete and the prospect of a holistic or integrated body of scientific knowledge on tourism appears to be a distant one. Some of the difficulties involved in this enterprise have been identified and discussed by Tribe (1997).

Identifying Tourists and Tourism

The World Tourism Organization Guidelines

The most general or inclusive view of tourism—one much broader than that taken by sociologists and anthropologists—derives from guidelines developed by the WTO. These are meant to standardize the collection of tourism information by the national tourism administrations of WTO member countries:

- *Visitor*—Any person visiting a country other than his or her normal place of residence, for a period not exceeding 12 months, and whose main purpose of visit is other than the exercise of an activity remunerated from within the country visited.
- *Tourist*—Any visitor staying at least one night in a collective or private accommodation in the country visited.
- *Same-Day Visitor*—Any visitor who does not stay at least one night in a collective or private accommodation in the country visited.

These definitions were later modified to accommodate domestic or intranational tourism, with *region* being substituted for *country*. Even with this modification, the WTO definition of tourist is uncomfortably broad. It would apply to the New York businessman in Tokyo to explore sales possibilities, the Princeton professor attending a three-day conference in Los Angeles, and the Seattle holidaymaker in Hawaii for two weeks of fun and relaxation. Although each of these visitors spends more than one night outside the normal place of residence and none is engaged in employment remunerated at the destination, wide motivational and behavioral differences exist between them. From a "common-sense" perspective, the visitor to Hawaii looks much more like a tourist than does either the businessperson or the university professor.

The distinction between tourist and same-day visitor, which hinges upon length of stay at the destination, also has limited value for researchers interested primarily in the behavioral aspects of tourism. If cruise ship passengers are same-day visitors when they spend a few hours ashore at Acapulco, what behavioral features distinguish them from those tourists who may be spending two weeks at this Mexican resort? We would probably observe more concentrated forms of sightseeing, shopping, and so on among the former, but little that would justify treating them as anything other than tourists. The distinction becomes even more problematic when we consider the situation of the passengers while they are actually on board the cruise ship, which is a floating hotel and leisure center as well as a means of transportation. Indeed, it could be argued that cruises represent a special form of escapist mass tourism, one in which travelers are encapsulated in luxury, insulated from the destination cultures, and taken on carefully scheduled forays ashore for superficial encounters with the locals.

We see, then, that the WTO approach is not especially helpful in providing a sociological or anthropological focus for tourism research. For a discipline such as geography, however, the WTO's broad definition of tourist poses few problems. A leading Canadian tourism geographer takes the view that tourism concerns all travelers visiting places away from home, whether for business, pleasure, or a mixture of the two, but feels that the excursionist or same-day visitor can safely be included in the tourist category (Murphy, 1983).

Tourism as Leisure Travel

Among sociologists and anthropologists tourism is typically viewed in the context of work-leisure relationships. In an influential article Nash (1981) suggested that the core of a touristic system is the encounter between working hosts and leisured tourists. Tourism is thus viewed as the activities of those who temporarily leave home while free of primary obligations (for example, gainful employment, study, family, and community responsibilities) and of those who serve them, whether at home (for example, travel agents), during the journey (for example, airline staff), or at the destination (for example, hotel and restaurant staff). A broadly similar approach is taken by British sociologist John Urry (1990), who recognizes the historical and sociological variations found in tourism but suggests that there are a number of "minimal characteristics" of the social practices we associate with tourism:

1. Tourism is a leisure activity presupposing its opposite, that is, regulated and organized work.
2. Tourist relationships arise from the movement of people to, and their stay in, various destinations.
3. The journey and stay are to, and in, sites outside the normal place of residence and work. There is a clear intention to return home within a relatively short period of time.
4. The purposes of the visits are not directly connected with paid work, and the visits normally offer some distinctive contrasts with work.
5. In order to cope with the mass character of modern tourism, new socialized (that is, organized group) forms of provision are developed. These distinguish tourism from individual travel.
6. Anticipation of pleasures from the visits is constructed and sustained through a variety of practices, such as film, television, magazines, or videos.
7. The tourist "gaze" is directed to things felt to be in some ways out of the ordinary. These are lingered over and often visually objectified and captured in photographs and postcards. By these means the gaze can be endlessly recaptured and reproduced.

8. The tourist collects "signs" (for example, a small English village becomes a sign for "real olde England").
9. Tourist professionals emerge to reproduce ever-new objects of the tourist gaze (pp. 2–10).

While most of these minimal characteristics are fairly straightforward, the fifth—tourism as a group activity and distinct from individual travel—is more contentious. It equates tourism with organized, mass leisure travel and excludes the lone, individual traveler from tourism's orbit. Other tourism sociologists—notably Cohen, whose ideas on this subject I discuss in chapter 3—would not agree. Interestingly, this kind of distinction between individual travel and collective tourism is also an element in the critique of tourism and tourists by certain kinds of travelers who do not wish to be mistaken for tourists.

Tourism as Commercial Enterprise

The conceptualization of tourism as leisure travel is clearly tourist-centered. The tourist is the central figure, with tourism being viewed as the activities of tourists and, by extension, of those who cater to tourists' needs. However, when tourism is regarded as an industry, a somewhat different conceptualization may be more appropriate. Smith (1988) points out that industries are normally defined by the products or services they provide and not by the characteristics of those who consume them. The sociological and anthropological conceptualizations of tourism are *demand-side,* emphasizing as they do the characteristics of tourists (the consumers). According to Smith, a more appropriate definition of tourism as an industry would have a *supply-side* emphasis. Accordingly, he offers the following "generic" definition:

> Tourism is the aggregate of all businesses that directly provide goods or services to facilitate business, pleasure, and leisure activities away from the home environment. (p. 183)

While this may be a reasonable approach to the study of tourism as an industry, it is not without its problems. Many businesses catering to tourists serve locals as well (for example, hotels, restaurants, taxis), and economists still disagree on the matter of which businesses, or parts of businesses, should be regarded as comprising the tourism industry. So it is hardly surprising that some economists are unwilling to regard tourism as a separate industry at all, noting the extremely diverse range of products and services being claimed for it, its highly fragmented nature, and the lack of systematic coordination among its various component businesses. These matters should not concern us greatly, for whether tourism is regarded as an industry or a partially integrated collection of businesses, the economic dimensions of tourism are extremely important and profoundly influence many of the things in which tourism sociologists and anthropologists are interested (see chapter 4).

Despite the existence of various rationales for the promotion and development of tourism, such as fostering international or national understanding, enhancing citizens' opportunities for travel and recreation, and so on, tourism promotion and development rest fundamentally on expectations of economic gains or benefits. This primary rationale operates in developed and developing countries alike. From the consumer's perspective, tourism may be regarded as a leisure activity offering opportunities for relaxation, recreation, or intercultural and interpersonal exchanges. From the producer's viewpoint, however, tourism is basically a system of commercialized travel and hospitality and this must be kept in mind when making any overall evaluation of its operation.

Tourists: Trivial Pursuers or Seekers of Authenticity?

Tourism has sometimes been described as an "unloved industry"—a means of generating foreign exchange, jobs, and development but also producing undesirable social and cultural side effects. And tourists themselves have often been portrayed in unflattering terms, including *gullible, exploitive, arrogant, naive, overbearing, frivolous,* and *insensitive.* Although he is critical of mass tourism, Krippendorf (1987) is also impatient with this kind of tourist snobbery, wryly noting that the tourist always seems to be "the other person."

The attitudes Krippendorf condemns can be found in a variety of writings, but are especially evident in the narratives of travel writers. Such writers normally do not consider themselves tourists, and their books are not designed to encourage tourists to visit the places they write about. They see themselves as "travelers," and seldom travel in groups. When they do, the group is usually cast as a band of resourceful adventurers or interesting eccentrics, rather than a humdrum collection of package tourists. They often journey to destinations off the main tourist tracks and generally try to avoid tourists as far as possible. Given the shrinking world in which we live, however, encounters between travel writers and tourists are almost inevitable. If the tourist in question appears experienced and independent, this may cause the travel writer some uncertainty about his or her own status as traveler-but-not-tourist. For example, while journeying by train through South America, Paul Theroux encounters a young German backpacker whose trip across the continent has been much more leisurely than his own. But after testing the German's memory on the places he had visited, the famous American writer is reassured, for the backpacker is able to recall only superficial impressions and is primarily interested in his own personal finances.

✺   ✦   ✻   ┽   ✺

Wolfgang

I thought that I was the only foreigner on the train. I should have known better. Experience had shown me that there was always a German in second class, slumbering on his pack frame and spitting orange pips out of the window. At Humahuaca, it was Wolfgang. He had boarded the Bolivian segment of the train in the cold downpour at Oruro, and he had suffered in second class ever since. I had not seen him, though he said he had seen me, buying tea from the Indian woman in La Quiaca. He had been traveling for months through Central and South America and had only the vaguest idea of where he was going. He was certain of one thing: if he did not have the luck to find a job in Buenos Aires, he would be in Argentina for the rest of his life. Frankly, he was eager to go home, he said.

Sometimes, in the presence of such a person—I had met many—I felt rather ashamed that I had traveled so swiftly from Boston. Two months before, I had boarded the Lake Shore Limited in South Station, and after a few snowy days I had been rattling under clear skies to Mexico. I had not been robbed or fallen seriously ill; I had seen pretty places and met pleasant people. I had filled hundreds of pages of my diary, and now I felt certain I would make it to Esquel in Patagonia, the small town I had seen on my map that had become an arbitrary destination. I had breezed through most of the countries, and was always brought up short when I met another traveler who said he was planning to spend a month in, say, Barranquilla or Cuzco. "I didn't like Ecuador," an American told me in Peru. "Maybe I didn't give it enough time." He had been there two months, which seemed an eternity to me.

Wolfgang's story was the same—a month here, a month there, two months somewhere else. He had been practically resident in these places; he was like a man looking for a new life. I knew I was merely skimming south, a bird of passage generalizing on the immediate. But because I had no camera and had written so much, my impressions of what I had seen were vivid. I could call up Mexico or Costa Rica by glancing at the conversations I had written, and from the peculiarities of the railway journey from Santa Marta to Bogota I felt I could reinvent Colombia. Travel was, above all, a test of memory.

So, partly to kill time—the train was still stalled at Humahuaca—and partly to relieve myself of the guilt I felt with someone who regarded me as no more than a tourist, I asked Wolfgang what he remembered of the places he had been.

"This is a quiz," I said. "I'll say the name of a place and you tell me what you remembered best about it. Pretend I'm someone who has never traveled anywhere—I want to know what these places are like. OK?"

"It's a good game," he said.

"Ready? Here goes. Mexico."

"Americans have a lot of trouble there."

"Guatemala."

"I missed the bus to San Salvador, but my pack was still on it, so my passport too. I spent three dollars on phone calls. It was terrible."

"Nicaragua."

"I should not have gone there."

"Costa Rica."

"Dull."

"Colombia."

"Lots of nice food in the markets, but I got sick there."

"Maybe it was the food," I said. "What about Ecuador?"

"One month I am there, trying to take the buses."

"Peru."

"Nice and cheap."

"Bolivia."

"All the people in Bolivia are stupid."

"Argentina."

"I will be there for some weeks or months," he said. "So? I have passed the test?"

"You flunked, Wolfgang."

He only became concrete when the conversation turned to the exchange rate. Here it was 670 pesos to the dollar, but there were towns where you could get 680. The difference was much less than a cent, but Wolfgang was the embodiment of the maxim I had devised earlier in this trip. It is the raggedest traveler who has the most precise notion of the exchange rate. Wolfgang wasn't looking for another life. Travel for him, as for many others, was just another way of saving money.

☀   ╬   ✳   ✦   ☀

Surprisingly, perhaps, stereotypical views about tourists are sometimes expressed by social scientists who specialize in tourism research. Smith, a tourism anthropologist who recognized and defined a number of different types of tourists, nonetheless characterizes charter tourists in a way that makes them appear mindless morons:

> Charter tourists wear name tags, are assigned to numbered buses, counted aboard, and continually reminded: "Be sure to get on the right bus." Given the requisite organization that makes charter

tourism a high-volume business, to avoid complaints tour operators and hotels have standardized the services to Western (or Japanese) tastes, and there are "ice machines on every floor." For charter tourists, even destination may be of very little importance, especially if they won the trip as part of an incentive sales program,
or it coincides with tax-free convention travel. (1989, p. 10)

However, as we shall see from the account of charter tourists' subculture given in
chapter 11, real charter tourists can function without name tags, know which bus
to get on, and appear to be no more stupid than most of us.

Denigration of tourists forms part of a more general condemnation of mass
culture and mass leisure that is particularly evident in the writings of conservative
or elitist critics of contemporary society. While their critiques take different forms,
they generally equate "good" culture and leisure with the interests and activities of
a refined or perceptive elite—a class of people with the time, wealth, and education
to devote to cultural excellence. From this viewpoint, the democratization of leisure and the rise of mass and popular forms of culture are matters to be deplored.
These processes represent a shift from refinement to vulgarity, and from world-
revealing leisure pursuits to mere entertainment and diversion. In other words, the
quality of culture—including leisure and leisure travel—is assumed to vary inversely
with its quantity and availability. A good example of this critical perspective applied
to tourism is represented by Boorstin's (1961) study of American popular culture.
Here the author is generally concerned with the phony and crass nature of culture
in the United States, but he uses the modern mass tourist to illustrate some of his
arguments. The passive, gullible nature of the modern tourist is contrasted with the
discriminating and intelligently curious traveler of former times. Whereas the latter was interested in the real world, the former seeks only illusions and manufactured "pseudo-events." While the latter sought enlightenment, the mass tourist seeks
diversion and escape. For Boorstin, therefore, modern mass tourism is essentially a
false system of contrived images and illusions. He does recognize the existence of
another kind of modern tourist—the "adventurer"—but finds little to admire here
either. The adventurer merely contrives situations or manufactures risks in order to
experience excitement. Such a tourist is a far cry from the sensitive, questing traveler of bygone times.

Criticisms of mass culture and mass leisure have also been leveled by radical or
neo-Marxist writers, who see capitalism and the growth of a "culture industry" as
the roots of cultural mediocrity and mindlessness in Western society. For such writers, leisure is not an area of free choice, but one of received options. Offering diversions, spectacles, and entertainments, leisure in capitalist societies becomes an
important vehicle of ideological hegemony (that is, a subtle means of reproducing,
reinforcing, and perpetuating the capitalist system). A fairly mild version of this
approach is adopted by MacCannell (1976), although he draws on a number of other
theoretical traditions as well. Like Boorstin, this sociologist also believes that much

of modern life is characterized by artificiality. But unlike Boorstin, MacCannell argues that tourism is an important means whereby people seek those things that seem to be lacking in their own societies. The modern tourist is in search of authenticity in his or her travels primarily because there appears to be little of this left in his or her normal environment. The tourist's motivation is not simply the desire to escape or to find diversions, but to satisfy a hunger for that which is largely missing in his or her ordinary life.

According to MacCannell, modern society has become organized, routinized, commercialized, and impersonal. Alienated from such an inauthentic world, the tourist is one who searches for authenticity and meaning in other places and other times. However, what the tourists seek has become more difficult to find. MacCannell argues that what is usually there at the end of the tourist trail is "staged authenticity," as the locals and the tourist establishment create situations, attractions, and events especially for tourist consumption. These are designed to look, sound, and feel authentic, but they are in fact contrived and inauthentic. Examples might be the Mexican fiesta, the Hawaiian luau, or the Greek fishermen's taverna draped with nets, floats, and other stage props. In the end, we see that MacCannell's tourist is no better off than Boorstin's, since both are consumers of illusions. But whereas Boorstin feels that illusions are what most tourists really want, MacCannell's argument is that the staged attractions reflect the commercial interests of tourism producers and the desire of locals to retain control of their authentic culture, which is only found "backstage," out of sight of the tourists.

These views about tourists, provocative as they are, fail to do justice to the variety of motives, interests, and behaviors one finds among contemporary tourists. Some tourists may resemble Boorstin's trivial pursuers while others may be more like MacCannell's authenticity seekers. In chapter 3 I will look at two of the best known attempts that have been made to develop typologies of tourists.

Chapter 2
Milestones

Premodern Tourism

Tourism in Ancient Times

Tourism, especially in its organized, mass commercial form, is usually regarded as a modern phenomenon whose key features, such as Urry's "minimal characteristics," began to emerge first in Britain during the second half of the nineteenth century. However, tourist-like travel has a very long history indeed and it is not difficult to find examples from much earlier periods in history. A number of examples of tourism in ancient times are given by McIntosh and Gouldner (1990), who suggest that the first journey made for peace and tourism was probably the cruise taken by the Egyptian Queen Hatshepsut in 1490 B.C. to the lands of Punt, which may now be modern Somalia. In ancient Greece a considerable travel industry centered on the Olympic Games, which were founded in 776 B.C. and attracted large numbers of visitors. And the ancient Romans utilized an elaborate network of roads—built in the course of imperial expansion—for journeys to Egypt, Greece, and Asia Minor. Among the attractions for Roman travelers were pyramids and other monuments, medicinal baths, festivals, athletic events, and theatrical productions. The authors also note that the fall of the Roman Empire and the consequent period known as the Dark Ages (476 A.D. to 1450 A.D.) virtually eliminated pleasure travel in Europe. Then, as now, travel was adversely affected by conditions of political disorder and instability.

The Pilgrimage

The religious pilgrimage has an interesting place in the history of tourism. Accustomed as we are to thinking about pilgrimages as purely spiritual journeys, it is sometimes difficult to conceive of them as forms of tourism. However, a special issue of *Annals of Tourism Research* (19[1], 1992) was devoted entirely to the subject of pilgrimages and pilgrimage tourism. As we shall see in chapter 3, Cohen's typology of tourist experiences helps to narrow the conceptual gap between the pilgrim and the tourist. In medieval Europe the pilgrimage displayed some of the features we now associate with tourism. We get a sense of this in Chaucer's *Canterbury Tales,* a long poem woven around the tales told by a group of English pilgrims journeying from Southwark to Canterbury. The tales vividly convey the earthy character and bawdy humor of the times, as well as the entertainments and diversions the pilgrims devised for themselves on their journey. Clearly, the pilgrimage could be a pleasurable form of travel as well as a serious spiritual undertaking. This is still true for modern pilgrims to holy sites, most of whom utilize the tourism establishment (for example, travel agents, tour operators, airline companies, hotel chains), buy souvenirs, or take organized side trips from holy centers to nearby places of interest. The link between tourism and pilgrimage has been given a new and perhaps ironic twist at the Canterbury Pilgrims' Way, where visitors to this heritage site in southern England are given the opportunity to play at being medieval pilgrims, retracing the steps of the various characters made famous by Chaucer.

Tramping

Elements of pleasure travel are also evident in other kinds of serious journeys, such as those directly connected with work. An excellent discussion of this is provided by Adler (1985), who suggests that the road culture of today's young middle-class drifter tourists has its roots in the tramping journeys of young European workers.

In England the tramping system emerged in the fifteenth century, mainly because of local unemployment, and it reached its peak in the early part of the nineteenth century. Most trades developed the practice of sending young unmarried members on tramp in search of work and provided travel funds to those who followed a prescribed circuit. Presentation of a membership card at craft society hostels entitled the *tramp* (the term did not carry the stigma that it later acquired) to a job and accommodation if such were available. The system operated as a form of labor exchange and unemployment compensation, as well as a means of gaining knowledge of regional variations in craft methods. In France and Germany four to five years' tramping was an integral part of the apprenticeship system, and it was required of those aspiring to master craftsman status. The tramps were expected to keep a log containing details of their travels and the jobs they held. Failure to present this log to local authorities on demand could lead to arrest under vagrancy laws.

Tramping afforded opportunities for pleasure and enjoyment as well as for work. That it did is evident from concerns regularly voiced by craft guilds and trade unions about young workers using the system mainly to get a cheap holiday. Fears were expressed about the tramps acquiring a liking for travel and adventure and of "working the ticket," that is, using the membership card to avoid work rather than to find it. The system of craft-organized tramping came to an end in the early part of the twentieth century. According to Adler, there were four main reasons for its demise: first, labor was increasingly concentrated in large, urban areas, making obsolete the practice of traveling between many small towns and villages in search of work; second, the development of the railways allowed workers to bypass small country towns and eliminated their dependence on craft hospitality; third, trades became increasingly mechanized, so that regional variations in craft practices began to diminish;

and fourth, unemployment benefits were introduced, making tramping unnecessary as a response to local unemployment. With these changes came a decline in the social status of the tramp. From being a legitimate and worthwhile activity, tramping came to be seen as a form of vagrancy, and the tramp became a marginal person or *transient*.

Middle-class fascination with tramping is evident in seventeenth- and eighteenth-century journals written by persons disguised as beggars. This tradition, as Adler points out, was continued in the writings of famous authors like Lee Merriweather and Jack London, both of whom used disguise to learn about the European poor and also to exploit, as tourists, working-class traditions of hospitality towards travelers. Today, middle-class interest in tramping has transformed it into a leisure activity, even if the wanderings of young Western tourists may sometimes be indirectly related to the search for employment.

The Grand Tour

Of major significance in the history of tourism is the so-called *Grand Tour,* which contained many of the seeds of modern tourism. Townley (1985) has provided one of the most intensive studies of the Grand Tour, analyzing documentary material on over 100 separate tours. These tours were undertaken between 1547 and 1840 and involved more than 200 tourists. The main points in Townley's study are summarized here:

- *Principal Features*—The Grand Tour began sometime in the mid-fifteenth century and ended, or developed into somewhat different forms, by the middle of the nineteenth century. It involved a circular tour of certain places in Western Europe and was undertaken mainly for education and pleasure. The route remained fairly constant throughout the period: Paris and the Court of Versailles; the lower Rhone Valley (Montpellier, Nimes, Arles); Northern Italy (Turin, Milan, Venice); the climax at Rome, Florence, and Naples; and then the return home via the German Rhineland and the Low Countries.
- *The Grand Tourists*—Most of the tourists were English, but by the middle of the nineteenth century other nationalities, especially Americans, began to appear in greater numbers. During the eighteenth century their numbers are estimated at between 15,000 and 20,000 annually, with members of the landed aristocracy predominating. Towards the end of the eighteenth century they were joined by people of different class backgrounds—lawyers, doctors, bankers, and merchants—and shortly afterwards aristocratic tourists began to seek more exclusive centers in Portugal, Greece, and the Near East. Until the latter part of the eighteenth century, students and their personal tutors made up a large proportion of the tourists. By the middle of the following century, this was no longer the case and the average age of the tourists was 42 years—compared with 23 years in the sixteenth century.

- *Major Changes*—Townley suggests that until the late seventeenth century, the tour had a primarily classical focus on antiquities and Renaissance art, with Italy as the main center. There was little interest in sightseeing as such, although humanized rural landscapes were admired. After this time, the tour developed a more romantic focus. There was growing interest in "wild nature" and in the picturesque features of things seen. The tour circuit underwent some modifications that reflected this shift in the tourist gaze, incorporating the Swiss Alps, the Jura Mountains, and the medieval towns of central Italy. The average length of the tour fell from 40 months in the mid-sixteenth century to four months in the middle of the nineteenth century. This shortening of the tour reflected the changing social composition of the tourists, as well as the unsettled political conditions in Europe following the French Revolution and the Napoleonic Wars. Speeding up the tour was achieved mainly by reducing the time spent at traditional long-stay centers, rather than by traveling faster on a daily basis.
- *The Grand Tour Industry*—Until the mid-seventeenth century tourists mainly used accommodations already established for pilgrims and traders along the major highways. A hundred years later tourist hotels had been created in places like Calais, Paris, Frankfurt, and Rome. At the same time, some palaces were converted into tourist lodgings as the fortunes of the European nobility declined, as in Venice and Genoa. In the early period, the tourists traveled along the major rivers and canals of Northern Europe, but by the mid-eighteenth century a regular coaching service was well-established, and by the middle of the following century it was possible to travel by rail from the Channel coast of France to the Swiss border. The tourists also utilized the services of a number of facilitators and intermediaries: hoteliers arranged transportation, and some offered package tours, which included food and lodgings as well as transportation; bankers were, by the late eighteenth century, offering currency exchange notes as well as assistance in hiring servants, forwarding baggage (the tourists did not travel light), and recommending suitable hotels; diplomats were an important part of the support system for English tourists traveling in Europe; and the arrival of grand tourists stimulated a growth in the numbers of guides, of whom there had usually been a few in places along traditional trading and pilgrimage routes.
- *Significance*—From Townley's account, we see that the Grand Tour contained embryonic forms of educational, scenic, and mass tourism at various periods in its history. Although it is often viewed by conservative writers as a model of desirable or worthy travel and contrasted favorably with modern mass tourism, it is clear that it was not exclusively travel for cultural enlightenment (Brodsky-Porges, 1981). In an amusing essay, Feifer (1985) shows that the tourists spent much time on gossip, flirtation, and fashions, and that harried tutors were often required to recover their young charges from brothels and taverns. In the course of its history, it underwent a degree of democratization

and a general reorientation of the tourist gaze. We see also a pattern that is repeated many times in the later history of tourism: the intrusion of lower status tourists into areas that were formerly the preserves of privileged groups, and the flight of the privileged towards less accessible places as the masses advanced. The growth of the Grand Tour encouraged tourism development on the European continent and provided the basis for a European tourism industry. It also provided much of the foundation upon which Thomas Cook established his travel empire during the second half of the nineteenth century.

Cook's Tours

It is generally agreed that tourism in a recognizably modern form first emerged in mid-nineteenth-century England, in large part because of the efforts of Thomas Cook. Cook was a printer by trade and was active as a lay preacher in the Baptist church. He was also a staunch supporter of the Temperance movement, which opposed the consumption of alcohol and its degrading effects, especially on the poor. Cook believed that leisure travel could provide a healthier and morally superior form of recreation to that offered by the public house or race track. This belief in the morally uplifting value of travel remained with Cook throughout his long career as travel entrepreneur from 1845 until his death in 1892.

Cook was undoubtedly a visionary with tremendous energy and formidable organizational abilities whose place in the history of tourism is assured. Yet it should be noted that a number of factors made the situation in mid-nineteenth-century Britain ripe for the developments in popular leisure associated with Cook's name. Industrialization brought with it rising incomes among the lower-middle class of clerks, shopkeepers, and independent artisans, and with this came a desire for temporary escape from the large urban industrial centers. It was also an era in which social reformers stressed the desirability of "rational" or "constructive" leisure, at least for the lower-middle and working classes (Cross, 1990). The growth of a national railway system also helped Cook's dreams of mass travel become a reality. And, as I noted previously, the Grand Tour in Europe resulted in the creation of some of the basic infrastructure, facilities, and positive attitudes (especially the idea that leisure travel was a worthy activity, rather than frivolous time wasting) upon which Cook could build.

Cook claimed to have formed the idea of organizing group travel while on his way from his home in the East Midlands town of Market Harborough to attend a Temperance Society meeting in the nearby city of Leicester. He decided to organize a special excursion by rail to take Society members to Loughborough, a town about 15 miles to the north. He managed to negotiate a substantially reduced fare and some promotional money from the Midland Counties Railway Company, and his idea was received enthusiastically by Society members. Some 3,000 wanted to make the trip, but only 600 could be transported. At their destination over 1,000 were fed and entertained, many having made their own way there. He followed up this first trip by organizing Temperance Society excursions to places of scenic beauty in the Midlands, and in 1843 successfully conducted a one-day excursion for 3,000 school-children from Leicester to Derby. Anyone who has ever tried to plan and conduct a successful excursion for only 30 schoolchildren will begin to appreciate Cook's organizational skills!

In 1845 Cook began to devote himself full time to commercial tour operating, organizing tours to Liverpool and North Wales, introducing tour guides, and publishing his own guidebooks. These ventures proved to be so popular that tickets for them were sold on the black market at greatly inflated prices. By 1851 he was primarily a travel promoter and organizer, with printing being an important adjunct of these activities. He introduced the first travel newspaper, *The Excursionist and Exhibition Advertiser,* which was distributed to workers and their employers. In it, he advanced various arguments in favor of permitting workers to attend the Great Exhibition to be held at the Crystal Palace in London that year. Arrangements were made for transportation, food, and lodgings for some 165,000 workers who visited the Exhibition. Bed and breakfast cost one shilling a night and the return fare was five shillings. The average weekly wage at the time was 20 shillings and the normal return fare was 15 shillings. Utilizing the valuable experience gained in 1851, Cook was actively involved in arranging excursions to the International Exhibition of 1862, which was also held in London. He catered for about 20,000 people, including members of the "select class" as well as visitors from France, Italy, and Germany. In the 1860s he also capitalized on the growing demand for trips to seaside towns after the health benefits of sea bathing had been proclaimed by medical quacks like Dr. Richard Russell.

Cook's earliest continental excursion was disappointing. In 1855 he tried to organize trips to the Paris Exhibition, but failing to secure favorable terms from French and Belgian railway authorities, he could only transport his customers as far as Calais on the French coast. Later that year he organized two circular tours of the continent with visits to Antwerp, Brussels, Cologne, Mainz, Mannheim, Heidelberg, Strasbourg, and Paris. These proved to be a great success with travelers, but Cook lost money on both ventures. Resuming again in the 1860s, Cook staged a six-day tour, which brought 1,673 people—mostly from the industrial towns of northern England—to Paris. This trip was perhaps the first large-scale European package tour, with all details prearranged and the Universal Coupon introduced for hotels, meals, and so on. Similar tours followed to Switzerland (1863) and Italy (1864), by which time Cook's tourists, or *Cookites,* as they were now called, were armed with guidebooks published by Baedeker, Chambers, Murray, and Cook himself. In many European centers, more privileged travelers often regarded Cook's tourists with the same kind of loathing that some travel writers have for today's mass tourists.

By 1866 Cook was offering tours to the United States and shortly thereafter began to organize tours of Europe for Americans. In order to relieve his tourists of the need to carry large sums of money around with them, he introduced his own traveler's check or "circular note" in 1873. With the opening of the Suez Canal in

1869, Cook became active in travel to the Middle East and Far East. He developed and popularized cruises on the Nile and built the famous Luxor Hotel by the river in 1886. By 1890 Cook's organization—now headed by his son John—had 15 steamers, designed as floating hotels, plying the great river. Its reputation as the world's leading travel organization was firmly established. In 1886 Cook's handled arrangements for the visit of Indian princes to the Colonial and Indian Exhibition in London; and in 1896 it organized Kaiser Wilhelm's tour of the Holy Land. Cook's resources and experience were also harnessed by the British army in 1899 in transporting troops and equipment during Kitchener's Sudanese campaign (Brendon, 1991).

Modern Developments

The Expansion of Leisure

During the twentieth century tourism continued to expand and it is now regarded as one of the world's largest and fastest-growing industries. Leisure travel accounts for approximately three quarters of all world travel by volume. The size of the travel and tourism industry is extremely difficult to measure accurately, for reasons alluded to previously. For example, in a study undertaken on behalf of American Express it was considered to be comprised of passenger-transport industries, hotels and lodgings, restaurants and bars, and recreational and cultural services. This made it the world's largest industry in 1987, although its size is somewhat exaggerated by the inclusive definition adopted, for it encompassed television and film production and distribution as well as the more obvious travel-related businesses. On the other hand, the study excluded such significant activities as retail sales of souvenirs and the underground economy of tourism (that is, the unofficial and unreported activities of people involved in tourism-related retailing).

The growth of tourism can be seen as a particular manifestation of the general expansion of leisure in Western societies. Growth in disposable incomes, increasing life expectancy, earlier retirement, and shorter working hours all contributed to this expansion. The mechanization of work made possible a reduction in work hours without a decline in productivity. British and American workers went on strike in 1919 to press for the eight-hour day or 48-hour week and this became the norm throughout much of Europe and North America shortly afterwards. By 1938 a 40-hour week had been accepted by most large employers in the United States, although it was not until the 1960s that this became the standard in Europe. In France a two-week paid holiday law was passed in 1936, while the number of British wage earners with paid vacation entitlement rose from 1.5 million in 1935 to 7.7 million in 1938 (Cross, 1990; Kelly and Godbey, 1992). For Western societies, future gains in leisure time may not be as great or rapid as those registered during this century. Already there are signs that globalization and increased international competition are helping to create a "leisure squeeze" that will probably have important repercussions for the tourism industry.

Less Free Time Means More Diversity in Tourism

Restraints on free time are making tourists evermore demanding of quality and diversity in holiday products. Consequently, the success of tourism businesses will depend on their ability to adapt to these new tendencies and to anticipate future changes. These were two of the main conclusions to emerge from the seminar, The Evolution of Leisure Time and Its Impact on the Development of Tourism, organized by the WTO Business Council on January 29 during the Spanish tourism fair FITUR.

WTO's Acting Chief of Statistics Agusto Huescar said tourism results for 1998 had demonstrated a clearly defined resistance to the turbulence in the financial markets and forecast that tourism would continue to show constant growth in the coming decades. Mr. Huescar said the forecasts predicted a growing diversity in tourism destinations. All the continents are now represented among the 15 principal destinations and although Europe still had the biggest quota—59%—it is losing ground to others. Current growth areas are in the development of tourism complexes and a movement towards people taking short breaks. Other expanding sectors included environmental and cultural holidays, those aimed at specific sectors of the population such as senior citizens, business trips, conferences, and cruising, he added.

The president of German consulting company IPK International, Rolf Freitag, said the European and North American markets showed an increase in demand for organized journeys, a search for sustainable tourism and a growing demand for quality at a lower price. Summarizing a report on leisure time trends conducted by World Tourism Organization Business Council (WTOBC) last year, Colin Clark, a director of consultants Horvath UK, said the main revelation was the reduction in free time in developed countries. The competitiveness of the world economy was acting as a brake against increasing leisure time, he said. In all the leading outbound countries, in Europe, the United States, and Japan, there was little hope of an increase in paid holidays in the near future. This would lead to a change in the way holidays are taken. They would tend to be shorter, more frequent and more intense, creating enormous possibilities in the industry to meet this growing diversification of demand.

WTO News Service, March, 1999. Reprinted with permission of the World Tourism Organization.

Improvements in Transportation

The twentieth century has also witnessed significant developments in the field of transportation that had important consequences for leisure travel. We saw that Cook's nineteenth-century travel empire depended heavily upon the railways as a relatively cheap, safe, and efficient form of tourist transportation. In the early part of the twentieth century, however, passenger traffic on American and British railways declined as the automobile became the major means of short-distance and middle-distance travel. The automobile helped free travelers from the schedules and fixed destinations that went along with travel by rail. The effects were especially marked in the United States, whose national parks became more easily accessible to large numbers of automobile tourists and which pioneered the standardized motor inn or "motel" along its major highways (Cross, 1990; Kelly and Godbey, 1992). In Europe the effects were felt somewhat later, but today the automobile is the form of transportation used most frequently by holidaymakers on that continent. The years following the end of World War II saw the demise of the great passenger liners, which were unable to compete with the new commercial airlines. In 1954 the introduction of the Boeing 707 prototype—which could move 189 passengers at speeds of 600 MPH—revolutionized international travel and set the stage for the jumbo jet era which was to begin in the 1970s. Some liner owners were driven to create a new North American market for cruises, especially to the West Indies. In doing so, they helped prepare the way for the subsequent development of Caribbean tourism packages (Burkart and Medlik, 1974).

In 1978 a major development in air transportation took place when the U.S. Senate abolished the Civil Aeronautics Board and deregulated the country's airline industry. This was meant to increase competition between airlines and thus make air travel more accessible for middle-class Americans. While deregulation achieved a considerable measure of success in these respects, it has not been an unmixed blessing. The larger airlines have consolidated their market positions and have succeeded in beating back competitors in their hub cities. Although there has been a drop in fares nationally, prices have increased on routes where the competition is weak, and large airlines' control of slots and gates at important airports can be used to limit access to smaller rivals. The larger airlines are also spending less on food, and there have been mounting complaints from customers about poor service and overcrowding, as well as sudden rescheduling and cancellation of flights (Holstein, 1999). A number of "no frills" airlines have managed to capture a share of the market, both in the United States and Europe, as recession in the early 1990s encouraged people to look for air travel bargains. Companies such as Southwest Airlines in the United States and easyJet in Britain are able to offer cheap fares by eliminating such things as complimentary in-flight service, reducing administrative costs, and selling directly to customers (Swarbrooke and Horner, 1999).

The Boom in International Tourism

The availability of relatively cheap, safe, and swift air transportation was a major reason for the rapid growth of international tourism after 1950. In some parts of the world the effects were quite dramatic: the Mediterranean resorts of Spain, France, and Italy quickly became meccas for northern Europeans; and British seaside resorts that were once popular with domestic, working-class holidaymakers entered a period of decline from which few of them ever recovered. The WTO estimated that international arrivals throughout the world increased from 25.3 million to 625.2 million between 1950 and 1998. About 75% of these arrivals involved persons who were engaged in leisure travel.

Although international tourism is often described as a global industry, the figures in Tables 2.1 through 2.3 show that it is a somewhat lopsided one, with Europe and the Americas having by far the largest share of tourist arrivals and tourism earnings. About 75% of global tourism's volume is accounted for by travelers from 20 countries (the most advanced industrial societies) and more than 50% of international tourist spending is done by the citizens of only five countries (Germany, Britain, France, Japan, and the United States). Table 2.4 (page 26) shows that Canada, Mexico, Japan, and Britain are the four largest suppliers of international visitors to the United States.

Most international tourist travel involves journeys between societies at roughly comparable levels of economic development, but travel to developing countries—so-called *North-South tourism*—has been increasing since the 1960s. The increase in travel to such destinations slowed down in the mid-1970s as several Third World governments became disillusioned with what seemed to them to be only modest economic gains and high social and cultural costs. At present a less sanguine but more realistic view of tourism's potential seems to be in evidence. The countries of the Caribbean, where disillusion was perhaps greatest, are once again energetically promoting tourism; and countries such as North Vietnam, Nicaragua, and Tanzania, where tourism was formerly shunned as a form of economic and cultural imperialism, are now trying to establish themselves in the international tourism market.

Table 2.1 International Arrivals, 1950 and 1998

Destination	1950 (millions)	*1998 (millions)
Europe	16.8	372.5
Americas	7.5	120.1
Asia-Pacific	0.2	91.9
Africa	0.5	24.9
Middle East	0.2	15.6
Total	25.3	625.2

*Estimate.

SOURCE: English (1986), World Tourism Organization Statistics Service.

Table 2.2 Leading Tourism Earners, 1998

Rank	Country	*Tourism Receipts (billions $US)	% of World Total
1	United States	74.2	16.7
2	Italy	30.4	6.8
3	France	29.7	6.7
4	Spain	29.5	6.7
5	Britain	21.2	4.8
6	Germany	16.8	3.8
7	China	12.5	2.8
8	Austria	12.1	2.7
9	Canada	9.1	2.1
10	Australia	8.5	1.9

*Estimate, excluding transport.

SOURCE: World Tourism Organization Statistics Service.

Lanfant (1995) reminds us that the growth of international tourism has not occurred spontaneously, but has been actively promoted and supported by major international associations such as the United Nations, UNESCO, the International Monetary Fund (IMF), the Organization of American States (OAS), the Organization for Economic Cooperation and Development (OECD), and the World Bank. She observes that these organizations have been involved in policy discussions and the formulation of global planning strategies, often in close cooperation with important tourism players like hotel chains and transportation companies. Besides cooperative agreements forged by these bodies, international tourism has also been encouraged by bilateral agreements between particular countries. These agreements

Table 2.3 Leading International Destinations, 1998

Rank	Country	*International Arrivals (millions)
1	France	70.0
2	Spain	47.7
3	United States	47.1
4	Italy	34.8
5	Britain	25.4
6	China	24.0
7	Mexico	19.3
8	Poland	18.8
9	Canada	18.6
10	Austria	17.2

*Estimate.

SOURCE: World Tourism Organization Statistics Service.

Table 2.4 Leading Countries of Origin of International Visitors to the United States in 1998

Rank	Country of Origin	Number of Arrivals (millions)
1	Canada	13.4
2	Mexico	9.3
3	Japan	4.9
4	Britain	4.0
5	Germany	1.9
6	France	1.0
7	Brazil	0.9
8	Italy	0.6
9	Venezuela	0.5
10	Argentina	0.5

Source: World Tourism Organization Statistics Service.

usually relate to the exchange of statistical information on tourism, support for vocational training and cultural exchange programs, and the coordination of entry requirements and procedures. Other bilateral agreements deal exclusively with air transport services, the United States having such agreements with more than 60 countries. Some of these are *Bermuda-type* agreements, which accept certain restrictions on the numbers of carriers and passengers, while others are of the *pro-competitive* type which permit each party to designate several airline carriers, allow fares to be determined by market forces, and prohibit the unilateral imposition of limits on flight frequency (Gee, Makens, and Choy, 1989). International tourism can also be affected by broader, multilateral agreements such as the 1994 North American Free Trade Agreement between the United States, Canada, and Mexico. Although tourism does not have a special section in this agreement, it is covered indirectly in those sections relating to trade in services, investment in finance and telecommunications, and temporary entry regulations (Smith and Pizam, 1998).

The face of global tourism will no doubt continue to change in the future. North-South tourism can be expected to grow in importance, although Africa, Asia, and South America may encounter stiff competition from Central and Eastern Europe— regions whose rich cultural and historical traditions, as well as their proximity to major tourist-generating countries, make them obvious candidates for rapid tourism development (Witt, 1998). New destinations will be "discovered" and developed and the international composition of travelers may change significantly as more residents of presently developing countries find the means and opportunities to travel abroad as tourists. And there are still untapped markets in some highly developed countries where the vast majority of people prefer to take their holidays at home. In this connection it is startling to realize that American tourists, who are the favorite targets of "tourist bashers" in Europe and much of the Third World, overwhelmingly prefer to vacation in their own country: 97% of U.S. tourism is domestic and only about 10% of Americans hold passports.

Postmodern Tourism?

New Escape Areas

Some observers have suggested that today's tourists have very different motivations and expectations from those of the 1960s, for most of whom travel abroad was a novel experience. Now tourists are said to be more experienced and knowledgeable and to want something more than organized escapes to sunny climes. According to this view tourists are becoming more discriminating and, at the same time, more environmentally and culturally sensitive travelers. These changes are believed to be largely responsible for the growth of interest in "alternative tourism" in the form of ecotourism, home-stay vacations, cultural tourism, educational tourism, and so on. It may also be significant that Arthur Frommer, best known for his popular but orthodox travel guidebooks, has in recent years been publishing an annual *Guide to Alternative Vacations*. Despite the growth of these more "serious" forms of tourism, it should be remembered that mass tourism destinations like Waikiki in Hawaii, Acapulco in Mexico, or Miami Beach in Florida remain tremendously popular; and the fastest growing tourist resorts in North America are Las Vegas and Orlando— places that offer visitors manufactured attractions in artificially constructed settings.

The deliberate manufacture of tourist places has been a particularly significant feature of tourism development since 1970. Rojek (1993) refers to these as "escape areas" and suggests they are organized around four major themes:

- *Black Spots*—These are places where celebrities or large numbers of people are buried or have met with sudden or violent death. The Dallas Tourist Board supports tours re-creating the assassination of President Kennedy, and the *USS Arizona* Memorial at Pearl Harbor is a major attraction for visitors to Hawaii. Other examples are Elvis Presley's home at Graceland, and the junction of Highways 488 and 41 in California, where the young actor James Dean was killed in an automobile accident. The tunnel in Paris where Princess Diana's fatal car crash occurred has also attracted large numbers of sightseers, while her burial place in Northamptonshire, England, is now firmly established on the English tourist circuit.
- *Heritage Sites*—These are places where attempts are made to re-create past events or lifestyles. Examples include old mining ghost towns like Virginia City, Nevada, and Barkerville, British Columbia. Sometimes the sites rest on very shaky historical foundations, as is the case at Nottingham in England, where the city's Robin Hood connection is exploited for tourism despite any convincing evidence that the famous outlaw ever existed.
- *Literary Landscapes*—These have been constructed in places associated with the lives of famous authors and fictional characters. Among the best known of these are "Hemingway Country" (Florida), "Bronte Country" (Yorkshire), "Catherine Cookson Country" (Newcastle and Tyneside), and "221B Baker

Street" (Sherlock Holmes). Sometimes these literary landscapes are fused with heritage sites, as in the village of Juffure in West Africa. This Gambian village is promoted as the ancestral home of Alex Haley, the author of *Roots,* as well as the birthplace of the real Kunta Kinte, the hero of the *Roots* saga.

- *Theme Parks*—These take many forms but usually include fantastic landscapes and participant attractions. Rojek suggests that, despite the parks' thematic variety, two prominent "meta themes" can be discerned: (1) *velocity*—this appears in the thrilling "white knuckle" rides common in many parks; and (2) *space-time compression*—this is found in attempts to construct "typical" representations of other lands, or cultures, such as in Disney's World Showcase pavilion in Orlando, or the Polynesian Cultural Center on Oahu, Hawaii.

These and other features of contemporary tourism are seen by some writers as reflecting new, "postmodern" cultural styles and practices. According to Sharpley (1994), the postmodern character of present-day tourism can be seen in a number of ways:

- *Tourism as Simulation*—Representations, rather than the realities represented, become items of touristic consumption. Much of the pleasure derived from such consumption requires the tourist to pretend that the representations are real, while knowing full well that they are not.
- *Tourism as a Game*—Going along with the pretense while scanning tourist brochures or participating in escape area activities involves an attitude of playful irony. Tourists understand that tourism is a game but can be enjoyed as such. The search for "authenticity" ceases to be a primary goal.
- *Tourism Fragmentation*—Because the opportunities for simulation are almost endless, tourist attractions and experiences become highly diversified and fragmented. The construction of tourist sites and attractions becomes possible almost anywhere, even in old industrial cities like Pittsburgh, Baltimore, Liverpool, or Manchester, which were formerly shunned by tourists.
- *Tourism as Collage*—Modernist distinctions between categories like work and leisure, past and present, performers and spectators, and so on, lose much of their former sharpness in conditions of postmodernity. In tourism the fusion of these categories is seen in a number of ways: places of work (factories or industrial areas) become objects of the tourist gaze; the past is absorbed into the present in re-created heritage sites; attractions from other places are reconstructed at culturally and historically disconnected sites (e.g., the Empire State building, the Eiffel Tower, and the Pyramids on the Las Vegas strip); and tourists become participants as well as spectators at pageants, tableaux, and various "hands-on" types of tourist attractions.

Needless to say, not all observers are convinced that contemporary tourism is significantly illuminated by a postmodernist perspective. It is still possible, perhaps, to regard current developments mainly as the continuation of an inventive tradition in the tourism industry as it tries to diversify its products in a highly competitive and segmented market. At the same time, we can see that the industry has often been able to successfully apply assembly line principles as it tries to cater to an expanding mass demand for its products (Ritzer and Liska, 1997). I shall return to these issues in my concluding chapter.

Chapter 3
Meeting Grounds

A Range of Possibilities

More than 20 years ago some of the more important factors underlying host-tourist relations were identified (UNESCO, 1976). While subsequent research has yielded additional insights, the earlier findings have generally remained valid (Nash, 1981; Robinson and Boniface, 1999). A review of the literature on this topic shows that numerous factors can influence and shape relations between locals and visitors in destination areas. The particular relevance of these factors also seems to vary from one touristic situation to another: some may be strongly influential in most destinations, while others may be of minor significance except in a few situations. Despite this qualification, these factors are still worth considering. They can be a useful checklist when examining particular case studies of host-tourist interactions in specific resorts or countries.

Transitoriness and Temporal Constraints

As a temporary sojourner or "bird of passage" the tourist is more likely than the host to experience the pressures of time shortage and to behave accordingly, for example, to try to see as many sights as possible, keep late hours, "hit the beach" immediately upon arrival, overdo the suntanning (some even "jump-start" this process at tanning studios prior to the holiday), and generally cram as much as possible into a limited vacation period. More importantly, perhaps, the tourist may seek immediate gratification of wants and express frustration and resentment over delays or unexpected hitches. An example of this kind of behavior was observed by me at the start of a two-week vacation in Mazatlan a few years ago.

Following an overnight flight from Vancouver, my group arrived at the hotel around 5 A.M. to find that the rooms, recently vacated by returning Canadian tourists, were not yet ready. Tired but anxious to get moving on the vacation—although it was still dark outside—the angry tourists besieged the front desk demanding immediate satisfaction and berating the travel company couriers. Within an hour all were accommodated, and shortly after daybreak most were at breakfast, while others were staking their claims to poolside lounge chairs (grab a towel and drape it on the chair, before going off), or making their first forays outside the hotel. The delay had been minor, but coming at the start of the holiday when the new arrivals had not quite adjusted to "tourist time," it was perhaps seen as a portent of awful things to come. For the hotel and travel company staff, however, the incident was a fairly regular occurrence, given the tight scheduling involved. It had happened before and would happen again. For them, the time frame was formed by the tourist season and not the two-week vacation period.

It is not difficult to imagine the potential for misunderstanding in situations of the kind described here. The twin perceptions—impatient tourist and indifferent host—are derived in part from differences between the time frames used by two different sets of actors. Moreover, the transitory nature of the encounter between tourists and hosts may influence the way they treat each other. It is probably easier to be uninhibited, rude or demanding with waiters one does not expect to see again. It is also probably easier to "rip off" a tourist who likely will go home before a thorough investigation can be conducted. However, the constraints imposed through time shortage do not always produce the kinds of behavior described here. Awareness that holiday time is short and precious can cause some tourists to downplay or ignore disappointments and get on with enjoying themselves. This "no time to grumble" response was observed among middle-aged English tourists in The Gambia (see chapter 10).

Spatial Constraints

In many destinations tourist areas are physically distinct and separate from those used by residents. In some cases, such as Club Meds and other self-sufficient resorts, the separation may be almost complete; in others, such as the coastal resort of Kihei on Maui, Hawaii, the separation is less marked, with tourists and locals sharing many of the same facilities and amenities and often living in the same condominium complexes. Even when tourist space is not physically demarcated from that of locals, it may be socially and psychologically separated through careful control and regulation by tour operators, hotel management, and others in the tourism establishment. In a recent visit to The Gambia I stayed in the capital, Banjul, at a beachfront hotel popular with British charter tourists. The hotel grounds border on a busy part of the city, but they are guarded by hotel security personnel who do not admit locals unless they have "legitimate business" to conduct there. Hotel residents are advised to use a hotel guide when walking into the city, as well as officially sanctioned local tour operators when making day-trips further afield. The result for most tourists and locals is a situation characterized by physical proximity and social distance.

The tourism literature often suggests that separation of tourists' and hosts' worlds is an undesirable condition because it gets in the way of genuine or meaningful encounters between tourists and residents. The physical, social, and psychological separation of tourists from locals may contribute to mutual misperceptions and to resentment on the part of locals who feel they are being shut out of the tourists' world. While the merging of tourists' and residents' spaces might provide greater opportunities for more natural forms of interaction and mutual understanding, a case can be made for some degree of separation. If one is interested in minimizing the disruptive sociocultural effects of tourists, it may be that a certain amount of tourist containment or insulation will be helpful in this respect. The sharing of common space can also foster resentment of tourists as intrusive competitors for local resources, as happens in some parts of Hawaii when tourists use the cheaper public golf courses instead of the more expensive ones at resorts, or use state subsidized public transportation instead of rental cars.

Work-Leisure Differences

These, along with sociocultural differences, are the factors most emphasized in sociological and anthropological studies of host-tourist relations, as I indicated in chapter 1. The fact that tourists are at leisure while hosts are at work can lead to different and sometimes conflicting interpretations of the relationship by both parties. Tourists typically expect waiters, hotel staff, and other paid hosts to serve their needs in a relationship that is one of commercialized hospitality. At the same time, these working hosts will usually be expected to act as if they too were on vacation— to smile and look happy, join in the fun, spend time chatting or socializing with the visitors, and so on. Hosts may reasonably expect tourists to be relaxed and friendly— after all, they are on holiday and not at work—but may sometimes find them irritable and fretful if things do not appear to be going as well as expected. The boundary between these two broad sets of expectations is usually fluid and shifting, and the management of boundary crossing is something requiring considerable sensitivity and skill. This is apparently easier in some touristic situations than in others. For example, in home-stay tourism in Cornish farmhouses in southwest England, the farm wives regularly leave their guests to baby-sit the kids while they go off for an evening at the local cinema. For the tourists this is all part of the "authentic" experience of life on a Cornish farm!

As I noted earlier, tourists' expectations may sometimes be extended to other kinds of hosts—those ordinary residents who are not personally involved in the local tourism industry, but who are expected to be kind, friendly, and courteous in their encounters with visitors. While these expectations are often met, especially in destinations where tourists are still something of a novelty, the situation can be quite different in places where tourism has grown too rapidly or too large. I shall return to this point later when considering the importance of resort life cycles.

Sociocultural Differences

These encompass a very broad range of differentiating factors and include language, religion, ethnicity, class, education, and cultural formalization (for example, manners and rules of etiquette) among others. Many of these can be influential in host-tourist interactions, especially in North-South tourism meeting grounds, or when Western types of destinations host tourists from developing countries (Reisinger and Turner, 1997). Together, they represent a fertile field for mutual misperceptions and misunderstandings, especially when other disturbing factors are present in tourism situations. These additional factors might include saturation or overloading of the destination, or local economic and political woes that make tourists convenient targets for scapegoating. Examples are not difficult to find: Jamaica in the 1970s and Egypt in the 1990s are situations that spring readily to mind.

These kinds of differentiating factors are not entirely absent from domestic tourism situations as well. In Ghana, for example, relations between local tourists (mainly well-to-do Ghanaians) and hotel staff are notoriously poor and are often marked by tourist arrogance and host resentment—behavior more commonly associated with encounters in international tourism situations. And many Ghanaians living in or near domestic tourism centers take an extremely poor view of hotels, which are often viewed as places where people spend valuable time and money "wastefully" and engage in "immoral activities" such as philandering with girlfriends or consorting with prostitutes. This view is sustained because the notion of leisure travel is not yet well-developed or accepted by the majority of Ghanaians, for whom travel has traditionally been associated with "worthwhile" activities like work, attending weddings or funerals, or dealing with family problems and other important matters (Adu-Febiri, 1988).

Economic Disparities

Given the relatively low wages typical of many jobs in the tourism industry, economic disparities between hosts and tourists can be a potential source of friction, even in domestic tourism situations. But they are likely to be much more significant in influencing host-tourist relations in North-South tourism. Here they can exacerbate work-leisure differences and cause other differences—for example, racial or ethnic ones—to assume greater significance. They appear to have been at the root of much of the resentment and hostility towards tourists in Jamaica. In Bermuda, however, which has a much higher standard of living than Jamaica, relationships between white tourists and black hosts have been generally good. It should be remembered that tourist spending usually assumes a concentrated or freewheeling form and tourists would become paupers very quickly if they spent like this at home. In some developing countries this kind of behavior may distort residents' perceptions of the magnitude of the economic gulf that separates them from the tourists.

Stages of Resort Development

It is important to avoid a static approach to host-tourist encounters and to recognize that the nature of these encounters may change over time. Some writers have suggested that predictable changes in host-tourist relations occur as tourism resorts move through different stages of their life cycles. A number of models of this process have been proposed. Three of the better known ones are described next.

Doxey's Irridex Model

This model postulates a five-stage developmental sequence of local attitudes to tourists, expressed in the form of an "irritation index." It is based on Doxey's own research in Barbados and Niagara-on-the-Lake, Ontario:

- *Stage 1—Euphoria*—Tourists are initially welcomed by enthusiastic hosts. Money flows in and there are new employment opportunities for locals. The feelings of satisfaction are mutual.
- *Stage 2—Apathy*—With an increase in the numbers of tourists, the local industry expands. Tourists are no longer a novelty and come to be taken for granted. They become targets for profit taking as their relationships with hosts become less personal and more formal.
- *Stage 3—Irritation*—Tourist numbers continue to grow to a point that local residents cannot tolerate them without improving or expanding existing facilities. The locals begin to feel squeezed out and become increasingly irritated.
- *Stage 4—Antagonism*—Tensions have mounted and the strain on local resources and infrastructure has become acute. Locals express irritation more openly. They now blame tourists for most of what has gone wrong. Mutual politeness virtually disappears. The tourist is now "justifiably" exploited.
- *Stage 5—Possible Outcomes*—If the resort or destination area is incapable of handling the problems manifested in the antagonistic stage, it will likely enter a period of decline as tourists seek more welcoming and trouble-free places. If, however, residents come to terms with the new reality—that their community will never be the same as it was prior to the introduction of tourism—they may find ways of salvaging the situation. This will likely involve attracting tourists who are very different in their expectations than those they so enthusiastically welcomed in the beginning. If the destination is capable of accommodating mass tourism and its residents can make the necessary mental adjustments, it will probably survive (Doxey, 1976).

Cohen's Three-Stage Model

This simple model condenses some general observations made by various investigators in a number of different destination areas:

- *Stage 1*—Tourists are accommodated within a preexisting system of local hospitality and are treated accordingly, as kin, neighbors, friends, honored guests, and the like. Cash payments may be relatively absent and tourists may compensate the hosts by making gifts or extending invitations to visit them.
- *Stage 2*—As tourist numbers increase, they are less welcome. Hospitality is no longer governed by traditional norms (including the norm of reciprocity),

but becomes more commercialized. This stage is marked by a certain degree of confusion as to how the tourist-host relationship is to be perceived. It is also marked by the emergence of a predatory attitude towards tourists and the beginnings of hostility and discrimination towards them.

- *Stage 3*—To counter the adverse effects beginning in the previous stage, local authorities promote the development of professionalism. This may be necessary to counter an adverse image and a possible decline in the number of visitors, for by now the resort may have become heavily dependent upon tourism. This stage sees the codification and enforcement of industry standards and various other safeguards, as well as the rise of different kinds of tourism professionals. The result may be an improvement in tourist-host relations, or it may simply put a professional gloss over a situation in which problems and friction continue (Cohen, 1984).

Butler's Resort Life Cycle Model

Similar in some respects to Doxey's irridex model, Butler proposes a seven-stage sequence, although his focus is somewhat broader insofar as it considers broader transformations in the local tourism industry as well as in host-tourist relations:

- *Stage 1—Exploration*—The resort is discovered by small numbers of adventurous travelers. Locals accept and treat them as guests and there is therefore little commercialization involved in their interactions. Relationships between hosts and tourists is close and personal, with balanced reciprocity in evidence.
- *Stage 2—Involvement*—The numbers of visitors increase and locals provide special facilities for them. Relations become more commercialized and some attempts are now made to deliberately market the destination. Nonetheless, relations between locals and tourists remain good.
- *Stage 3—Development*—With the continued increase in tourist numbers, local people begin to lose control of the industry. Externally owned hotels and tour organizations appear, while mass tourists replace the more independent travelers of the exploration stage. Host-tourist relationships become more commercialized and impersonal.
- *Stage 4—Consolidation*—The destination has now lost many of the unique or unspoiled features which attracted the earlier tourists. It has come to resemble many other mass tourist resorts, with a tourist enclave separated from residential areas. Tourists' interactions with locals are now mainly confined to commercialized encounters with those employed in the tourism industry.
- *Stage 5—Stagnation*—Industry marketing has now led to a situation in which the destination's carrying capacity has been reached. Growth in tourist numbers has peaked, investors are looking for opportunities elsewhere, and facilities, amenities, and infrastructure deteriorate. In order to attract tourists, the local industry is forced to lower prices and target low-budget mass tourists.

- *Stage 6—Decline*—Encountering stiff competition from other destinations which are at earlier stages in this cycle, the resort fails to attract enough tourists. Hotels and businesses dependent on tourism close. Buildings become derelict or are converted to other, nontouristic purposes. Some tourism activity continues, but relations between hosts and tourists remain formalized and commercialized.
- *Stage 7—Rejuvenation*—The decline is arrested by creating new attractions and a new destination image. As the potential of this reorientation begins to be realized, and tourists once again show interest in the destination, investment capital returns (Butler, 1980).

Although these sequences may be followed in the development of tourism in particular places, they need not necessarily occur everywhere. Barbados and Niagara-on-the-Lake may well have undergone the kind of transformations suggested in Doxey's irridex model, but others have not. In places like the Himalayan country of Bhutan the initial stage of development was one in which locals took a guarded "let's see how this goes" attitude, rather than one of naive enthusiasm. Some destinations manage to rejuvenate themselves by creating new attractions for new tourists: a good example of this is Atlantic City in the United States, which responded to the competition from Florida by introducing legalized gambling casinos (Craig-Smith and French, 1994). However, many British seaside resorts were unable to halt the process of decline and decay and are now mere shadows of their former selves.

One leading tourism geographer suggests that, while Doxey's developmental sequence seems to have been followed in places like Cape Cod and the Scottish Highlands, the evidence does not support the view that it is an inevitable process for all tourism destinations (Pearce, 1989). In Maui (see chapter 9) many residents are opposed to tourism development, but direct their anger and resentment at local authorities and industry leaders, rather than at tourists, with whom relations are generally good. Even when a country undergoes rapid and massive growth in numbers of visitors, it will not necessarily become an arena for host-tourist conflict. International tourist arrivals in Spain soared from only 80,000 in 1946 to almost 48 million in 1998, yet host-tourist conflict in that country has been relatively minor (Barke, 1999).

Types of Tourists

We saw earlier that Boorstin and MacCannell approached the subject of tourism with two very different conceptualizations of the tourist in mind. But both writers tended to treat tourists as homogenous groups, largely ignoring the differences among them. However, tourists are not all alike, and different kinds of tourists may form different kinds of relationships with their hosts. A number of attempts have been made to identify tourist types and the ways in which they relate to local conditions in tourist settings (Lowyck, Van Langenhove, and Bollaert, 1992). I will discuss only two of the best known formal typologies of tourists, both of which were developed by Erik Cohen.

Novelty and Familiarity

The first of Cohen's typologies develops one of Boorstin's basic ideas—that tourists often seek novel experiences but want these in familiar and secure surroundings containing such things as comfortable hotels, familiar food, or reliable transportation. Cohen suggests that different types of tourists seek different mixes of novelty and familiarity in their tourist experiences; and that these types can be arranged along a continuum, ranging from those for whom novelty is paramount to those who want familiarity above all else. The result is a fourfold typology of tourists:

- *Organized Mass Tourists*—These are the least adventurous kinds of tourists, people who prefer to stay mainly within an "environmental bubble" throughout their tour. The prototype here is perhaps the package tourist on a guided tour in an air-conditioned bus, or the cruise ship tourist making brief scheduled stops at exotic destinations (Foster, 1986; Gorman, 1979; Holloway, 1981; Schuchat, 1983). The tourist buys a vacation package and makes few important decisions thereafter. Familiarity is maximized and novelty is minimized. Tourists of this type are the favorite targets of serious travel writers or filmmakers.
- *Individual Mass Tourists*—This type of tourist makes most major arrangements through a travel agent, but is not bound so tightly to a group and exercises more control over itinerary. The environmental bubble is again maintained, and occasional ventures outside it do not usually lead much farther afield than those of the organized mass tourist. Familiarity is still dominant, but less pronounced. There is a greater experience of novelty, but this is often of the routine kind involving forays into well-charted territory.
- *Explorers*—These tourists make all or most arrangements alone and try to get off the beaten tracks. Nevertheless, they will seek comfortable accommodation and reliable transportation. More willing to leave the environmental bubble than either of the two previous types, explorers try to establish closer contacts with locals. But they make sure that the bubble is still within reach and that it can be returned to fairly easily if the situation warrants it. Here novelty dominates, but explorers do not become completely immersed in the local community.
- *Drifters*—Drifters go farthest from the beaten tourist tracks, avoiding contact with the tourist establishment and with other types of tourists. They may live with the locals, adopt many of their customs, and share in their way of life. There is no fixed itinerary or clearly defined travel goals. With immersion in the host culture, novelty is at its highest and familiarity is almost absent (Cohen, 1972).

The first two types involve institutionalized tourist roles, which are fairly tightly integrated into the tourist system of travel agents, tour operators, hotel chains, and so on. The last two Cohen regards as noninstitutionalized tourist roles, since they are more autonomous and are only loosely attached to the tourism system. Organized and individual mass tourists have been the main objects of investigation in tourism research, while comparatively little attention has been given to explorers or drifters. However, Cohen suggests that the importance of these latter types may be out of proportion to their numbers, which are thought to be small in comparison with mass tourists. Explorers, for example, may find new places of touristic interest and pave the way for later, more commercialized forms of tourism. Drifters, who normally travel on tight budgets and are constantly on the lookout for bargains in food and accommodation, may in some senses be more exploitive of locals than many mass tourists (Riley, 1988). It appears that drifter tourists have already begun to develop their own fairly elaborate support systems, involving exchange of information among themselves and the use of special guidebooks such as those in the Lonely Planet series. In other words, it appears that this tourist role is also undergoing a process of routinization and institutionalization.

Alienation and Authenticity

In a more complex attempt to sort out basic differences among tourists, Cohen utilizes MacCannell's concept of authenticity but suggests that not all tourists are equally concerned about this in their travels. This, he argues, is because they do not all experience the same sense of alienation from their own societies. These two variables—alienation and authenticity—will be directly related: the greater the sense of personal alienation, the more intensive will be the tourist's quest for authenticity. This leads him to propose a fivefold typology of tourists focusing on the kinds of touristic experiences they seek. Cohen also borrows the concept of center from the work on pilgrimages by anthropologist Victor Turner (1973). In Cohen's usage, the individual's center is the source of his or her ultimate moral values—those things and ideas that give life meaning and reality, structure, and direction. It is not necessarily the place where an individual normally resides. For the pilgrim, for example, the center is somewhere "out there" (for example, Mecca, Jerusalem) and the pilgrimage involves a journey from the periphery (for example, London or Los Angeles) to this center. For most contemporary international tourists, however, the journey usually involves a movement from a center "here" to a periphery represented by the tourist destination. Cohen's five types are:

- *Recreational*—This is associated with the travels of people who sense little or no personal alienation from their society. Tourism is a means of recreation and a form of entertainment or idle pleasure. Recreational tourists have little interest in the authentic, and tend to accept things pretty much at face value.

They enjoy the touristic experience in much the same way as they do a television show or a film—as relaxing, entertaining make-believe. For them the journey represents a temporary move away from the center, but serves to reinforce their attachment to it.

- *Diversionary*—Tourists of this type are people who have begun to experience some degree of alienation. For them, life has become somewhat meaningless, and touristic travel is a source of diversion. The search here is not for an alternative, more meaningful center "out there," but for temporary escape and comfort. The experience can provide some solace, but it does not re-create the individual. It merely serves to help the person cope with alienation by making it more tolerable.

- *Experiential*—Here we are among tourists whose sense of alienation is more profound. With a growing awareness of the futility and meaninglessness of normal life, they search for meaning in the lives of others in an attempt to recapture authenticity. The person feels that somewhere—out there but not here—is a better, more genuine or meaningful society, culture, or way of life. However, the tourist is still aware of the otherness of these places and is not converted to this different way of life. The tourist is still a stranger among the authentic, experiencing it but not adopting it.

- *Experimental*—With this type of tourist the sense of alienation is so strong that he or she can no longer derive moral or spiritual sustenance from his or her own society. He or she participates actively in the authentic life of others but does not make a complete or final commitment to it. In extreme cases, the experimental search may itself become a way of life and the tourist becomes an "eternal seeker"—losing the ability to make final choices and unable to make the leap to a new, elective center.

- *Existential*—Existential tourists are people who have finally found an alternative center of meaning and have made a commitment to it. Normally, they will shuttle regularly between the two worlds—the meaningless world of everyday life and the meaningful world of the elective center. This type of tourist now resembles the pilgrim who travels regularly to the center that offers moral and spiritual sustenance. In extreme cases, he or she may form a permanent attachment to this new center and take up residence there. At this point they cease to be tourists.

The first two types seem to identify the kinds of tourists implied in Boorstin's treatment of the modern mass tourist, with the emphasis on escape, diversion, pleasure-seeking, and so on. Of particular interest here is Cohen's suggestion that such tourists are not particularly interested in authenticity and are quite able to suspend critical faculties when confronted with "staged authenticity." For them, it matters little if the Hawaiian hula dance performance is genuine, or if the Mexican fiesta is really being conducted along traditional lines. Recreational and diversionary tourists don't really care very much, which is rather different from being cultural dopes.

With the experimental tourists, we begin to recognize some of the characteristics of MacCannell's authenticity-seeking tourists, these characteristics becoming more pronounced as we move down the typology. Experimental tourists look fairly similar to Cohen's drifters, or to the young North American, European, and Australian backpackers on the trail to Katmandu or on visits to ashrams, kibbutzim, or other communes. Existential tourists are probably the rarest, but fairly close approximations may be found among those who make annual visits to a kibbutz or undertake regular "roots" journeys to ancestral homes.

It is important to note that Cohen recognizes individuals whose touristic experiences do not closely resemble any of the five types. There are *humanists* who have a broad conception of the center, who see themselves as "citizens of the world," and who do not feel alienated from a particular society. There are also *dualists* who can feel equally at home in two different societies and for whom there may be two corresponding centers.

In teaching courses on tourism to sociology and anthropology students, I have found that the subject of tourist typologies sometimes generates skeptical, critical, and even heated reactions. Much of this seems to stem from a fairly natural aversion to being labeled, and a conviction that tourists—especially us—are individuals and not occupants of convenient little boxes constructed by some tourism theorist. This reaction may miss the point of typologies devised by Cohen and others. The *abstract* nature of these typologies needs to be kept in mind. They are designed as analytical tools, more rudimentary than those "ideal types" formulated by Weber in analyzing types of capitalism, types of authority, or types of administrative organizations, but similar in purpose (1947). They are different from inclusive sets of categories, such as might be used to classify a population by age or income levels. In these category sets, nobody is excluded—every individual belongs to one category or another. In Cohen's typologies of tourists, however, no claim is made that all individual tourists must conform to the specifications of one type or another. In their behavior and aspirations some tourists may closely resemble the various types, while others may not. The types are best regarded as modal points on a logical continuum, and the typologies can serve as tools for analyzing such things as historical changes in the composition of tourists, the different ways in which tourists relate to hosts, or the different effects different kinds of tourists can have on host economies, social structures, and cultures.

All this does not mean that the typologies are beyond criticism: one might suggest, for example, that Cohen's fourfold typology requires further development and the inclusion of more modal points; or that, in his fivefold typology, the causal connection between a sense of alienation and a search for authenticity is by no means obvious. With his fivefold typology in particular, we see that the focus is on individual tourists who have individual expectations and who make individual travel decisions. Since a good deal of traveling is done by small groups of people, such as friends, married couples, families, and so on, one wonders how the typology might accommodate the kind of compromises or "give and take" that goes on when people decide to travel together. Could it accommodate, for example, the authenticity-seeking wife who goes to Las Vegas with her hedonistic husband this year, on the clear understanding that they will both visit Outer Mongolia or the Brazilian rain forest next year?

Types of Hosts

Perhaps the main weakness of the resort development models discussed earlier is their tendency to treat local residents as a fairly homogenous group reacting positively, negatively, or indifferently to the presence of tourists. Although no formal typologies of hosts have been developed, it is well-recognized that in many tourism destinations reactions and attitudes to tourism and tourists can vary greatly among the people living there. Studies of resident attitudes in a number of resorts show a fairly consistent pattern: more positive attitudes are expressed by those directly involved in or dependent upon the tourism industry. A notable exception is Hawaii, where Liu and Var (1986) found no significant differences between the attitudes of those who worked in tourism and those who did not. The generally favorable attitudes were attributed mainly to the maturity of Hawaii's tourism industry and to local recognition of its importance in the state's economy. Similarly, some researchers have noted more favorable attitudes among residents with greater knowledge of tourism, and emphasize the importance of tourism education in creating a positive public climate for tourism development.

Some "adaptancy platform" studies stress the need for direct resident involvement in local tourism planning, but this can be problematic when residents themselves are sharply divided on tourism issues. It is now clear that approval of or opposition to tourism are not simple reflections of people's perceived economic relationships to the industry, but are often linked to differences in the ways residents define their community and see its future. In Maui, Hawaii, it was found that many of the most vocal and active opponents of tourism were people who had moved to the island from the U.S. mainland. Like Cohen's existential tourists, they had discovered a new, elective center that seemed like paradise and had decided to settle there, only to see their dreams of paradise evaporate in the face of continued tourism growth (Wyllie, 1998a, 1998b).

The Demonstration Effect

This term refers to the ways in which tourist behavior can generate new wants and aspirations among the host population, especially among the young. Discussion of this topic has tended to emphasize local striving for symbols of wealth and status associated with tourists, for example, ready cash, transistor radios, sunglasses, imported food and drink, and so forth. Most writers have described the demonstration effect in generally negative terms. In poorer countries, the effect may be mainly to introduce aspirations that cannot be easily or swiftly realized; and if locals mistakenly believe that tourists' free-spending behavior is typical of the way they behave at home, their own feelings of social and economic inferiority may lead to frustration and resentment. Difficulties in realizing these new consumer goals may cause some locals to seek escape to Western societies through alliances or friendships with tourist sponsors. This behavior has been noted among Thai women and young Gambian males, as well as among people in a number of other international tourist destinations. In assessing the demonstration effect, one must be careful not to overestimate the naivete of members of the local population. A UNESCO report (1976) suggests that while young people are especially vulnerable to the demonstration effect, most adults soon overcome an initial sense of inferiority and learn how to profit from tourists' weaknesses. Since tourists are rarely the only sources of new consumer values and social aspirations (other sources include local elites, expatriate communities, films, and other mass media) it is usually difficult to assess their demonstration effect with any degree of accuracy.

The demonstration effect is sometimes viewed more broadly to include wide-ranging changes in local values and morals that may accompany tourism development. Again, these changes are generally viewed negatively by most observers, especially when manifested in such things as increasing crime, gambling, begging, prostitution, and the like. Other tourist-induced changes are more difficult to assess in positive or negative terms. These include changes that threaten established patterns of authority based on gender or age discrimination. The difficulty here may be illustrated with reference to student reaction to a documentary video shown in one of my tourism courses. The video dealt with the effects of hill-trekking tourism in the Himalayan kingdom of Nepal and showed, among other things, how some Nepalese women had begun to question existing patriarchal relations in the household and in society at large. Some of the women, impressed by apparently liberated young Western female tourists, sought greater economic independence from their menfolk and wanted to keep part of their tourism earnings for their own personal use, rather than hand it over to their husbands or fathers. Some had adopted a more relaxed attitude towards premarital and extramarital sex, and others expressed a desire to visit the West and experience the "good life" represented by the tourists.

In the seminar discussion following the film, some students expressed a "hands off" reaction. ("Our ways aren't for everyone." "I couldn't put up with what these women do, but their society seemed to work OK before the tourists came in with their new, disruptive ideas." "The tourists are acting as agents of Western cultural imperialism—women are no happier in the West than these women were before tourism came along.") Others rejected this relativistic approach and suggested that values such as freedom of the individual, equality between the sexes, emancipation of women from patriarchal control, and so on, were universally valid—whether in Nepal or in Canada. ("It's hypocritical to say Nepalese women should be treated as second-class citizens just because they are Nepalese." "How can you say that we

Canadian women should be treated like human beings, but then say the Nepalese women shouldn't?") Others felt the issue was largely irrelevant. ("Big deal. If the tourists hadn't introduced the new ideas, they would have come about eventually anyway.")

Keeping Things in Perspective

The nature and dynamics of host-tourist relations are influenced by a large number of factors, several of which have been discussed in this chapter. The complex interplay of these factors makes it extremely difficult to generalize about host-tourist relations, or to predict with confidence the ways in which they will develop over time in actual tourism destinations. Neither tourists nor hosts can be regarded as homogenous categories, and the variety of types and subgroupings within each category has to be constantly kept in mind. It is also important to emphasize that it is not only people who interact in host-tourist encounters, but cultures as well. As Rojek and Urry remind us, while people tour cultures, cultures and objects also travel (1997). I shall have more to say about the nature and consequences of cultural encounters in tourism in chapter 6.

In our discussion of host-tourist interactions, we have looked at a few of the factors that can shape their character. Almost inevitably, perhaps, this has the appearance of a catalogue of things that can go wrong when locals and tourists come together on destination meeting grounds. We also read newspaper stories of tourists being murdered, robbed, raped, ripped off, or otherwise victimized. All this can create the impression that touristic travel today is a dangerous or risky business and needs to be approached with great caution. One can argue, however, that this is far from being the case. We need to remind ourselves of the tremendous scale and volume of contemporary international tourism (see Table 2.1 in the previous chapter), with millions of people annually crossing national and cultural boundaries. The overwhelming majority of these tourists experience no serious breakdowns in their relations with hosts, and most encounter nothing worse than occasional rudeness, overcharging, or poor service from some hosts.

Wide sociocultural gulfs between hosts and tourists are often amicably bridged, however temporarily, especially in encounters between young drifter tourists and the locals they associate with in their travels. Such contacts are not entirely unexpected, given the drifter's impulse to get to know the people and the fact that residents in drifter destinations are often still enthralled by tourist strangers from the outside world. Even in mass tourist destinations, where tourists remain for relatively short periods and have few opportunities to acquire an in-depth appreciation of local cultures, the bridging of sociocultural differences is not unknown. These differences may be "bracketed" or suspended during the vacation period, and points of commonality established between tourists and hosts. An example of this is provided in the following vignette, based on my observations of tourists and waiters in a Gambian hotel. The tourists were English, mostly from northern industrial cities such as Manchester, Leeds, and Sheffield; the waiters were young Gambian males, most of whom were Muslims from small towns and villages in the interior of the country. Relations between the two groups appeared excellent—as smooth as one might hope to find in any mass tourist destination—despite wide social and cultural gulfs.

❊   ✦   ✳   ᐨᕀᐟ   ❊

Abdul and the Yorkshire Tourists

Near the end of dinner in the hotel restaurant the dessert trolley is wheeled to the table occupied by Mr. and Mrs. Hodgkins from Sheffield and Mr. and Mrs. Hargreaves from Leeds, both couples in their sixties, who had struck up an acquaintanceship during the holiday. "What would you like for dessert this evening, ladies and gentlemen?" asks Abdul the waiter in mock-formal tone. "Eee! Listen to 'im, will ye!" exclaims Mrs. Hodgkins, "He's coomin over all posh t'night, in't ee?" Abdul, a young man in his twenties, grins broadly and runs through the list of desserts. There is a good deal of joking and bantering; and it is clear that a kind of surrogate mother-son relationship has developed between Mrs. Hodgkins and Abdul. "Ah'l joost 'av a bit o' that gateau, Abdul luv—not too mooch, mind you—got to watch me figure, y'know." More banter and then a discussion of Sheffield Wednesday's win that day in the English Premier soccer league. Abdul is well up on this—like most young Gambian men, he is an avid soccer enthusiast and knows a great deal about English and other European teams and players. There are more friendly exchanges, then Abdul moves on to the next table.

❊   ᐨᕀᐟ   ✳   ✦   ❊

In this encounter, the sociocultural gulf is bridged, primarily through a shared interest in soccer—a truly international sport—and Mrs. Hodgkins' extension of her working-class "mum" role in "adopting" the young Gambian. The point here is not the sincerity of the parties in what is essentially a commercial transaction. It is, rather, that major differences can be bridged or circumvented in these short-term host-tourist relationships. Nowadays one has to go very far afield to find locals who know nothing at all about the world the tourist comes from. Ordinary people like the Hodgkins and the Hargreaves make up the vast majority of contemporary Western mass tourists; and a good many of them, it seems, have no difficulty in seeing beyond obvious sociocultural differences to establish workable relationships with other ordinary people like Abdul in tourist destinations all over the world. Among contemporary English tourists, people like the Hodgkins and Hargreaves are probably encountered more frequently than those like Jeanette and Duggie, the dreadful tourist couple portrayed in the film, *Shirley Valentine*.

If contemporary international tourists are indeed more experienced travelers than were those of the 1960s, it is also likely that they take in their stride some of the things that upset or outraged some of these earlier visitors, for example, "funny" food, "skunky" beer, "wonky" toilets, and so on. It must be remembered that the vast majority of international tourist visits are not to Third World destinations, but to places with well-established tourism industries and, in many cases, with cultures which are similar to those of the tourists themselves. And the growth of tourism as an industry has involved the development of techniques and personnel training programs designed to manage or alleviate potential difficulties in host-tourist interactions. Finally, we should remember that not all tourism is highly commercialized or revolves around encounters between strangers. So-called *VFR tourism* (visiting friends and relatives) has received little attention by tourism researchers, although for multicultural societies like Britain, Canada, and the United States it probably accounts for a large segment of the tourism market (Seaton and Palmer, 1997).

Chapter 4
The Bottom Line

Tourism as an Industry

I have already noted the disagreement among economists on the question of whether tourism can properly be regarded as an industry. Clearly, people in control of the production and marketing of travel and hospitality goods and services would like it to be regarded as an industry. Something that can be presented in this way, rather than as a motley collection of different businesses, may stand a better chance of winning public respect and government support (Davidson, 1998). What then are the kinds of businesses that are typically claimed as part of the tourism industry? According to Lickorish and Jenkins (1997) "tourism trades" are of three kinds: (1) the *primary trades* of transport, travel trade (e.g., tour companies, travel agencies), accommodation and catering, and tourist attractions; (2) the *secondary trades* of retail shopping (e.g., crafts and souvenirs), banks and insurance, entertainment and leisure activity, excursions and admissions, and personal services (e.g., newsagents, hairdressers); and (3) the *tertiary trades* of public sector services, publishing and printing, food and fuel, manufacture and wholesale, and travel industry infrastructure and support. Smith (1988), whose supply-side approach was mentioned earlier, believes that tourism is a retail service industry. It consists of Tier 1 businesses, which are closely related to the demands of travelers and can be viewed as "pure tourism" (for example, airlines, hotels); and Tier 2 businesses, which are "mixed" in the sense that they are important to both travelers and local residents. Tier 1 businesses, such as airlines, would cease to exist if there were no travel. Tier 2 businesses, such as restaurants, would continue to exist if there were no travel, but their trade would be at significantly reduced levels. Even some Tier 1 business hotels, which sometimes cater to local residents, exist to serve travelers. If travel ceased, hotels would disappear.

Smith's arguments have been challenged by Leiper (1990, 1993), who believes that tourism is a system that is only partially industrialized. His view is that, in practical terms, an industry is a collection of businesses that produce similar or related goods and coordinate their activities in the process; and even competition within an industry will occur within collaborative frameworks. For Leiper, tourism does not quite fit the bill in these respects: the goods and services are often quite dissimilar or not closely related; and many organizations in the so-called *industry* derive direct benefits from tourism but do not themselves promote it or collaborate with those that do.

We may leave these arguments for the economists to settle. However, we should remember that tourism's economic dimensions have profoundly influenced the research agendas of tourism sociologists and anthropologists. High on these agendas are the examination of relations between hosts and tourists, and the effects of tourism development on the broader society and culture. These principal areas of interest have their bases in the peculiar production-consumption relationship that operates in tourism. In order to consume the product tourists have to spend time at the site of production (the tourist destination or resort). This makes the relationship between producers and consumers very different from those one might find in, say, a forestry or mining community. Because numbers of consumers do spend time at tourism production sites, the effects of their presence and behavior in such places go far beyond anything that might result from the visits of a few buyers' representatives in forestry or mining communities. It is also difficult to think of another industry that makes the kinds of demands tourism does upon people who are simply residents at the sites of production, but who themselves are not employed in the tourism industry. In tourism communities ordinary residents are often expected to be unpaid tourism agents and exhorted to be kind, friendly, or helpful to tourists. They may even be expected to become part of the tourism product, allowing themselves to be photographed by tourists, or to dress and behave in ways that conform to tourists' expectations. And Article 1(3) of the WTO Global Code of Ethics for Tourism urges them to respect tourists and familiarize themselves with tourists' lifestyles, tastes, and expectations (see Appendix). We see too that many social and cultural effects of tourism are rooted in economic transformations wrought by the industry. For example, the movement of people from agricultural to tourism occupations can lead to changes in family structures and patterns of community life. New job opportunities created by tourism can also lead to changes in traditional gender and age group relationships, while the influx of tourist dollars can generate new material aspirations and values among people living in or near tourist destinations.

Tourism as Big Business

To people who are not professional economists, the question of whether tourism is an industry or something else may appear academic in the worst sense of the term. For sociologists in particular, so often accused of inventing definitions and quibbling over them, it may be heartening to see their more hardheaded colleagues in economics wrangling over such issues. Whether tourism is an "industry," a "system," "the world's largest industry," or "the world's largest partially industrialized system," it remains the case that tourism is an activity of great and growing economic significance. For convenience, we will continue to use the term *industry*, while recognizing that there are arguments about tourism's structure and size.

Tourism is a growth industry and is likely to remain so for the foreseeable future. It has proven attractive to companies whose business interests were formerly peripheral to tourism and some of these companies have become major tourism players. A good example here is Britain's Bass PLC, which was originally strictly a brewing company, but whose hotels and resorts division is now one of the world's largest and includes Inter-Continental Hotels, Crowne Plaza, Holiday Inn, and Holiday Inn Express. American companies moving into tourism resort development and ownership include Northwestern Mutual Life Insurance, American Factors (AMFAC), and Dole Foods, all of which have been prominent in the recent development of Hawaii's tourism industry (see chapter 9).

International tourism has performed well compared to many other export-oriented industries. The tourism market is also relatively free. Governments in more developed countries—the main tourist-generating areas—are unlikely to impose restrictions on their citizens' rights to travel (the U.S. ban on travel to Cuba is an unusual situation), or on how much they can spend while traveling. This freedom makes tourism different from many other exports, which are often subject to quotas and tariffs. And since tourism products are largely consumed "on-site," there are opportunities for adding value to services offered in the destination areas.

According to *The Economist*, average tourist spending in 1996 was $559 per capita, a figure expected to increase by 8% annually until the year 2000. This rate of increase is a little higher than it has been in recent years. It cites World Travel and Tourism Council (WTTC) estimates of the value of goods and services attributable to tourism as being $3.6 trillion in 1996, a figure equal to about 10.6% of the world's gross product. WTTC also reckons that tourism supports more than 1 in 10 of all paid jobs, provides employment for 225 million people, and could well provide another 130 million jobs by 2006 (*The Economist*, 1998). A key aim of the WTTC is to lobby on behalf of the industry and persuade governments to provide financial and infrastructural support for tourism.

Canada introduced a tourism satellite account in 1994, and the government's spending on tourism has increased significantly since then, totaling $130 million in 1996. Over the same period revenues from tourism increased by about 25%, to just over $12 billion. A tourism satellite account has recently been developed by the WTO. This should provide a more realistic measure of tourism's economic significance and, as the following vignette suggests, help the industry secure more backing from governments and financial institutions.

❋   ✦   ✳   ❊   ❋

The Tourism Satellite Account

The World Tourism Organization's new approach to measuring the economic impact of tourism won wide support by more than 650 delegates attending an international conference in Nice, France, from 15–18 June. The World Conference on the Measurement of the Economic Impact on Tourism, organized by WTO, attracted representatives of 120 countries, including some 25 ministers of tourism or economy and 12 international finance agencies. Its aim was to attain international backing for a Tourism Satellite Account that measures the industry's true contribution to national economies and to the global economy. "With the satellite account and its results, we anticipate that tourism will at last be taken seriously in every country that develops such a system, as well as by the international community," said WTO Secretary-General Francesco Frangialli. "We expect that tourism will—finally!—receive from governments and financial institutions the respect and consideration that its leverage in national economies justifies."

The Tourism Satellite Account sets a series of global standards and definitions for evaluating the tourism industry in terms of its contribution to GDP; jobs; capital investment; tax revenues; and the role of tourism in a nation's balance of payments. In compliance with United Nations recommendations, it runs alongside national accounts and provides internationally comparable data developed by a country's own statistical institutions that puts tourism for the first time on an equal footing with other economic sectors. "Tourism Satellite Accounts are not just an instrument of statistical comparison or economic analysis, but also a tool for policymaking and this is where its true value lies," said World Travel and Tourism Council President Geoffrey Lipman, who endorsed the approach presented in Nice.

According to the World Tourism Organization, 635 million people traveled to a foreign country in 1998, spending US$439 billion. International tourism receipts combined with passenger transport currently total more than US$504 billion—making tourism the world's number one export earner, ahead of automotive products, chemicals, petroleum, and food. But international data does not begin to explain the full impact of the tourism industry. The Tourism Satellite Account will for the first time begin to measure domestic tourism and employment in the tourism industry.

Several countries presented their work on developing Tourism Satellite Accounts at the conference. Canada was one of the first nations to develop the system and a great deal of the international Tourism Satellite Account is based on Canada's groundbreaking work. It determined that in 1998 tourism accounted for 4.1% of Canadian GDP and was responsible for 518,000 jobs. "Before the TSA, we relied on passion and persuasion to get a reasonable hearing and to disguise the fact that our numbers were soft. But now we have the ability to make a hard economic case for tourism with credible numbers," said Tourism Industry Association of Canada President Debra Ward. France, the world's number one destination, also carried out early studies on the impact of tourism on the national economy. It determined that tourism accounts for about 7.3% of the country's GDP and nearly 600,000 direct jobs. "Tourism is an activity that cuts across numerous areas of the economy, such as transport, construction, and public works, as well as culture, leisure, and most sectors of consumption," explained French Secretary of State for Tourism Michelle Demessine. "Its complexity makes it difficult to appreciate the true impact on the economy and difficult to obtain the means needed to fully exploit its positive effects." Other countries that have already produced a Tourism Satellite Account or are in the process of doing so include Norway, Sweden, Spain, Switzerland, the Dominican Republic, the United States, Mexico, and Chile.

WTO News Service, June 1999. Reprinted with permission of the World Tourism Organization.

☀   ⌗   ✳   ✦   ☀

Tourism as Export Industry

Mathieson and Wall (1982) suggest that tourism has a number of features that make it different from more conventional industries:

1. It is an invisible export industry, with no tangible product being moved from one place to another.
2. The consumer collects the service personally from the place where it is shipped.
3. The exporting destination incurs no freight costs outside its borders, except where the transportation used by tourists is owned by the destination area.
4. Ancillary goods and services are required (for example, transportation facilities, water supplies, sewerage systems).
5. The tourism product is fragmented (for example, hotels, shops, restaurants, recreational facilities, souvenirs) and is thus linked with many other sectors of the local economy.
6. Tourism is a highly unstable export, the demand for which is subject to a variety of external and internal forces.

However, while these are all important characteristics of tourism, they are not all peculiar to tourism: for example, international banking and insurance services are also intangible exports; ancillary services will be required for many other industries besides tourism; and the demand for tangible commodities, such as sugar or cocoa, may also be subject to a variety of external and internal forces.

Tourism's Economic Benefits

Research studies suggest there are five main kinds of economic benefits that are expected to result from tourism: increased foreign exchange earnings; creation of new employment opportunities; multiplier effect of tourism expenditure on other sectors of the economy; generation of government revenues; and promotion of regional development (Mathieson and Wall, 1982; English, 1986; Pearce, 1989). Domestic tourism cannot secure the first of these benefits, although it can be a way of conserving foreign exchange. The other benefits may accrue from both domestic and international tourism. Let us look briefly at each one of these.

Foreign Exchange Earnings

Here it is important to remember that the most desirable forms of foreign exchange are *hard* currencies like the Swiss franc, the U.S. dollar, the German mark, or the British pound. These currencies are freely available and can be exchanged without restrictions. *Soft* currencies like the Ghanaian cedi or the Gambian dalasi are not freely available and are subject to severe exchange restrictions outside their countries of origin. Hard currencies are generally those of the most highly developed countries and the most widely used in international trade (Mathieson and Wall, 1982).

Foreign exchange represents an especially important kind of earnings for developing countries, one that enables them to purchase overseas goods and services necessary to promote economic development. As we saw in chapter 2, it is the larger countries with big tourism industries that generally secure the lion's share of foreign exchange revenues. So, while countries like the United States, France, Spain, and Italy each earned more than $25 billion from foreign tourists in 1998, all African countries combined earned only $9.5 billion, and all Middle East countries earned $9.1 billion. However, in most developing countries, these tourism revenues account for a much larger share of total export earnings than they do in highly developed countries.

Employment Creation

Tourism is widely regarded as a labor-intensive industry, especially in developing countries. But even in a country like Britain, the capital-per-worker ratio for the tourism sector may be only half that for the economy as a whole (British Tourism Authority, 1982). An important implication of this is that tourism can be a particularly important source of employment generation in poorer countries with high rates of unemployment and underemployment. The fact that many jobs in the tourism industry are relatively unskilled is another important factor here. Tourism-generated employment can take three main forms:

- *Direct*—In businesses selling goods and services directly to tourists, for example, hotels, restaurants, shops, transportation.
- *Indirect*—Stimulated by tourist spending in activities supplying goods and services to tourists, for example, manufacturing, wholesale distribution.
- *Investment-Related*—In construction and capital goods industries (Mathieson and Wall, 1982).

I have already noted the various trades that are thought to comprise the tourism industry, but what kinds of occupations and careers are involved in its operation? Given the breadth and heterogeneity of the industry, it is hardly surprising to find a correspondingly broad and diverse range of tourism jobs. Gee et al. (1989) list some 188 different occupations, ranging from flight attendant and tour escort to restaurant cashier and cruise ship refrigeration engineer; and no fewer than 50 for air transportation alone, including some less obvious ones like upholstery mechanic, plumber, and food service porter. As an information-intensive industry, tourism has made extensive use of advances in information technology (Sheldon, 1997). Information technology applications in tourism include computerized reservation and global distribution systems, computerized airline operations, and flight information display systems. These kinds of applications have helped create new job opportunities in tourism for people trained in computer programming and related fields.

The Multiplier Effect

The multiplier effect refers to the stimulating effects of tourism spending on other sectors of the economy. As Pearce (1989) explains, this involves a relationship between three kinds of expenditures:

- *Direct*—Tourist spending on goods and services; tourism-related investment (so long as both spending and investment initially remain in the destination area).
- *Indirect*—Local responding in successive rounds of business transactions. Leakages occur in each round until there is little or no responding possible.
- *Induced*—Further consumer spending generated by additional personal income.

As with foreign exchange earnings, estimates of the size of the multiplier effect done in the 1960s were somewhat optimistic, but are perhaps more realistic today. The multiplier effect is still a contentious issue among tourism economists and is exacerbated by the fact that different types of multipliers are calculated (for example, income, output, sales, employment multipliers) and no single methodology for calculating them has been universally adopted. Income multipliers are probably the most widely used, and a simple way of calculating them has been described by Pearce as follows:

$$K = A \times \frac{1}{1 - B\,C}$$

K = Income multiplier.
A = % tourist spending remaining in region following first round leakages.
B = % income of local residents spent on local goods and services.
C = % expenditures of local residents accruing as local income (1989 p. 207–208).

Therefore, if A were 50%, B 70% and C 40%, the income multiplier would be:

$$K = 0.5 \times \frac{1}{1 - 0.7 \times 0.4} = 0.69$$

Obviously, the size of the tourism income multiplier is greatly affected by the size and complexity of the destination area's economy. Archer (1982) estimated Hong Kong's tourism income multiplier to be 1.02, while that of the British Virgin Islands was only 0.58. Two final points are perhaps worth noting: there will be internal variations of the multiplier effect between different components of the tourism industry, for example, between accommodations and transportation; and there is no reliable evidence that the tourism income multiplier is consistently greater than those of other economic sectors.

State Revenues

In many developing countries, direct taxation cannot be a major source of government revenues. Levying taxes may be difficult because the labor force is too small, or because the majority of people are engaged in agriculture at or near subsistence levels. This low-level employment base is too small to generate substantial revenues through direct taxation of incomes. In some countries, tourism can be a major contributor to government revenues, through taxes on goods and services. For example, in Bermuda and the Bahamas the governments do not directly tax personal or company incomes.

Tourism contributes to state revenues in the following ways:

- *Taxes*—Corporate, sales, income, and property taxes.
- *Overseas Earnings*—spending by international visitors, fees from foreign airlines, and so on.
- *Reduced Social Charges*—Reductions in such things as unemployment benefits payable.
- *Industry Profits*—From hotels and other tourism enterprises owned or partly owned by the state (Pearce, 1989).

Again, we find wide variations between countries in the extent to which tourism contributes to state revenues. In countries such as Australia and the United States it is likely that less than 5% of state revenues will come from tourism, while in places like Bermuda and the Bahamas tourism probably generates over 60% of state revenues (World Tourism Organization, 1983).

Regional Development

Many countries have regions or districts where the range of alternative economic development possibilities is extremely limited. Examples include the Scottish Highlands, the Australian Gold Coast, the Borabur temple complex in Java, the Swiss

Alps, and many coastal areas throughout the world. In such areas, the promotion of tourism can be an ingredient in policies aimed at correcting regional imbalances. The results of such efforts have been mixed. Fairly positive illustrations come from the coastal tourism projects in Languedoc-Rousillon (France), the Scottish Highlands and, until recently, in Croatia. The development of Alpine tourism in Europe appears to have brought about a per capita increase in revenue, but it has not triggered a general process of economic and cultural development. In India, attempts to reduce regional disparities through tourism have met with little success; the four main metropolitan centers still attract more tourists, who also spend more and stay longer (Pearce, 1989). In Hawaii, the spread of tourism beyond Waikiki, on the island of Oahu, to the neighbor islands of Maui, Kauai, Lanai, and Hawaii (the Big Island) has met with considerable success. But in Maui, as we shall see in chapter 9, vocal and organized opposition to continued tourism development has been heard, albeit from a minority of the island's residents.

Economic Costs and Drawbacks

While the previously mentioned economic benefits are all possible from tourism development, they represent only one side of the ledger, and have to be balanced against a number of economic costs and obstacles. The most important of these are import costs, opportunity costs, occupational hazards, and inflationary pressures. I shall look briefly at each one of these debits.

Import Content

In estimating the importance of tourism as a means whereby countries—especially less developed ones—can earn valuable foreign exchange, it is not enough simply to calculate the spending of foreign tourists. We also have to take into account foreign exchange leakages, or the "import content" of a country's tourism. In this way we can get closer to an estimate of how much of the tourist revenues actually accrues to the tourism destination. If we subtract the import content from tourist revenues, we discover what the net foreign exchange earnings of a country are. The main leakages or components of tourism's import content are now well-recognized, unlike the situation in the 1960s, when they tended to be ignored or underestimated. They are:

- *Costs of imported goods and services consumed by tourists.*
- *Foreign exchange costs of capital investments in the tourism industry.*
- *Payments abroad.* For example, capital remittances and profits by foreign tourism companies; wage remittances by expatriate workers; interest payments on payments on foreign loans; fees for franchises (for example, hotels), management services, foreign travel agents, and tour operators.
- *Overseas promotion and advertising.*

- *Costs of training tourism personnel overseas.*
- *Expenditures on additional imports sought by local residents.* These might include expenditures by those whose earnings have come from jobs in the tourism industry, or people whose tastes as consumers have been influenced by tourism's demonstration effect (International Union of Official Travel Agents, 1975; Pearce, 1989).

Tourism's import content can vary considerably from one country to another. Generally speaking, it will be higher in small developing countries—especially small island states—whose economies lack most of the resources necessary to service and maintain the industry.

It should be noted that industries other than tourism can involve foreign exchange leakages as high as, or higher than, those listed in Table 4.1 (Pearce, 1989). However, for governments of some developing countries, the magnitude of tourism industry leakages came as a nasty shock and generated disillusionment and pessimism about tourism's place in economic development. More recently tourism has fallen back into favor in such countries, who now take a less sanguine and more realistic view of its potential benefits and costs.

Opportunity Costs

These are the costs of using scarce resources for tourism that might possibly be used more productively in other sectors. Factoring in these costs leads to an estimate of the "net social gain" from tourism, that is, income earned above (or below) what would have been generated by the same resources in their next best alternative employment (English, 1986). This gain or loss is extremely difficult to calculate in a precise way, since the exercise typically involves estimating the potential earnings of resources were they to be used for purposes other than tourism. In developing countries tourism development will often require extensive involvement of public administrative and technical personnel, which may come at the expense of other important sectors of the economy, such as agriculture (Bryden, 1973; English, 1986). Where there are few viable alternative economic uses for existing resources, such as beaches, mountains, or historical sites, a poor performance by a tourism industry based on such resources might still be better than could be registered by some other economic activity involving these same resources.

Occupational Hazards

While there is little doubt that tourism has been a major generator of employment worldwide, questions have been raised about income levels, seasonality, and related issues. As with other aspects of tourism's impacts, survey results are highly variable. In Britain, Australia, Germany, and the former Yugoslavia, wages in the tourism industry are significantly lower than those in most other employment sectors, while

---

Table 4.1 Tourism's Import Content for Selected Countries

Country	Import Content
Bahamas	72.0%
Antigua	60.0%
Aruba	58.0%
Fiji	56.0%
Nepal	47.0%
Indonesia	44.0%
Hong Kong	41.0%
Sri Lanka	26.0%
Morocco	19.0%
New Zealand	12.0%

SOURCE: English, 1986; Pearce, 1989.

---

the opposite appears to be the case in Greece and Sri Lanka (Pearce, 1989). And one of the most striking cases is the Indonesian island of Bali, where tourism has generated the highest income-per-capita levels of all 27 provinces in the country (Holden, 1984; Pearce, 1989). Seasonality is a feature of tourism employment in most tourist-receiving countries, but seems to be especially pronounced in winter-sun destinations. In The Gambia, for example, seasonal workers account for nearly 70% of all hotel employees, while the corresponding figure for Barbados is about 40%.

Other aspects of tourism employment are subject to more qualitative assessments. Some observers have stressed the "menial" character of many tourism jobs (such as waiter or waitress, hotel maid, or porter) and the degrading qualities of some tourism-related occupations (such as prostitute, pimp, hustler, or black marketeer) compared with more "noble" economic activities like farming and fishing. These contrasts rest essentially on moral distinctions which often seem to involve the *white knight* syndrome—an attitudinal complex that, while well-meaning, may ignore the preferences and feelings of those who are to be rescued (English, 1986). It is surely not stretching credulity too far to imagine that some Mexican waiters, for example, might actually prefer tooling around a comfortable, air-conditioned hotel bearing food and drinks, to toiling away in the fields under a broiling sun. Insofar as many tourism jobs require their occupants to "perform" on tourism stages (and not simply to deliver the goods), they often seem to demand behavior of a kind not usually associated with other kinds of employment. The performative character of tourism employment is discussed by Crang (1997). Tourism employment is also usually characterized by relatively low levels of unionization, a high degree of functional flexibility demanded of workers, and a disproportionate number of females in lower level jobs.

I noted earlier that information technology applications have created new job opportunities in tourism. But these same applications, together with an increased use of information technology by prospective tourists, is threatening one of tourism's traditional occupations, the travel agent. Major airlines have begun reducing the commissions they pay agents, while Internet sales of tickets by companies such as Travelocity and Expedia were valued at $800 million in 1997 and are expected to be worth $8.9 billion by 2002 (*The Economist,* 1998).

Inflation

Tourism development can have an inflationary effect for a number of reasons. Increased demand for goods and services in destinations may, especially in the early stages of their development, outstrip supply and push prices upwards. Normal seasonal shifts in the price of food may become more extreme as a result of pressures from tourist demand. Hotels and restaurants catering to tourists are often more willing and able to pay higher prices for food and other necessities than are local residents. The price of land and accommodation can also increase sharply as developers cater to the demand for holiday accommodation and houses for workers in the industry. The issue of "affordable housing" has become a prominent one in Hawaii, especially on the islands of Oahu and Maui, where tourism development has proceeded farthest.

Tourism Development
and the Jafari Thesis

In promoting tourism as a component of national economic development policies, governments and planners in Third World countries have concentrated primarily on international tourism. Jafari (1986) has argued that this emphasis is misplaced in many cases and that the economic benefits often fall far short of expectations. His thesis is that countries which have not yet fully embraced international tourism development should concentrate on creating a sound domestic tourism industry. Ghana, a West African country with a fledgling domestic tourism industry and significant natural and cultural resources for international tourism, provides an ideal test of the Jafari thesis. Here I outline the five interrelated arguments comprising the thesis and consider their possible application to Ghanaian tourism development (Wyllie, 1993, 1994b):

1. *Domestic tourism should have priority, at least initially, over international tourism.* Here the argument is that domestic tourism should be developed and consolidated prior to embarking on the attempt to exploit the foreign market. If a viable domestic industry can be established, a country can gradually and effectively enter the international tourism trade later. The former would constitute a training ground for the latter. Locals can learn the arts of receiving, accommodating, and servicing domestic tourists. The industry would gain the strength, experience, and infrastructure for eventual entry to the international market.

Application to Ghana. This argument has a special appeal through its logic of "one-step-at-a-time" or "walk-before-you-run." As a strategy for tourism development in Ghana, however, two kinds of problems present themselves:

- *The problem of practicality*—Ghana's tourism producers and planners have shown a reluctance to put their plans "on hold" in this way. They have long believed that viable overseas markets exist: for Ghana's beaches as a winter destination for northern Europeans; for the historic forts and castles as a basis for roots tourism for middle-class African Americans; and its game reserves and national parks as attractions for nature lovers and ecotourists.
- *The problem of benefit-transfer*—The assumption that development of a domestic tourism industry will benefit the subsequent development of international tourism is just that—an assumption. Much depends on how good the local industry becomes and how demanding and discriminating Ghanaian domestic tourists become. As yet, facilities and amenities are generally of mediocre quality and domestic tourists do not exert much pressure for improvement. Domestic tourism in Ghana does not appear to provide an adequate preparation for entering the international market. Practices and standards currently prevailing in the industry could not be transferred to international tourism without seriously damaging Ghana's destination image.

2. *Domestic tourism can save foreign exchange and redistribute personal wealth.* This is a two-pronged argument. International tourism is aimed primarily at earning foreign exchange, but domestic tourism can be a way of saving it. The domestic tourism industry can attract a segment of the affluent, local population who would otherwise choose overseas holiday destinations. Since unskilled tourism jobs are mainly filled by people from the lower economic layers, domestic tourist expenditures would involve a direct transfer of wealth from the relatively rich to the relatively poor.

Application to Ghana. Domestic tourism could conserve foreign exchange and redistribute wealth only under certain circumstances. Ghana's domestic tourism products would have to become attractive *alternatives* to those offered by foreign travel. This has not happened. While there are no reliable statistics on domestic tourism in this country, Adu-Febiri (1988) discovered that local leisure travel is quite popular among affluent Ghanaians. However, the kinds of trips taken—mainly weekend visits to coastal centers like Cape Coast or Elmina, to Lake Volta, or to relatives elsewhere in the country—are not really alternatives to overseas travel. They are essentially brief escapes from workaday routines, frequently taken in conjunction with family reunions of various kinds or with the performance of family obligations; and they do not always involve the use of facilities such as hotels, restaurants, or public transportation. Their overseas trips, on the other hand, tend to be of longer duration, involve a greater amount of sightseeing and related tourist activities and often entail visits with family members working or studying abroad. For many, such journeys are also an opportunity to obtain consumer goods which are either more expensive or more difficult to buy at home. Besides, overseas travel still has considerable prestige value for those who can afford it and the Ghanaian who has been abroad is often referred to as "been-to" or "hamburger" in local parlance. It is unlikely that international travel will lose such comparative advantages over domestic travel in the foreseeable future. Thus, it may be some time before domestic tourism could produce the foreign exchange savings and redistribution of personal wealth which Jafari anticipates. And since a major portion of the local industry would be owned by relatively wealthy Ghanaians, the transfer of personal wealth from the rich to the poor may be subject to a good deal of siphoning off.

3. *Domestic tourism can be developed with mainly local resources and man-power and can aid in the spread of national economic development.* Here it is argued that, to a greater extent than is possible for international tourism, domestic tourism can be developed with local resources such as construction materials, local food and drinks, and so on. These are more acceptable to local than to foreign tourists, who usually prefer imported products. Local people can be prepared fairly quickly for employment in the domestic tourism industry and there is less need for expatriate managers—this reduces one form of foreign exchange leakage. Unlike foreign tourists, local tourists will be more willing to visit the less popular centers. And since most would come from the urban areas, their visits would bring a flow of investments and touristic commitments from the metropolitan to the less developed areas.

Application to Ghana. While the general drift of Jafari's argument here is probably correct, its persuasive force is blunted somewhat when we remember that we are talking mainly about domestic tourism for local elites—the only people with sufficient discretionary income to engage in it to any significant degree. The origins of construction materials matters little to affluent Ghanaian tourists, so long as the building itself satisfies expectations of comfort and value for money. And there is no evidence that local products are more acceptable to well-heeled Ghanaians than to overseas visitors. Indeed, a common complaint among foreigners visiting the capital, Accra, is the lack of good African restaurants in that city. Eating out in restaurants is something ordinary Ghanaians cannot afford and, equally importantly, something which seems to them a needless extravagance. For affluent Ghanaians, on the other hand, a visit to a restaurant makes little sense unless it offers a change of fare—Chinese or Indian, usually. As far as affluent Ghanaians visiting less popular local destinations is concerned, there is little evidence of this at present.

4. *Domestic tourism can produce several sociocultural benefits.* Jafari argues that a number of positive sociocultural results may flow from domestic tourism development. Tourists will gain a keener appreciation of their country and develop greater national awareness. Social barriers will be eroded as they associate with people of different regions, ethnic groups, and religions; traditional urban-rural barriers will be lowered. A process of acculturation would be fostered in the exchange of ideas and practices between tourists and hosts. The metropolitan language, which is often the language of national government, will also be further popularized.

Application to Ghana. The various sociocultural benefits Jafari expects from domestic tourism are, in a sense, the microcosmic version of the macrocosmic scenario sometimes projected for international tourism. As such, their realization is subject to many of the same kinds of constraints that beset international touristic situations. As I noted in chapter 3, tourist-host encounters among Ghanaians are far from being problem-free and hotels are in some areas viewed with suspicion. Although not all tourist centers are characterized by negative reactions to Ghanaian visitors, it is nonetheless evident that the local hospitality industry has something of an image problem at present. This constitutes an impediment to the kind of bridge building Jafari anticipates from domestic tourism. Since the majority of domestic tourists come from the more urbanized parts of the country, the acculturative exchange of ideas and practices is bound to be somewhat one-sided. The demonstration effect operates in domestic tourism contexts as well as international ones. The promotion of a Ghanaian national culture through domestic tourism can be an exercise in metropolitan domination. It can also lead to a diminution of that cultural variety and heterogeneity—including linguistic—which is one of Ghana's most attractive features and is probably an important ingredient in the country's appeal for foreign visitors.

5. *Domestic tourism can provide a basis for the enjoyment of leisure by the majority of citizens.* Here Jafari suggests that, as the general state of the economy of the country improves, more leisure time and paid holidays become possible for the majority of residents. If domestic tourism is properly promoted and developed, it will be in place when needed by the mass of the population as their opportunities for leisure and recreation increase.

Application to Ghana. Although Jafari is not explicit on this point, it is implied throughout that tourism for the relatively poor and underprivileged (often referred to as *social tourism*) should come after tourism for the relatively affluent. In Ghana, it would make more sense to have both forms—elite and social—develop simultaneously rather than sequentially. There are various reasons why low-cost, subsidized tourism for ordinary Ghanaians should be taken just as seriously as elite tourism: improvements in general levels of health and well-being; the tonic effect of a holiday away from home,

especially upon morale in the workplace; and a reduction in the risk of resentment and frustration inherent in a program of domestic tourism development mainly for the rich.

It would appear, therefore, that it could be a serious mistake for Ghana to recoil
from the problems involved in developing international tourism and to concentrate
exclusively or heavily on domestic tourism instead. Both forms of tourism present
special opportunities as well as difficulties and might best be developed in tandem.
On balance, it may be that a greater emphasis on the development of a viable international tourism industry would be the better course of action, one which could
also aid in the expansion and improvement of the country's domestic tourism facilities. As we shall see in chapter 7, this seems to be the direction Ghana's tourism
development has begun to take.

Conclusion

Arguments over whether tourism is an industry or simply a collection of businesses
hinge primarily on questions concerning the nature of the products and the degree
to which the various tourism sectors are operationally interconnected. Critics of
the tourism-as-industry position usually stress tremendous product heterogeneity
and weak integration of supposed tourism businesses to support their views. Those
who do believe tourism can legitimately be called an *industry* typically point to
extensive product complementarity, the functional interdependence of tourism businesses, and the rise of national, regional, and international organizations representing the collective interests of many tourism businesses and agencies. While we
chose to sidestep this issue and to use the term *tourism industry* as convenient
shorthand, we nevertheless recognize the social and political dimensions of the debate. For many persons centrally or directly involved in tourism-related businesses
or organizations, the debate has less to do with semantics than with establishing
legitimacy, with being taken seriously, with gaining public recognition and esteem,
and with strengthening claims for government support.

My principal aims in this chapter have been to reveal something of the complexity and dynamism of tourism from a supply-side perspective, and to provide a
summary assessment of some of tourism's main economic benefits and costs. It was
seen to be a rapidly growing, multifaceted enterprise, embracing many trades and
hundreds of different occupations. It has attracted new and important players in an
enterprise that, despite numerous periodic setbacks, appears to be headed on a course
of continued growth.

However, while tourism can be a useful means of earning foreign exchange,
creating jobs, promoting economic diversification, or of strengthening economies
threatened by decline of traditional industries, dependence on tourism as an economic mainstay can be extremely risky. Demand for tourism, though rising globally, is highly variable between different destinations and can be adversely affected

by a variety of factors. Political events such as attempted military coups in developing countries can have an immediately negative effect on demand. The possibility of terrorist attacks on airports during the Gulf War in 1991 is believed to have been primarily responsible for the sharp reduction in the number of Japanese visitors to Hawaii at that time. Murders of foreign tourists in Florida have led to a determined campaign by that state's tourism authorities to convince people that it is still a safe place to visit. Demand can also be affected by changes in currency exchange rates, by reduced opportunities for discretionary spending in major tourist-generating countries, or by changing fashions in tourist tastes. While the global prospects for tourism look good, this can be small consolation for countries or regions having to face problems of the kind just mentioned.

Chapter 5
Culture by the Pound?

Cultural Commoditization

As noted in chapter 1, most of the earlier anthropological studies of tourism in small-scale communities were highly critical of tourism's effects. Investigators saw tourism as leading to cultural commoditization (or commodification), a process in which cultural forms and practices are given a monetary value and sold as commodities in the tourist market. In tourism, as elsewhere, the selling can take different forms, ranging from outright sales of items such as carvings or jewelry, to selling rights to view cultural centers or activities, such as religious shrines or dance performances. Why would this be a cause for concern among anthropologists and others worried about cultural commoditization? After all, it is extremely unlikely that the particular carvings or pieces of jewelry will be priceless, irreplaceable national treasures. So where's the harm in selling these easily reproducible things to tourists? And if the religious shrine or dance performance still remains after the tourists have had a look, who loses? Isn't this just another version of the same old story—paternalistic anthropologists trying to protect "their" people from the present and freeze them in some ethnographic past, or about their annoyance at having to share cultural access with "ignorant" tourists? The answer will depend on what you make of the first half of this chapter, as well as on your own value position on the issues involved.

A brief statement of the case against cultural commoditization in tourism might be useful at this point. Simply put, it can be argued that when culture is commoditized it loses its authenticity and much of its former meaning for people. For producers, the production of masks and jewelry for tourists does not have the same meaning as the production of such items within the traditional cultural fabric. Torn from this fabric, they are produced in volume only for money, so that their quality deteriorates, and there is a decline in the number of highly skilled producers remaining outside the tourist market. Likewise, performing for tourist outsiders is very different from performing for oneself. Not only do the tourists have little understanding of the cultural meaning of the performance, but the touristic situation is often governed by time constraints and schedules into which only a highly condensed version of the performance can fit. The result will be a simplified, truncated, and choreographed affair offering *staged authenticity*—that is, an inauthentic performance presented to tourists as if it were authentic. As these hollow fabrications become an important source of income for people in tourist destinations, they come to replace the cultural realities they so inadequately represent.

Commoditizing Cultural Performances

Northern Spain

One of the sharpest anthropological critiques of tourism as cultural commoditization was that made by Greenwood in his famous essay, "Culture by the Pound" (1989). Greenwood expressed what many anthropologists felt about tourism at that time, and his paper is an archetype of the anthropological attack on tourism in the 1970s. While his focus was on one public festival in a particular community, he believed that the situation he described was fairly typical of the undesirable effects of tourism on local cultures. As an oft-cited study in discussions of cultural commoditization in tourism, "Culture by the Pound" is worth looking at fairly closely.

Greenwood describes the Alarde, a major public festival held annually in Fuenterrabia, a Basque town in northern Spain. It commemorates and re-creates events of 1638, when the town successfully withstood a siege by the French. All sections and classes of the community had stood together during the siege, and the Alarde recaptures and reaffirms this unity by involving residents of the old walled city, the six town wards, members of all occupational groups, men and women, young and old. Following mass in the early morning, contingents representing various sections of the community assemble outside the old citadel and parade through the streets to the strains of martial music and the cheers of onlookers. They are followed by the mayor and local councilmen on horseback, who then take their places on the town hall's balcony to review the parade. Armed groups from each ward fire a salvo in unison, and the entire procession congregates in the plaza, where another salvo is fired in unison. Then all the guns are fired until the ammunition has been exhausted, and the people disperse to rejoin their families and stroll down to the fishermen's ward for food and drink. Greenwood emphasizes that the Alarde enacts the sacred history of Fuenterrabia and is not performed for the benefit of outsiders. It is, he insists, a performance for the participants and not a "show."

The Alarde takes place at the height of the tourist season, and the town is popular with visitors who come to see the old fortifications, watch the boat races, and savor various other local attractions. The Alarde is by no means the main attraction, but it has been publicized in tourism promotional literature as part of the local color to attract tourists. However, Greenwood suggested that tourism had begun to threaten the Alarde at the time of his field research in Fuenterrabia in 1969. In that year the Ministry of Tourism and Public Information completed remodeling of the fortress of Charles V in the plaza, converting it into a tourist parador (a hotel-restaurant-bar combination, usually moderately priced). The facility was opened by the Spanish dictator, Francisco Franco, and received national publicity in newspapers and on television. The municipal authorities wanted to capitalize on this publicity by having the Alarde enacted twice in one day, since the narrow streets could not accommodate the large numbers of spectators who wanted to see it. This kind of thinking involved a redefinition of the Alarde as a public show for outsiders, who were entitled to see it because of their economic importance as visitors. Although the wishes of the municipal authorities were not realized, Greenwood tells us that their intentions caused considerable disillusionment and cynicism among the townspeople. When Greenwood returned to Fuenterrabia in 1971, he believed that interest in participating in the Alarde had waned to the point where municipal authorities were considering paying people to take part, that the meaning of the ritual had gone and had been transformed into a performance for money.

Given its importance in the debate on cultural commoditization in tourism, it is surprising that Greenwood's essay has been treated so gently by critics. His methodology is unclear, we do not know who his informants were or how his interpretations were arrived at, and a good deal of what he tells us has to be taken on trust. No evidence is offered to support his view that the presence of outsiders was unwelcome and that participating in the Alarde became an obligation to be avoided. If the townspeople did, in fact, become less interested in participating in the event, how can we be sure that this was due to the (unrealized) wish of municipal leaders to make the event a public show for outsiders? What is the source of the information that local authorities were contemplating paying the townspeople to perform, and how seriously was this considered? And since this too seems to have been an idea that was not implemented, what grounds are there for concluding that the Alarde had actually become "a performance for money" and that its meaning for Fuenterrabians had gone?

Greenwood's essay, which first appeared in 1977, was subsequently reproduced in its original form, together with an "Epilogue" in which he reflected upon his earlier interpretation of the Alarde (1989). He maintained that the anthropological critique of tourism as cultural commoditization remained generally valid, but acknowledged its ideological dimensions. He acknowledged that all cultures change and may be understood differently by different members of society; that it was a matter of "external judgment" when anthropologists claimed to have identified a culture's true or authentic forms; and that tourism need not always be destructive, but could sometimes transform and stimulate a culture (1989).

Bali

In Bali (Indonesia) customary rituals and dance performances have been commoditized and presented for tourist consumption, sometimes in abbreviated, choreographed forms. McKean (1976) suggested that these performances have three different audiences—the gods, the villagers, and the tourists—and that the presence of the latter has not spoiled the performances for the performers or the other two audiences. The tourist audience is valued for the economic benefits it brings, and these increase the possibility that such cultural practices will be conserved. McKean (1989) also used the term *cultural involution* to describe the process whereby Balinese, in order to secure the funds necessary for modernization, have been encouraged by economic necessity and conservatism to retain their traditional skills as musicians, dancers, carvers, and so on. More recently, however, another researcher has suggested that McKean's conclusions were too optimistic, that tourism has neither revived Balinese culture nor degraded it, and that its main contribution has been to make the Balinese realize, for the first time, that they possess something valuable called *culture* (Picard, 1995).

Southern Ghana

In performing for tourists, Balinese have used their rituals as forms of self-representation before interested outsiders, something the Basques of Fuenterrabia were apparently not very interested in. A powerful interest in self-representation is very much in evidence in the Aboakyer or deer-hunting festival in Winneba, a fishing community in southern Ghana (Wyllie, 1968, 1994a). Here the picture is strikingly different from that observed by Greenwood in Fuenterrabia. The Aboakyer is a weekend event held annually to commemorate the founding of Winneba some three centuries ago. Formerly an affair of purely local interest, it has become a mass spectacle attracting approximately 25,000 to 30,000 visitors, and it is publicized by the Ghana Tourist Board. It involves an exciting deer-hunting contest between Tuafo and Dentsifo, the town's two Asafo companies (former military regiments), to which nearly all residents now belong. The contest takes place on the outskirts of the town, with each company working its own designated section of the hunting ground. The deer has to be captured alive and uninjured for sacrifice to the local deities. The ritual core has remained virtually unchanged for as long as anyone can remember, but around it has developed a superstructure of festivities, and it is shown on national television as well as reported in the national press.

The growth of the festival as a visitor attraction has not dampened local enthusiasm for the event. The vast majority of Winneba's residents eagerly look forward to it and revel in the spotlight cast on their town during festival weekend. They acknowledge that the temporary invasion of their community brings with it some problems, such as public drunkenness, altercations and fights in bars, and the depredations of street pickpockets. These are all attributed mainly to youth gang members from Accra and are regarded as only minor inconveniences. Most visitors are well-behaved and seem to enjoy their stay in Winneba, although their presence at the end of the dry season sorely taxes the town's water supply. Here again, however, the problem is viewed as a passing one, and there are some residents who believe that the increasing popularity of the Aboakyer may eventually compel the government to improve the water supply and other local amenities. Such a view is held not only by members of the festival's organizing committee, but also by traditional priests and Asafo company leaders.

Whether or not such long-term benefits materialize, most residents regard the festival as an important cultural resource that generates economic benefits. They know that some of the visiting dignitaries—especially foreign diplomats—make parting gifts to the community. While these are usually in the form of medical or educational supplies, sometimes direct financial assistance is given for local community projects. Similar considerations underlie local support for increasing the numbers of foreign visitors to the festival, for residents think foreigners are more interested in its cultural aspects and more likely to interest themselves in local problems. Winneba's merchants, bar owners, food sellers and other street vendors clearly recognize the short-term economic benefits of the festival and support it wholeheartedly, offering prizes to the victorious company. The town's three small hotels and one beach resort complex are fully booked weeks in advance of the festival, whereas their normal occupancy rates seldom exceed 40%; from this quarter too, the Aboakyer receives unqualified support.

The positive attitude towards Aboakyer visitors is only partly based on local understandings and expectations of economic benefits. In interviews with traditional priests, Asafo leaders, festival committee members, local merchants, market women, street vendors, and other residents, two themes were prominent. One was that the Aboakyer was a centuries-old tradition that had survived and could continue without the presence of large numbers of visitors, but that visitors made it more enjoyable. "They make it more interesting, more exciting" (Dentsifo leader); "If visitors don't come it will not affect the success of the festival, only that it will not be interesting enough" (priestess); "Even without visitors we know that we are celebrating the Aboakyer to pacify our gods as our ritual duty; the visitors don't help in that respect, but they help make the occasion more interesting and enjoyable" (priest). The other theme was that the festival's attraction for visitors helped maintain and enhance Winneba's reputation in Ghana and abroad: "It is proper that they (visitors) come in their good numbers, for they will sell the good reputation of Winneba when they go home" (Tuafo leader); "The visitors enrich the festival by making it known outside Ghana" (priestess); "Foreigners take pictures and videos of the festival and raise its image in other countries" (female teacher/petty trader); "The participation of whites in the Aboakyer means that we will be known everywhere" (female fishmonger).

The case of the Aboakyer appears to support Cohen's conclusions that commoditization does not necessarily destroy the meanings of cultural products, that old meanings may remain salient for an internal public, and that tourist-oriented products may serve as vehicles of self-representation before external publics. It seems unlikely that the Aboakyer will in the near future encounter the kinds of problems associated with the Alarde of Fuenterrabia. In Winneba, authorities are prepared to risk inconveniencing and disappointing visitors by terminating and rescheduling the Aboakyer when the hunt fails to result in the capture of a deer, a course of action which has been taken on a number of occasions. A "staged" hunt prepared and orchestrated for such an emergency is out of the question, since this would violate the understandings between gods and locals that still underpin the Aboakyer's ritual core. As with the Balinese ritual performances discussed by McKean, the Aboakyer has three different audiences—the divine, the local, and the touristic—and the expectations and understandings of the latter do not invariably take precedence over those of the first two.

Ghana plans to promote international tourism as a major source of foreign exchange earnings, and it is difficult to predict the likely effects of tourism growth on the Aboakyer. The present timing of the festival in early May places it in what would probably be the beginning of the low season for most European visitors. This might mean that the Aboakyer would not be significantly affected by an increase in the numbers of international visitors. However, there could conceivably be some pressure to move it forward to February or March, and thus present an interesting test of people's commitment to satisfying the divine audience. Even if international tourism growth does not make a major impact, no doubt new ways will be found to exploit the economic value of the Aboakyer. It may be that the possibility of charging a visitor fee, discussed and eventually rejected by the festival organizing committee in 1990, will again be considered, for its rejection was not based on distaste for cultural commoditization, but on the grounds that it would be extremely difficult to collect and might discourage many visitors from attending.

Residents themselves express confidence in the future of the festival and do not consider an increase in visitors to be a serious threat. Of greater concern in this respect is the spread of farming in the hunting ground. It has resulted in the gradual elimination of the trees and thickets providing natural cover and protection for the deer. This issue has been raised with the central government, and the Department of Game and Wildlife is considering the feasibility of designating the area as a regional park. Some uncertainty has also been caused by a claim by the neighboring Gomoa tribe on a section of the hunting ground. Even if this claim is successful, it is unlikely to create a situation that would place the Aboakyer in jeopardy. Had the festival remained a small, exclusively local affair, instead of becoming a major tourist attraction, these kinds of problems might well have signaled its demise.

Commoditizing Arts and Crafts

Mathieson and Wall (1982) provide a concise summary of anthropological views on how traditional art forms have changed as a result of outside contact, especially contact with tourists. The authors identify three main phases of change:

1. The disappearance of traditional artistic designs and art and craft forms, particularly those with deep religious and mythical affiliations.
2. The growth of a degenerate, unsophisticated replacement, which develops in association with mass production techniques.
3. The resurgence of skilled craftsmanship and distinctive styles of incorporating the deeper cultural beliefs of the host society. This phase is a response to

the deleterious consequences evident in phase 2 and also to the gradual decline in the symbolic meaning of traditional arts which also occurs in the second phase.

The American anthropologist Nelson Graburn (1984) has examined the effects of tourism on indigenous art, noting a movement away from the production of "functional traditional art" to the production of souvenirs and novelties for the tourist market. The former was rooted in the religion and culture of the producers, and its production was therefore satisfying for the artist. Tourist art, however, is said to be divorced from traditional cultures and its production is therefore less satisfying. As tourist market pressures come to dominate art production, traditional art forms become "museumified" or separated from the lived culture, and those who produce traditional art are themselves marginalized. A somewhat different view is taken by Jules-Rosette (1984) in her study of tourist art in Africa. She noted that the producers of such art responded to market pressures by standardizing and simplifying many of their works, but they also developed new designs and new combinations of different artistic styles.

Tourism has generated pseudo-traditional arts, mainly stylized, poorly executed work produced in volume to suit tourist tastes. These are what are commonly referred to as "airport art." But it has also stimulated work of exceptional quality, not only in the Third World and the Fourth World (for example, Inuit and Haida carvings), but also in mass tourism destinations like Hawaii, where there is a close relationship between marine art and the environmentalist movement, as we see in the paintings by Casay, Lassen, Nelson, Wyland, and others. The study of tourist arts is still a fairly undeveloped area of research, but a special issue of *Annals* (20, 1993) is devoted exclusively to this subject.

In her important and timely article, Valda Blundell (1993) examined the issue of cultural appropriation as it relates to the production of "native-type" souvenirs, such as replicas of totem poles, feather headdresses, Inuit hunters, and so on, for visitors to Canada. Canadian aboriginal peoples derive few economic benefits from the souvenir trade, for while some inexpensive items of this kind are sold to tourists by aboriginal producers, most are mass produced by nonaboriginals from Canada and other countries. When these are sold in retail outlets, they are not usually presented as symbols of Canadian aboriginal cultures, but rather as something distinctively Canadian and as reminders of the tourist's visit to Canada. As such, they form part of Canada's "borrowed identity," and lose their uniqueness as symbols of particular aboriginal groups. In many cases the tags or labels on these souvenirs are designed to create the impression of authenticity. Apart from the question of misleading advertising, these practices also raise the issue of the right of nonaboriginals to use the material image base (the cultural motifs, aesthetic styles, and so on) of aboriginal peoples, and to employ stereotypes in misrepresenting the reality of aboriginal culture as it is lived today.

Blundell's article is interesting and well-argued, but the issues she raises are far from simple. One might argue that most contemporary cultures include elements that have been borrowed or stolen from others. These include words from other languages, songs from other musical traditions, forms of government from other political systems, sports from other sporting traditions, and many more. Cultures are dynamic rather than static, and an important source of cultural change is the interaction between cultures. Contemporary aboriginal culture also borrows from outside: the famous "Indian" sweaters produced by the Cowichan band on Vancouver Island are the result of a combination of traditional aboriginal motifs or designs and Western Scottish knitting techniques; and the touristic offerings of several Canadian aboriginal peoples now include rodeos, trail rides, and casinos, none of which is particularly "aboriginal" (Amoakohene, 1997). Stereotypical misrepresentation of other peoples is also widespread, and there are few ethnic or national groups whose cultures or cultural traits have not been distorted by others. The key issues, it seems, are economic and power relations—historical and contemporary—between those who do the appropriating and those whose cultures are being appropriated, between those who misrepresent and those who are misrepresented. If these economic and power relations are fairly balanced, then cultural borrowing, stealing, and misrepresentation can go on without causing a great deal of concern. If they are not—as in the situation described by Blundell—cultural appropriation and stereotypical misrepresentation are likely to be regarded as expressions of a longstanding and continuing pattern of exploitation.

Commoditizing the Past

The Heritage Industry

A major focus of recent research has been on a process referred to as the "commoditization of the past," which has given rise to a "heritage industry" that sells tradition and history in a tourist-driven market (Hewison, 1987, 1996; Urry, 1990). This orientation to past or vanishing culture is seen not only in the consumption of Third and Fourth World arts and artifacts, but also—and perhaps even more strikingly—in the heritage tourism of many Western industrial societies. This kind of tourism is particularly important in Britain, which specializes in the creation of tourist experiences based on the country's history and traditions. Foreign visitors seldom visit coastal resorts but tend to follow the so-called *milk run* whose itinerary connects various important heritage centers, such as London, Stratford-on-Avon, Oxford, Cambridge, and Edinburgh (Turner and Ash, 1975; Urry, 1990). More recently my home town of Stirling in central Scotland has come to occupy a particularly significant place on the heritage route. As a former Scottish capital, with an imposing castle, many buildings dating back several hundred years, and numerous battlefields in the immediate vicinity, the town's historical importance has been recognized for a long time. But the publicity generated by *Braveheart,* a film dealing with William Wallace and the Scottish struggle for independence from England, has attracted many more visitors and necessitated rapid expansion of local tourism infrastructure and facilities. The town and surrounding area are now promoted and sold as *Braveheart Country,* a term no resident had ever heard of before the film appeared.

As I have already observed, heritage sites are often based upon events that are part myth, part history. In Nottingham, the "Tales of Robin Hood" center was opened in 1989 and has enjoyed considerable success as a tourist attraction, despite doubts about the reality of the outlaw hero. Like Stirling, Nottingham's touristic appeal has been greatly enhanced by the success of a major commercial film. What Mel Gibson did for Stirling, Kevin Costner did for Nottingham. The Canterbury "Pilgrims' Way" from Southwark to Canterbury is based upon more solid historical ground, but it is inspired by Chaucer's *Canterbury Tales.* This tourist offering is interesting as an example of tableau form, which, according to Rojek (1993), may be the next main growth area in heritage tourism. It also does what so many of these attractions now do, that is, offer opportunities for visitors to "participate" in history by interacting with paid actors in the re-creation of scenes and events from the past. The tourist becomes a "pilgrim" here or an "outlaw" at Nottingham or a "Viking" at the Jorvik site in York. This technique is also applied in heritage tourism in other Western societies: for example, at the Plymouth Plantation Center in New England or, in a much more demanding way, in the six-day cattle drive beginning at the MW Ranch in Colorado (Rojek, 1993).

In Britain, heritage tourism has been constructed not only around sites and events linked to remote periods in national history. There has also been a remarkable growth of interest in the more recent and grimy industrial past, as evidenced in "The Way We Were" site at Wigan Pier in Lancashire, the Black Country Museum site at Dudley in Staffordshire, or the Quarry Bank Mill site at Styal in Cheshire. The center at Wigan Pier offers visitors such experiences as a trip down a coal mine, a re-creation of the terrible Maypole mine disaster, and a visit with a "miner's family." The Black Country museum features displays of industrial craft skills—brass founding, nail making, and so on. And the Quarry Bank Mill center tries to recapture the lives of nineteenth-century textile workers and their families (Urry, 1990).

How do we explain this urge to travel into the past? The popularity of these forms of tourism has led some observers to speculate that tourists' motivations may be undergoing profound changes. For example, Urry (1990) has suggested that holidays are now no longer so sharply contrasted with learning and education as they once were. From this postmodernist perspective, contemporary tourism is taking on some of the characteristics of the Grand Tour. It is perhaps too early to say if Urry's assessment is correct. We may indeed be witnessing the emergence of a new kind of "serious" tourist, one who has grown tired of escaping for two weeks of fun in the sun and wants something more from the holiday experience; or it may be that what we are dealing with here is yet another form of escape, fuelled by nostalgia for things of the past—a nostalgia that has been successfully exploited for some time by

Western filmmakers and television producers in such productions as "Happy Days," "The Waltons," "Upstairs Downstairs," *American Graffiti,* and so on (Dann, 1998).

Re-Creating Ethnicity

Ethnic cultures have also been commoditized for sale as local color or as sources of exotic sights, sounds, and smells in a number of Western industrial societies, with the Chinatowns of places like Vancouver and San Francisco being fairly obvious examples. In Britain, the Asian communities of Bradford and Manchester have become part of the package of attractions for visitors to these industrial cities; and in Birkenhead, near Liverpool, a Black Heritage center has been opened (Urry, 1990). Where social and cultural changes have virtually eradicated ethnic subcultures that were formerly unique and vibrant, tourism has been a factor in a process usually referred to as the re-creation or reconstruction of ethnicity. Two of the more interesting studies of this process as it appears in tourist settings are summarized here.

Ethnic Tourism in Brittany (MacDonald, 1987)

Brittany is a mainly agricultural region of northwestern France, with a population of over 2.5 million. The region accounts for some 11% of France's agricultural output and is the country's second most important tourism region in the country after the Cote d'Azur. About one-half of the region's residents speak the Breton (Celtic) tongue, although not necessarily as their first language. Brittany is the center of a Breton ethnic movement concerned with the fate of Breton language and culture in the face of French cultural dominance. Most members of this movement are well-educated middle-class or professional people.

As a tourism region, Brittany is marketed as a place of unspoiled charm and rural traditions, and appeals to both general vacationers and more "serious" tourists. Its tourism takes two main forms:

- *Coastal Tourism*—This is located primarily in the southern part of the region, which has a more favorable climate. It is more tourism-intensive and has more Breton attractions—for example, folklore festivals, costume parades—the demand for which is tourist-driven. Here a Breton "tradition" has been created by Celtic intellectuals and the tourism authorities. The everyday reality, as MacDonald points out, is very different—high-tech agriculture with stereo-equipped tractors, and so on.
- *Inland Tourism*—This is a somewhat later development and has become a hotbed of ethnic tourism. It attracts more serious tourists, especially those who are anxious to experience "genuine" or "authentic" Breton culture. This type of tourism features, among other things:

    + *A National Regional Park*—Here some locals radically changed the character of their dwellings, installing modern kitchens and bathrooms and generally copying the style of the smart, Park Office facilities. Others, however, had restored their houses to traditional, Breton farmhouse style and were selling these to "back-to-rural-roots" enthusiasts. Some merely rented their restored houses to tourists, while they themselves lived in the cellars or in modernized homes they had purchased.

+ *Eco-Museums*—These were usually lodged in traditionally restored houses. At first these re-creations of the past were resented by many locals, who felt embarrassed by visitors seeing how humbly they had lived not so long ago. As tourist enthusiasm grew, however, many began to express pride in having lived in such houses when they were young.

+ *Language Courses*—These are mainly organized by members of the Breton Movement. The tourists come to stay with a farm family and perform farm work in exchange for Breton language instruction. The hosts, however, may normally speak French at home and return to it after the tourists have gone.

+ *Night Festivals*—These are Celtic festivals of music and dance (known also as *ceilidhs* in the Scottish Highlands). They had almost disappeared until they were revived by Celtic scholars and members of the Breton Movement. Some tourist participants are seen to be more competent Breton dancers than their hosts.

The situation in Brittany then is one in which economic forces unconnected with tourism have wrought fundamental changes in Breton society. Tourism and the Breton Movement have helped to foster among locals a sense of pride in their cultural traditions. But while tourism has helped to preserve cultural elements that might otherwise have become moribund, it has not revived these as part of a living culture, for locals show no interest in making these part of their ordinary, everyday lives.

Cajun Tourism in Louisiana (Esman, 1984)

Tourism is a thriving Louisiana industry, the state's third largest and surpassed in importance only by agriculture and petrochemicals. Many visitors to the state are from other countries, but most are domestic tourists who generated $2.8 billion in 1980. In that year *Acadiana,* or Cajun country—an area in the southern part of the state—accounted for just under 10% of domestic tourism revenues. The Cajuns (or Acadians) themselves stem from a number of different ethnic groups—Louisiana Indians, Africans, French and Spanish Creoles, and others—but the French element has been the strongest part of their culture. French exiles from Acadia (now Nova Scotia and New Brunswick in Canada) journeyed to settle in Louisiana near the end of the eighteenth century. The settlers developed a distinctive hunting, fishing, and trapping culture adapted to the local environment with its swamps and marshes.

Since the middle of the twentieth century, this part of Louisiana has undergone rapid and dramatic changes, primarily as a result of new roads, television, the oil industry, and the arrival of increasing numbers of newcomers. The old swamp culture has almost vanished, its main traces being the camps and cabins used for weekend sport fishing and hunting. Although some traditional values remain, the Cajuns have now become virtually indistinguishable from other U.S. residents. However, the French language enjoys semiofficial status: its use is optional in legal documents, and it is encouraged in public schools as a second language. Festivals and dances featuring Cajun-style music and the use of Cajun slogans in commercial advertising are other ways in which the region is presented as a unique cultural enclave. Much of the interest in a revival of Cajun culture comes from external Francophone areas: France, Belgium, and Quebec subsidize bilingual education programs and support Cajun musicians.

Tourism development in Cajun country began in the 1960s alongside a renewal of interest and pride in Cajun ethnicity. Outsiders seemed to be interested in the "foreign" flavor of the region. Among the principal attractions are the old community of St. Martinville—the alleged setting of Longfellow's epic poem, *Evangeline* (a Cajun heroine)—and a reconstructed swamp village. Many Cajuns do not know the Evangeline story, and few people live in the swamp today, but for outsiders these are "signs" for Cajun-ness. Festivals, most of which are of recent origin, celebrate the Cajun love of a good time and emphasize Cajun food and Cajun music. Few Cajuns actually listen to Cajun music at home, and it is heard mainly in bars and other places frequented by tourists and local university students.

Esman (1984) suggests that McKean's concept of "cultural involution" applies to the Cajun situation as well. The locals' desire for modernization, progress, improvement, and so on runs into conflict with visitors' desire for past traditions. The solution is to retain certain traditional cultural features for tourist purposes, but within a modernizing context. However, while people in many parts of the world provide tourists with a "front region" to protect the integrity of their "backstage" private worlds, Cajuns do so for a different reason—to allow them to follow standard American middle-class practices and values in their everyday lives.

Cultural Commoditization Revisited

At the beginning of this chapter we saw that the problem of cultural commoditization was rooted in the belief that tourism causes a loss of cultural authenticity and meaning. In the discussion that followed, the term *authenticity* was treated as if its meaning was clear and unproblematic. This, indeed, was the assumption made by many anthropologists in their critiques of tourism during the 1970s, after which time the concept came under closer scrutiny. The writer who did most to challenge this assumption was Cohen (1988b), who developed further some of the ideas presented earlier on types of tourist experience, and argued that our understanding of the concept of authenticity needed to be modified. He suggested that criticisms of the kind made by Greenwood and others rested on a static or conservative view of culture. According to this view, cultural forms and practices were deemed to be authentic only if they retained their "traditional" and precommercial character. Cohen, however, points out that this is only one of several ways of recognizing the authentic, and suggests that it is an overly rigid approach to the issue—one taken by ethnographers and museum curators, for whom authenticity is a quality of traditional life before "contamination" by modern influences. These cultural experts, he argues, are usually among the most alienated members of their societies; and as such, they are both more serious in their search for authenticity and more stringent in their use of strict criteria for identifying it.

As against this "purist" view of authenticity as a primitive given, Cohen argues that its meaning is socially constructed or negotiable. This means that the criteria employed in its recognition can vary widely between different individuals and groups in society: some, for example recreational tourists, will have modest or vague criteria, insofar as they are interested in authenticity at all; others, such as existential tourists, ethnographers, or museum curators, will have more stringent requirements. In other words, there is no single test of authenticity that must be universally accepted. Cultural authenticity is not only something whose meanings are varied and negotiable at any particular time and place, but is also something that cultural items can "acquire" over a period of time. A cultural product might originally be regarded as inauthentic because of its contrived, fabricated, or foreign attributes, but in time might come to be viewed as an authentic cultural representation. Cohen uses the term *emergent authenticity* to describe this process and suggests that this is what happened with Haida argillite carvings and Inuit soapstone carvings. Perhaps it applies also to the evolution of the Cowichan knitted sweater as an "authentic" cultural representation. Looking ahead, Cohen also considers it quite likely that a contrived attraction like Disneyland might one day soon be generally regarded as an authentic representation of contemporary American popular culture.

Having tackled some of the problems inherent in the conventional understanding of authenticity, Cohen then questions whether cultural commoditization necessarily leads to a loss of cultural meaning. While he concedes that such losses do occur, he points out that these are not the inevitable consequences of commoditization. Folk and jazz musicians perform for money, but remain committed to their art and delight in playing for an audience appreciative enough to pay for the pleasure of listening to them. There is no sound reason, he thinks, for assuming that the same kind of thing cannot happen in commercialized performances for tourists. As for the tourists themselves, Cohen is not convinced that they are "shortchanged" or deceived by cultural commoditization. He suggests that many tourists have notions of authenticity that are much less rigorous than those of cultural "experts." They may even recognize inauthenticity in what they are offered, but be nonetheless willing and able to playfully enjoy the products and experiences.

But how successful has Cohen been in clearing up the confusion and orienting us toward a more sociologically realistic concept of authenticity? Is it enough to adopt the postmodernist view that all values are "fictive" and so each person's notion of what is authentic is as valid as everyone else's? Does it make sense to consider the authenticity of a cultural item without also considering the claims made for it by those who produce, present, or sell it? If no one actually claims that the facsimile of an Italian palace on the Las Vegas strip is "really Venice," does authenticity then become a nonissue? Are such tourist artifacts no more than *authentic replicas,* or is this term itself an oxymoron?

Chapter 6
Close Encounters

Tourism and Sex

Along with sun, sand, and sea, sex is one of the most pervasive elements in modern tourism imagery. The hint of sexual adventure may be suggested indirectly and in oblique ways, as in travel brochure pictures of bikini-clad women, swaying hula dancers, rugged lifeguards, or handsome cruise ship officers. The suggestion may be made more directly, but stop short of a promise, as it did in most Club Med advertising until recently, when this organization began to target families and middle-aged tourists as well as "swinging singles." In the rest of this chapter, I look beyond mere hints and suggestions to forms of tourism where sex is the main attraction and is sold as a commodity.

The association between tourism and prostitution has been observed and examined in a variety of different societies, including resort areas in Western societies, for example Nice (France), Las Vegas and Atlantic City (United States), and Brighton (England). It is in Third World tourism settings, however, that sex tourism has attracted the greatest attention and evoked the strongest criticisms. While there are probably many reasons for this response, it is likely that prostitution for wealthy foreigners is a particularly powerful symbol of the commoditization and exploitation of human beings. It expresses, in a way that is concrete rather than abstract, the crux of the analogy that "tourism is whorism"—that is, that tourism is mainly about poor countries selling themselves to rich ones in order to survive. I will return to this analogy later.

Research Problems

As Cohen (1982, 1986) has pointed out, discussion and analysis of sex tourism are complicated by a number of methodological difficulties that are often glossed over in the literature. Among the more obvious of these are:

- *Difficulties in measuring the extent of prostitution and sex tourism.* Since prostitution is often illegal and informal, obtaining reliable data on the activity is not easy. The stigmatization of prostitutes can make them reluctant to give out information on their activities to researchers. Authorities may also be unwilling to cooperate with research workers and may even refuse to acknowledge the existence of prostitution as a widespread activity or problem. Despite these difficulties, most writers feel obliged to produce figures, which are often crude estimates whose sources are left unexplained. The problem is then compounded by continuous reproduction of the same figures by subsequent writers, so that what began as an informed guess can acquire the status of compelling fact. We need to keep in mind that these estimates are "ballpark" figures, whose size may be influenced by the ideologies and moral values of the writers.

- *Difficulties in isolating and assessing the actual influence of tourism on the commercialization of sexual services.* Isolating tourism would involve some analysis of local historical and cultural traditions concerning gender relations and sexual behavior, as well as the roles of various modernizing agents besides tourism, such as the military, the mass media, local elites, and so on. It would also involve trying to delineate the ways in which a country's sex industry is divided physically, economically, and organizationally between local and tourist markets.

- *Difficulties in treating the commercialization of sexual services in a dispassionate, morally neutral or "value-free" manner.* Prostitution is an activity that many people view as morally questionable or reprehensible, even when it occurs outside tourism contexts. When prostitution occurs in the context of North-South tourism, this view may be held even more firmly, and influence the analyses and interpretations offered.

- *Difficulties in weighing the ideological content of the literature.* In light of the previous point, it is not surprising that much of the literature on sex tourism has been produced by writers with strong personal or institutional views on the subject. These views are not necessarily incorrect, but it is always worth noting their ideological roots. It is also difficult to assess the degree of ideological influence at work in apparently "neutral" discussions of sex tourism. These may well turn out to be reasonably successful attempts to lay aside personal biases or moral convictions, but it is also possible that such "value-free" approaches mask ideological positions, for example, liberal-humanism, hedonism, or Eurocentrism.

- *Difficulties in evaluating various advocacy positions adopted by researchers.* Much of the writing on prostitution and sex tourism takes the form of advocacy, with writers claiming to represent or speak for victims who are thought to be powerless, inarticulate, or not fully aware of their situations. Advocacy of this kind may well be required, but ideally one would want to hear more from the people directly involved. As with most analyses of tourism's human consequences, this ideal is not often attained.

Sex Tourism in Southeast Asia

By far the greatest share of research attention on this subject has gone to Southeast Asian countries, especially Thailand, the Philippines, South Korea, and Taiwan. Feminist perspectives have informed much of the analyses and interpretations of Southeast Asian sex tourism, and a useful summary of feminist writing on this has been presented by Graburn (1983). This summary deals especially with research undertaken by members of the International Feminist Network (Rome) and the Asian Women's Association (Tokyo). Also active in this area of research are a number of religious bodies who have combined their efforts under the umbrella of the Ecumenical Coalition on Third World Tourism (ECTWT).

In his distillation of feminist writing on Southeast Asian sex tourism, Graburn outlines the basic thesis presented in this body of literature. It is that women have been forced into prostitution because of a number of factors, principally:

- *A widespread, deeply rooted patriarchal attitude to sexuality.* This attitude casts women in the role of either "Madonna-virgin" or "whore." It is one shared by both foreign male tourists and local men, including fathers and other male figures of authority.
- *The "tainting" of women who are considered to have violated certain norms.* These "violations" include having been seduced, raped, or abandoned by husbands or boyfriends. The tainted women are cut off from other employment opportunities and have to join the ranks of the "tainted unemployed or underemployed."
- *The crisis in agricultural and cottage industries.* This crisis is the result of capitalist intrusion, ecological degradation, and population increases. It forces women to move to urban areas in search of employment.
- *The discrimination against women in business and industrial jobs.* As a result young, poor, uneducated women are forced or trapped into or "willingly enter" various forms of prostitution, especially those catering to apparently wealthy foreigners, such as tourists and members of the military.

Graburn offers only mild criticisms of the feminist literature on sex tourism in Southeast Asia, noting that it neglects Western societies where tourism and prostitution go hand-in-hand, as well as the phenomenon of male prostitution for female or male tourists. However, his general assessment is that, despite the "ideological cast" of the studies, they provide more than enough evidence to support both the facts and the interpretations they present. He concludes by pursuing the "tourism is whorism" analogy in the context of a patriarchy-imperialism analytical framework. Like many prostitutes, poor countries have few economic alternatives at their disposal, and have little to sell but their physical attractiveness. The men of such societies are often forced into the role of "cultural pimps." At a psychological level, poor countries are forced into the "female role" of servitude, of being "penetrated" for money, often against their wishes. By contrast, the outward-going, pleasure-seeking "penetrating" tourists of powerful nations are cast in the "male" role.

The thesis just summarized is not very different from the socio-historical interpretation offered by Hall (1992), who outlines a four-phase developmental process in sex tourism:

- *Phase 1—Indigenous Prostitution*—A situation in which women have been subjected to bonded prostitution (sold as sexual slaves to pay off loans or reduce debts) or concubinage within the patriarchal structures of their communities.
- *Phase 2—Economic Colonialism and Militarism*—A situation in which prostitution has become a formalized expression of dominance and a way of meeting the sexual needs of occupying forces. This stage marks the beginning of a process whereby the host society becomes economically dependent on the sale of sex as a means of economic development.
- *Phase 3—Substitution of International Tourists for Occupation Forces*—As traditional economies undergo restructuring in the postwar period, sex tourism becomes an organized system for earning foreign exchange. The promotion of sex tourism is made easier by the authoritarian nature of governments—the denial of individual rights can support the view that human beings are sexual commodities to be used in furthering national economic development.
- *Phase 4—Rapid Economic Development*—This has led to a general improvement in living standards in most countries of the region. Hall is not sure how this will affect sex tourism, but he suggests two possible scenarios: higher living standards may gradually reduce female dependency on sex tourism; alternatively, insatiable demand for consumer goods may help maintain female dependence on sex tourism well into the future.

Since Hall's essay was published, several countries in Southeast Asia have encountered serious economic problems, including the collapse of major financial institutions and drastic devaluations of national currencies. These recent events may make Hall's two scenarios irrelevant, at least for the time being. It is more likely that a period of economic hardship is in store, and that female dependency on sex tourism will not be reduced. We should not view Hall's developmental sequence as a "natural" process of evolution, leading irrevocably from traditional prostitution and concubinage to contemporary sex tourism. The convergence of prostitution and tourism to form a packaged commodity is the result of a number of supply-side and demand-side factors. While the former are now fairly well understood, the latter are much less clear. It is fairly easy to see how many young women in Southeast Asia end up working in the tourism sex trade, given the shortage of alternative economic opportunities and the comparative disadvantages of some of these alternatives, such as lower earnings and inflexible working hours (Truong, 1983). However, it is not quite so easy to explain why large numbers of men take the trouble to travel to Southeast Asia to buy something they could as easily obtain in their own countries. So, how are we to explain the apparently large and increasing demand for sex with Southeast Asian prostitutes?

Obviously, there is no single, straightforward answer that can be given to this question, especially since research on sex tourism's demand-side factors is far from exhaustive. However, a number of demand-generating factors have been identified by researchers (Cohen, 1986; Hall, 1992; Kruhse-MoundBurton, 1995; Leheny, 1995; Sanghera, 1987):

- *Accessibility*—It should be noted that many tourists visiting destinations in Southeast Asia are from other countries in the region. In Thailand, for example, Malaysian and Japanese tourists ranked first and second among international visitors in 1992. Men make up 75% of Japanese arrivals in Thailand. The region is also popular with tourists from Australia, while the introduction of jet travel and relatively cheap charter flights and package tours have brought the region well within the "pleasure periphery" for European and North American tourists.

- *Advertising and Promotion*—Sex tourism has been successfully advertised and promoted by travel agents and tour operators in a number of countries. The development of the Internet has also provided a new vehicle for sex tourism advertising and promotion. Advertising ranges from fairly subtle, suggestive hints about the sexual delights awaiting the male visitor, to provision of information about the prostitutes—who are usually referred to euphemistically as escorts or hospitality girls—available as part of the holiday package.

- *Value for Money*—The costs of sexual services are generally much lower than those charged for comparable services in the countries from which the sex tourists come. Moreover, the range of services openly available is usually more varied than would normally be the case back home. The prostitutes themselves often combine qualities such as delicate features, small physique, and submissive attitudes that Western sex tourists seem to find especially attractive. They are also often adept at camouflaging the commercial relationship with tourists, so as to create the illusion of affection, romance, or even love. These attributes and behaviors of the prostitutes can make the "product" seem very different from anything available in the sex tourists' own countries. So it might not really be a matter of going a long way for something readily obtainable at home.

- *Confirming Male Identity*—As gender relations change and women in Western societies experience improvement in their status and enjoy greater sexual freedom, some men may feel they are losing out in the "battle of the sexes." An annual sex tour cannot alter this perception in any lasting way, but it may present an opportunity for them to act as "King for a Day," and to perform temporary repairs on their threatened male identities.

These factors relate to very general kinds of circumstances that can affect demand for sex tourism. However, not all male tourists become sex tourists, just as not all economically and socially oppressed Southeast Asian women become prostitutes. Why *particular men* go on these sex tours, or *particular women* enter the sex trade, is a question that sociology is ill-equipped to answer. An understanding of these individual actions and motives requires in-depth analysis of the personal circumstances, life histories, and personalities of those involved. Truong (1983), however, suggests that heterosexual male demand for prostitution services is conditioned by personal codes of sexual conduct, circumstances that prevent the establishment of a regular heterosexual relationship, or lack of satisfaction with an existing heterosexual relationship.

Sex Tourism in Thailand

Thailand is generally regarded as the world's largest center of sex tourism and much of the writing on Southeast Asian sex tourism focuses on this particular country. Most of what we know about sex tourism in Thailand is due to the researches of Erik Cohen, who has spent several years working in this country, and whose knowledge of Thai social and cultural conditions is probably unmatched by any other contemporary Western sociologist. Cohen's work is especially interesting because his interpretations and theoretical propositions are sometimes controversial. In this section, I will draw on some of his better known studies of sex tourism in Thailand.

Most writers agree that concubinage and prostitution have been longstanding and commonplace features of Thai society, sanctioned by patriarchal Buddhist culture. This traditional background is thought to have provided a basis for the subsequent development of sex tourism. The number of prostitutes may have increased from about 400,000 in 1964 to around one million in 1980, although not all of these service tourists. Most Thai prostitutes are from poor rural households in the northern and northeastern provinces. Remittances from these young women and girls are often crucial for the survival of economically marginal rural households.

According to Cohen, prostitution, concubinage, and sex-for-sale have long been familiar elements of Thai society and were not created by tourism. However, commercial sex never approached its present scale until foreign demand for it soared in the mid-1960s. The earliest sexual liaisons between Thais and *farangs* (white foreigners) were between Thai males and foreign women. The present pattern began with the arrival of American military men in 1962. Tourism expanded rapidly after the Vietnam War, and among tourist arrivals males have outnumbered females by a ratio of about two to one. The precise share of tourism-related prostitution in the total prostitution scene is unknown. It appears that the great majority of prostitutes still serve a local Thai and Chinese clientele, while a minority works with European, Australian, Japanese, or American tourists. It would appear, however, that tourists constitute a majority of the clients of the higher quality establishments.

The Bangkok prostitutes interviewed by Cohen were mostly in their twenties, and many had small children from previous marriages or cohabitation with Thai men. Some were formerly house girls or factory workers who had faced unemployment or whose incomes were insufficient for their needs. Most lived alone, working intermittently as prostitutes, and several expressed a strong aversion to Thai men. Some may have had boyfriends who lived off their earnings but who did not act as pimps. Most had no formal training in English or any other foreign language, but still managed to work the bars and coffee shops successfully.

Cohen suggests that there is no clear-cut separation in Thai society between emotional and mercenary sexual relationships. These tend to form a spectrum from premarital, marital, and extramarital love relations; through permanent or protracted liaisons between relatively wealthy men and poor concubines, mistresses, or minor wives; to short, commercialized, sexual encounters in brothels and massage parlors.

Tourism prostitution is thus seen to be incompletely commercialized; and so, according to Cohen, the relationships between prostitutes and tourist partners are riddled with ambiguities. The prostitute's initial primary motive may be to earn a large amount of money quickly, but this can be complicated by two other considerations: the interest and excitement in meeting strange or attractive foreigners, and the hope of marrying a foreigner and escaping her present predicament. Some prostitutes stay with a tourist for the entire period of his visit, and many maintain contact with their tourist friends through correspondence. Some eventually manage to go abroad as wives or girlfriends.

Based on his observations in Bangkok, Cohen proposes a typology of tourist-prostitute relationships:

- *Mercenary*—A form of "pure" economic exchange. There is a clear understanding on both sides that sex is being exchanged for money. Personal involvement is neither demanded nor feigned. This type of relationship is usually of short duration.
- *Staged*—A form of economic exchange camouflaged as social exchange or even love. Each side interprets cues given by the other according to his or her own cultural premises. Hence, this is an inherently unstable relationship, subject to tensions and breakdowns. The tourist may suffer from "staging suspicion," or interpret his partner's willingness to stay with him without payment as a sign of her sincerity. His partner, however, is likely to consider money from her *farang* as a gift rather than as a payment.
- *Mixed*—This type of relationship involves a highly variable mixture of economic exchange and social exchange. Again, it is an unstable relationship, since it is based on conflicting emotions.
- *Emotional*—This is based on love, intrinsic gratification, and social exchange. It is less conflict-ridden and unstable than the other types of relationships. However, its stability depends essentially on the strength and duration of the mutual emotional involvement of the partners.

Cohen believes that the kinds of tourist-oriented prostitution he observed do not usually solve the problems that induced the women and girls to enter the profession in the first place. Some may indeed achieve unusual "success" by marrying a foreigner, while others may achieve a more limited degree of mobility. Many Thai prostitutes who succeed in going abroad may end up working as prostitutes in various tourist-generating countries. For most, however, it usually means a career characterized by long periods of economic and personal insecurity, broken by brief periods of temporary affluence. This kind of career, he argues, can inflict considerable social and psychological damage on the women and girls who pursue it (Cohen, 1982).

The often ambiguous relationships between tourists and prostitutes was explored from a different angle by Cohen when he examined the correspondence between sex tourists and their Thai girlfriends (1986). Cohen analyzed over 100 letters written by mainly Western tourists to prostitutes they had associated with during their visits to Thailand. Since the prostitutes were usually unable to read English, or any of the other languages in which the letters are written, they made use of local intermediaries to act as scribes. The scribes interpret the letters for the prostitutes and, with guidance from the latter, write suitable replies. Cohen's analysis of the *farangs'* letters is designed to reveal the nature and working out of three "dilemmas" in the tourist-prostitute relationship:

- *The Dilemma of Intimacy and Distance*—Obviously, the postvacation relationship between tourist and prostitute is different from that operating when they were together. During the vacation, the *farang* operates in a "buyer's market," while the prostitute is one of many sellers competing for the *farang's* custom. When the tourist goes home, however, the situation is transformed dramatically. He becomes dependent on the prostitute's willingness to continue the relationship at a distance, while she is free to enter new relationships with other tourists. According to Cohen, a yearning to maintain intimacy-at-a-distance is evident in many of the letters, for example, "I die a little bit every day I don't hear from you." "I would volunteer to come back. Even if it was to fight a war, but if that gets me to see you sooner then I go fight." "Oh, my God! He knows how much I miss you . . . too much. . . ."
- *The Dilemma of Trust and Suspicion*—The tourist who wants to maintain or extend the relationship formed during his vacation needs to believe that his Thai friend thinks likewise. However, the circumstances of their fairly brief encounter in Thailand, and awareness of her activities as a prostitute, provide grounds for mistrust and "staging suspicion" on his part. Unable to verify the truth of the prostitute's assurances of faithfulness, but wanting badly to accept them as true, he will sometimes indicate his ambivalence or press for reassuring information, for example, "but Darling, before you start to speak to me (during a long-distance telephone conversation), some guy count some numbers on the line, in German, maybe another telephone operator, right?"

"I hope you are serious about this (marriage) and not playing a trick to get money out of me. I will trust you till I have found out you have lied to me."

- *The Dilemma of Love and Money*—Since the letters of the prostitutes usually contain requests for money, the tourists have to respond to these somehow. Apparently, most tend to display greater generosity in sending money immediately after they return home, or in the weeks just prior to a return visit. The basic problem, according to Cohen, is that the prostitutes generally prefer money while the tourists prefer love. Tourists' anxiety over this comes through in several letters, for example, "I do not want you to feel that you care for me because of the money. I will send you the money. . . ." "Don't love me because I give you things, love me because I am me, OK." "[Y]ou will lose a great deal more than me (if she is dishonest with him). If you are good and honest you can win it all."

From Cohen's data, one might easily conclude that sex tourists are, to put it charitably, a little out of touch with reality. This view was expressed by one female student who, in a seminar discussion of this article, summed up the feelings of many of her classmates when she exclaimed, "Are these guys crazy, or what? Don't they remember that the girls are prostitutes?" However, we do not know if the letter writers were representative of sex tourists in general, or even if they were representative of letter-writing sex tourists. Nor can we be sure that the letter writers were always being completely serious in their correspondence with the prostitutes. Is it possible, perhaps, that just as the prostitutes were writing—through their scribes—what they thought the tourists wanted to hear, so too some tourists were writing what they thought the prostitutes wanted to hear? Some male students in the seminar felt that this was probably the case in many instances. As one student said, "No, I don't think these guys are crazy at all. I think they are just saying and doing what they think they need to, so that the girl will be lined up for them when they get back to Bangkok. Better to spend a bit of time writing this stuff and sending them a few bucks than go through a big rigmarole when they hit Bangkok." This student hastened to assure the seminar that he was not "speaking from experience," but just from "common sense."

Although Cohen makes no claims as to the representativeness of the tourists whose letters he analyzed, his methodology is still somewhat controversial. For example, the letters were a convenient repository of data, having been left by prostitutes in a house occupied by an English-speaking Thai. Should the contents of such documents, written as private and personal communications, become public research data without the consent of the writers? For most students, however, the main sticking point proved to be Cohen's argument that, at the *macro* level, sex tourism was the manipulation and exploitation of prostitutes by the sex tourists, but at the *micro* level it involved the manipulation and exploitation of individual sex tourists by individual prostitutes and their scribes. Some students—mainly males—

thought this was a plausible interpretation, while others—mainly females—thought that this was just the same old story of "blaming the victims."

Although the 1960 Prostitution Act made prostitution illegal in Thailand, the government has done very little to eradicate sex tourism. Brothels and massage parlors are registered as eating houses and charges under the law are easily evaded by bribing police and other officials. Thai authorities have become concerned about their country's global image as Southeast Asia's leading sex tourism destination. But they are also aware that sex tourism is a major earner of foreign exchange. There are some signs that the AIDS epidemic may be forcing Thai authorities to reorient their tourism policies and to refurbish Thailand's destination image—an image that has served it so well for so long.

AIDS appeared in Thailand in 1984 at a time when the tourism industry there was undergoing rapid expansion. The early cases suggested to the general public and the authorities that the disease afflicted only foreign homosexuals or Thai homosexuals who had contracted it overseas. In 1986 the official line was that Thailand had only 36 HIV carriers and that tests on female and male prostitutes, intravenous drug users, and blood donors had detected only one HIV carrier, a male prostitute. Thai journalists mounted a critical attack on the official position in 1987, voicing suspicions that the extent of the epidemic had been played down to protect the country's tourism industry. By early 1987 authorities were presenting a rather different picture, one that showed 128 HIV carriers and 11 cases of full-blown AIDS. However, there was a relatively low incidence of the disease among female sex workers, which apparently encouraged the authorities to be more open in releasing information on HIV and AIDS in Thailand. This openness, in turn, helped to increase public awareness of the disease.

The belief that foreigners were the main sources of infection led, according to Cohen, to the growth of a "mild but widespread xenophobia," manifested in a growing opposition to sex tourism and demands that all foreigners entering Thailand should be tested for HIV. Some sex establishments banned foreign customers, and others came under heavy pressure to do so by local customers. This may be having the effect of resegregating the tourist-oriented and locally oriented segments of the sex industry. Tourists themselves appear to be more aware of the risks, and recent arrivals indicate a reduction in single-male tourism and an increase in family tourism. The inauguration of "Visit Thailand Year" in 1987—the year of the King's sixtieth birthday—provided an opportunity for authorities to redesign the country's tourism image. Their efforts involved the promotion of Thailand's natural and cultural attractions and the de-emphasizing of its sex tourism (Cohen, 1988a). Between 1986 and 1987 the number of tourists visiting the country increased by a staggering 24% (Leheny, 1995). Cohen notes the irony of this situation, in which a deadly disease was responsible for bringing about changes that appeals to morality could never have achieved.

We must be careful not to assume that this change in marketing strategy signals the end of sex tourism in Thailand. There is no clear evidence to date that there has been a decline in the numbers of sex tourists visiting the country. Recent Internet reports from ECTWT and similar bodies campaigning for an end to sex tourism have suggested that the fear of AIDS may be redirecting the sex tourist gaze towards younger and presumably "safer" girls, so that we can expect a marked increase in child prostitution for tourists. Leheny's (1995) belief is that a decline in Southeast Asian sex tourism is most likely to come as a result of quite different factors influencing demand. In particular, he stresses the growing importance of Japanese women in the region's tourism market. They represent a potentially lucrative market segment for countries like Thailand, but at present they tend to avoid destinations that are associated with sex tourism. However, Japan's economic problems will likely dampen its citizens' demand for overseas travel, and it may be difficult for Thailand to cultivate this particular market segment. Bishop and Robinson (1998) believe that, just as Thailand's "economic miracle" was built on sex tourism, the country's recovery from recent economic collapse will also depend heavily on this activity.

Child Prostitution

I have alluded to child prostitution previously. Although much less is known about this than adult prostitution, there seems little doubt that it has become an important part of the sex tourism industry in several countries. One watchdog group, End Child Prostitution in Asian Tourism (ECPAT), estimates there are probably one million children involved in tourism-related prostitution in Asia alone. Child labor in general is quite common throughout much of the Third World, and is now being exploited for the new tourism market. It has been observed that traditional acceptance of child labor is being combined with the traditional custom of "deflowering" young girls to promote new forms of sexual entertainment for sex tourists. It has been available as part of the package in Thailand, where the price for deflowering is around 4,000 baht (about $200), and a young virgin may be obtained by a procurer for about $300. The procurer can expect to recover two-thirds of his investment in only one transaction with a tourist. In view of the rigor of child labor in factories, children may sometimes expect sexual labor to be less onerous and may be attracted by the superficial glamour of the sex tourism industry.

There are possibly over 10,000 child prostitutes at work in Thailand and 3,000 to 5,000 in the Philippines. They are sometimes sold into prostitution by poor parents, many of whom may imagine that their children will quickly find desirable jobs in the city. Of the children who arrive in Bangkok in this way, about 50% appear to enter prostitution immediately, while another 10% do so within a year. Bangkok's child prostitutes are expected to service an average of three customers a day for between $2 and $6 a customer, with their earnings being divided between them and the brothel owner. Children who are pawned, that is, given to another in repayment of a debt, receive nothing. Others may receive an allowance of $1 a week. The situation is similar in the Philippines, where young boys are being drawn into the sex industry in increasing numbers (Sanghera, 1986).

In 1997 the WTO was instrumental in helping to form the Tourism and Child Prostitution Watch task force, an industrywide alliance of governmental and private organizations dedicated to the eradication of child prostitution in tourism. The following vignette describes the task force's campaign objectives and strategies.

❋   ✦   ❂   ❖   ❋

WTO Campaign to End Child Prostitution

On the initiative of the World Tourism Organization, the first meeting of the Tourism and Child Prostitution Watch task force was held on March 8 at the ITB tourism fair in Berlin. "It takes a lot of courage for the tourism industry to tackle this problem, because we would prefer to always present a positive face—but we felt it was our duty to bring together the different partners who are in a good position to do something," said WTO Secretary-General Francesco Frangialli in opening the meeting. Two weeks later in Paris, the Secretary-General presented a new logo adopted by the task force to unite the tourism trade in its fight against child prostitution. "This logo can be used to identify all organizations and tourism businesses that have joined together for the initiative," he told a news conference during the Salon Mondial du Tourisme travel fair.

The logo is part of a worldwide public awareness campaign designed to warn travelers about the exploitation of children. It is intended to be used in travel literature and window displays to identify organizations and businesses that are actively working to prevent and eliminate child prostitution. Accompanied by the words, "NO Child Sex Tourism," the international logo was provided by Brazilian national tourism board EMBRATUR, which developed it as part of a national campaign against child prostitution launched in February. In Brazil, the logo is already being used on airline ticket jackets, brochures, television ads, T-shirts, and hang tags for hotel doors.

The international campaign will be coordinated by the Child Prostitution and Tourism Watch task force sponsored by the World Tourism Organization as a coalition of governments, tourism industry groups, and international organizations. The first meeting of the task force reviewed actions already undertaken by individual countries and tourism organizations. The task force also agreed on a series of first actions, including:

- Recommendation that countries set up hotlines to denounce cases of child sex tourism.
- New research to measure the size of the problem and where it is occurring.
- A data base of legislation and national campaigns to stop child prostitution.

- Establishment of a Web site on the Internet for the campaign.
- Cooperation with airlines and in-flight magazine articles, to inform passengers about the exploitation of children in sex tourism.
- Designation of national and industry focal points to monitor the campaign.

The sexual exploitation of children was first brought to public attention by the Bangkok-based action group ECPAT (End Child Prostitution and Trafficking). According to ECPAT statistics, some one million children in Asia alone are involved in the sex trade and many of those children are exploited by foreign tourists. "Organized sex tours don't really exist anymore. The travel industry has managed to handle this problem very well," ECPAT founder Ron O'Grady told the meeting. "Today's sex tourists are generally individuals or people travelling on holidays in pairs who find out where to go from information provided on the Internet," he said. This is why the task force decided that its campaign would focus primarily on public awareness, both in destinations and in tourism-generating countries.

Ghana, Egypt, India, Venezuela, Germany, Sri Lanka, Brazil, and Thailand were among the countries represented at the meeting. International organizations included the Universal Federation of Travel Agents' Associations (UFTAA), the International Hotel and Restaurant Association (IH&RA), the Federation of International Youth Travel Organizations (FIYTO), and the International Federation of Women's Travel Organizations (IFWTO). Nongovernment organizations included ECPAT, Tourism Watch (Germany), and Save the Children (Denmark).

WTO News Service, May 1997. Reprinted with permission of the World Tourism Organization.

Sex Tourism for Women?

We have seen that some prostitutes in Southeast Asia operate on a part-time or casual basis, although they seem to be a minority. In certain tourist destinations, informal or casual prostitution appears to be the most prevalent form. This is often the case when female tourists have sexual encounters with local males, in relationships whose commercial aspects are either minimized or heavily camouflaged (Dahles and Bras, 1999; Karch and Dann, 1981). Is this simply sex tourism socially constructed as "romance" to suit a female clientele, or is it really fundamentally different from the kinds of tourist-related sexual activity we have discussed thus far? A look at the Gambian and Jamaican situations may throw some light on this question.

Gambian Bummerboys

The Gambia, whose tourism experience is discussed in chapter 10, is a West African country with a fairly well-developed tourism industry oriented to mass charter tourists from European countries—primarily Britain and Scandinavia. Prominent in the informal tourism sector are so-called *professional friends* or *bummerboys*—young Gambian men who try to make a living through relationships with visitors in the main tourist areas. They have been studied by the Swedish anthropologist, Ulla Wagner and her student, Bawa Yamba, who focus mainly on the bummerboys' efforts to "escape" to Europe with tourist assistance. Although the authors do not situate their discussion in a sex tourism context, it would appear that many bummerboys are engaged in part-time prostitution for a tourist clientele, and that they enter into relationships with tourists that seem to fit Cohen's "staged" or "mixed" types. Like the lovelorn *farangs* in Thailand, the bummerboys' tourist friends often want companionship and affection as well as sex; and their comparative wealth allows them to exercise considerable, if not absolute, control of the relationship. In short, there appear to be no good reasons for regarding this as anything other than a form of sex tourism that is as yet relatively unorganized, casual, and incompletely commercialized.

Congregating around hotels and other establishments in the coastal tourist area, the bummerboys offer services ranging from bag carrier, through guide on shopping or other excursions, to sexual services for mainly female tourists. Apart from the expectations of short-term economic gain and excitement from associating with tourists, the young men also hope to find a patron who will send them gifts from her home country, or a sponsor who will help them to travel overseas for work, education, or "the good life." In this respect middle-aged Scandinavian women appear to be among the more generous and sympathetic tourists. If the women are married, the bummerboys' expectations are usually limited to securing money, gifts, and entertainment opportunities in exchange for sex. With women who are unmarried, divorced, or separated from their husbands, the bummerboys may set their sights somewhat higher and cultivate the relationship so as to travel abroad. If they succeed in this, however, the results are not always what they hope for, and the relationships formed with tourists in The Gambia are often difficult to sustain in a new and very different social and cultural environment (Wagner and Yamba, 1986).

Jamaican Hustlers

Relationships between Jamaican men and Euro American female tourists have been examined by Pruitt and LaFont (1995). These authors believe that mass tourism has expanded the opportunities for Western women to negotiate new gender roles and identities. Traveling independently of men and freed from the constraints of their own societies, they seek intimate relationships with local men for sex, companionship, romance, and cultural experience. Pruitt and LaFont argue that Jamaican "romance tourism" is not simply sex tourism with the roles of men and women reversed. We are told that neither the tourists nor the men think they are involved in prostitution, although other Jamaicans believe they are; that the relationships are "constructed through a discourse of romance;" and that those involved stress courtship rather than commercialized sex. The men are not regarded simply as sex objects and this, together with the women's desire for a culturally enriching experience, is felt to make romance tourism something quite distinct from sex tourism. Mutual attraction is fostered by the different cultural scripts both parties bring to the relationship: in Jamaica fair skin, straight hair, and Caucasian features are often admired, and many Jamaican men feel foreign women are more "tender" and "emotional" than local women; the female tourists, for their part, generally regard Jamaican men as more "natural," attentive, and passionate than those back home. Many of the women stay in Jamaica for extended periods, and several are repeat visitors.

While the relationships just described are heavily overlain with romantic imagery, they also display a number of features which render them similar, in certain important respects, to those described by Cohen in his work on sex tourism in Thailand. Most obvious, perhaps, are the sharp differences in economic and social status between the parties. The men come mainly from poor rural areas and have limited opportunities for economic advancement. The tourists are from rich countries, are wealthy enough to take regular, extended vacations, and often have good jobs and excellent career prospects. As financial providers, the women possess greater power in defining and controlling the relationships, and the men often regard them as fickle or unreliable and feel that they are being used. While relationships with foreign women require little or no financial outlay on the part of the men and are a source of status among peers, dependence on women conflicts with their need to be "in control" of women. Like Bangkok prostitutes, the men also appear to be adept at staging or feigning love and take great pride in their ability to "sweet talk" the women, who are known to value such affirmations of longing and affection. "Rasta" men (Rastafarians) attract unusual interest from foreign women, who regard them as more "natural," "spiritual," or "independent," so men hoping to form relations with female tourists sometimes adopt the Rasta hairstyle (dreadlocks) and language style. Their phoniness is recognized by other Jamaicans, who refer to them as "rent-a-dreads." It would seem that these kinds of relationships, like those in Southeast Asian sex tourism, also serve to reproduce and reinforce existing patterns of racial and cultural superiority and domination. However, in some places Western female tourists in search of romance may find the local males to be at least as wealthy and well-traveled as themselves. This appears to be the case in Otavalo valley, high in the mountains of Ecuador (Meisch, 1995).

Some Loose Ends

While the academic literature on sex tourism has grown steadily in recent years, much more work remains to be done. For fairly obvious reasons, sex tourism usually comes under close scrutiny in places where its magnitude is such that it has attained the status of a social problem. Research then involves the examination of its present structure and operation, and the reconstruction of its historical development. It would be interesting, however, to have more information on the transitional or formative periods in sex tourism when the basis is being laid for its subsequent development. This would mean looking at destinations like Ghana, which is in an early stage of tourism development. This West African country is not an international tourist destination of any significance at present, although its tourism industry is growing quite rapidly. Prostitution in Ghana is found mainly in the hotels, bars, and nightclubs in the larger urban areas. What we see in Ghana is prostitution in an essentially pretourism stage and a foundation upon which tourist-oriented prostitution could develop if Ghana's efforts to attract more international visitors are successful. Already, hotels are viewed as places of immorality by many ordinary Ghanaians, who associate them with wastefulness and the philandering activities of Ghanaian married men. Many respectable Ghanaian women hesitate to visit a hotel on their own, for fear they will be mistaken for prostitutes or girlfriends of hotel guests (Adu-Febiri, 1988). There are many other countries that are also in the beginning stages of tourism development. What we badly need are studies that reveal some of the processes of sex tourism formation and the factors that shape supply and demand for sex as a tourism commodity.

Tourism per se does not cause prostitution, since the latter clearly predates the former. But there is little doubt that tourism development is associated with the growth of prostitution in many parts of the world. There are, however, a few exceptions to the general rule that tourism development encourages prostitution development. If we can understand why some countries have been able to avoid tourism-driven prostitution, we may, in the process, see more clearly why others have not. Studies of Bermuda and Cyprus have revealed no significant increases in prostitution following tourism growth. The reasons for this are not entirely clear as yet, but in both Bermuda and Cyprus poverty is not as acute as it is in most Southeast Asian destinations. And it appears that the economic benefits of tourism have been distributed widely enough to minimize a sense of relative deprivation or hopelessness on the part of locals. In Bermuda, the overall standard of living (literacy, educational levels, life expectancy) is higher than in many Western societies. In Cyprus, tourism has created opportunities for female employment not only in menial and low-paying jobs, but also in such categories as tour guides, hotel receptionists, and managers (de Kadt, 1979).

The situation in Swaziland is somewhat different. Prostitution was recognized as a problem in this African country as long ago as the late 1930s, before the development of tourism. A 1956 commission of enquiry into juvenile delinquency and associated problems addressed the issue of prostitution, but found that the customers were mainly Swazi migrants returning from spells of employment in the Republic of South Africa. In 1970 another report suggested that a few hotels had become centers of prostitution and that most of the customers were non-Swazi, although the evidence here was far from conclusive. At present, the extent of prostitution and the composition of the clientele is difficult to determine, but there is no reliable evidence that prostitution has increased as a result of international tourism development. One observer has suggested that the main issue is perhaps not prostitution but the stigmatizing of local women who prefer the company of foreigners with more wealth, more status, and a more caring attitude than most Swazi males, noting that a similar process of stigmatization was experienced by British women who associated with American GIs during World War II (Harrison, 1992b).

Sex tourism and romance tourism connect with the much broader topic of gender relations in tourism. These have received scant attention by researchers so far, probably because most investigations of tourism (and, indeed, of most other social science topics) have been conducted by men. As more women become involved in tourism research they have turned their attention to a number of hitherto neglected subjects, including historical and contemporary inequalities between men and women in their opportunities for leisure travel, qualitative differences between men's and women's touristic experiences, the negotiation and formation of gender identities in tourism, and the masculinized character of tourist sites and the tourist gaze. A special issue of *Annals of Tourism Research* (22, 1995) is devoted to gender issues in tourism, and excellent discussions of this research area are found in Kinnaird and Hall (1992) and Morgan and Pritchard (1998).

Since sociologists and anthropologists have seldom rubbed shoulders with real mass tourists, preferring instead to view them from a safe distance and organize them into various abstract types, it is hardly surprising that we know little or nothing about the formation of sexual or romantic relations *between* tourists who were formerly strangers to each other. Would these relations fall outside the context of commoditized sex, or could they be considered part of sex tourism in its broadest sense (Oppermann, 1999)? Are the stories one hears of Club Med affairs and "love boat" cruise romances mainly myths or products of the fevered imagination? This is an area that would surely repay investigation.

Chapter 7
A Tourism Paradox?

Tourism and the Environment

We have already seen that tourism is in certain respects a rather peculiar industry. It successfully encourages vast numbers of people to spend a good deal of money and time on a product that is hard to define exactly. It persuades millions of these people that they must travel quite long distances to obtain this product, since it cannot be brought to them. And it also convinces many people in tourist destinations to do unpaid work on behalf of it, or to become willing objects of the tourist gaze. Another remarkable aspect of contemporary tourism is its relationship with the physical environment. This relationship often seems paradoxical: maintaining a high-quality physical environment should be a major priority in tourism development, since failure to do so could lessen the appeal of destinations; yet tourism is increasingly charged with environmental degradation, and tourists themselves are not always discouraged by the physical deterioration of resorts. In this chapter I consider some of the issues surrounding the tourism-environment relationships. I look at ways of assessing tourism's environmental effects, outline some abbreviated case studies, and examine ecotourism as a development option. My focus is on the physical (rather than the social and cultural) environment, with most attention being given to the natural and seminatural environments in which tourism has been developed.

Evaluating Tourism's Environmental Effects

Cost-Benefit Analysis

The conventional approach in the literature evaluating tourism's global environmental impacts normally involves fairly routine *cost-benefit* balance sheets, in which tourism's negative effects are listed, along with a (usually much shorter) list of environmental benefits. The discussion of environmental impacts by Mathieson and Wall (1982) takes this approach, although the authors give more attention than most to the effects of tourism on the built environment. Among the negative or harmful effects cited by Mathieson and Wall are destruction of vegetation; air and water pollution; undermining wildlife privacy and disturbing the predator-prey relationship; extraction of unique rock formations by souvenir hunters or suppliers; soil erosion in mountain areas; ribbon development; traffic congestion; and architectural pollution. They credit tourism with some environmentally beneficial effects: the rehabilitation of existing historic sites, buildings, and monuments, as in places like Cape Cod in Massachusetts and Williamsburg in Virginia; the rehabilitation of old, disused buildings into new tourism facilities, as in London, where derelict warehouses were transformed into discos and pubs; the conservation of natural resources, through the development of national parks and game reserves in various parts of the world; and the introduction of planning and administrative controls at various historical sites such as Stonehenge in England and the Parthenon in Greece.

Although Mathieson and Wall acknowledge that it is difficult to accurately weigh the pros and cons of tourism's effects on the physical environment, they conclude that all too often tourism and the environment are in conflict and that planners must change their emphasis from planning the environment for tourism to defending the environment from tourism's negative effects. A similar conclusion is reached by Australian tourism researchers Craig-Smith and French (1994). These verdicts appear reasonable, in a very general way. But a number of caveats have to be entered:

- *There is no scientifically valid, global balance sheet for tourism's environmental effects to support the conclusion that these are on balance positive or negative.* It is extremely difficult, if not impossible, to objectively compare such things as traffic congestion in Rome and the rehabilitation of Williamsburg. It seems more appropriate to apply cost-benefit analysis to a particular destination, for example, Rome or Williamsburg, or to a particular environmental resource, such as East African wildlife or Australia's Great Barrier Reef.
- *Environmental damage may result from "alternative" forms of tourism as well as from conventional mass tourism.* If these forms, such as drifter tourism or hill-trekking, are not carefully managed and regulated, their effects can be just as deleterious (sometimes more so, given the often fragile ecosystems utilized) as those of mainstream tourism. The situations in Boracay and Nepal, which are discussed later in this chapter, are examples of this.
- *Some aspects of the accounting process involve the use of subjective criteria that cannot be scientifically validated.* While most environmental effects can be measured and assigned positive or negative ratings in a fairly noncontroversial way (for example, air pollution, water pollution, soil erosion, wildlife preservation, historic site restoration, improved public sanitation, and so on), others may be less clear-cut. The transformation of old warehouses into pubs and discos may not be to everyone's liking. *Visual pollution,* of which architectural pollution is but one form (advertising billboards and neon lighting may be others), can be evaluated only with reference to aesthetic values or criteria, about which people may have very different opinions. "Dr. Beach," whose rankings of America's best beaches appear in travel magazines such as

Condé Nast Traveler, usually gives top billing to fairly secluded beaches in settings where signs of human settlement are either absent or effectively screened from view. In 1997 the top two were Lanikai and Kailua beaches in Oahu, Hawaii, although the ocean at both places is not particularly good for swimmers. Waikiki, Oahu's most famous beach, never makes the top 10 for reasons that include its "ugly backdrop" of high-rise hotels and condominiums. However, what is ugly to Dr. Beach may be beautiful or exciting to others. Many modern resort projects have followed certain principles of architectural appropriateness, which emphasize the harmonizing of buildings and landscaping with local architectural styles and features of the natural landscape. While this writer also favors such an approach, others may find nothing jarring or unsightly about an eclectic mix of architectural styles or landscapes.

- *The environmental costs of tourism need to be weighed against the costs of alternative industries.* While we can agree with Mathieson and Wall's view that the environment should be defended against tourism impacts, some environmental costs are also likely to result from alternative types of economic development. If there is no need to exploit a particular set of resources for economic development, the issue of environmental costs becomes irrelevant. If there is such a need, however, the key questions become: What are the relative environmental costs of the various kinds of economic developments under consideration? and Are the environmental costs bearable in light of anticipated benefits?

The first question reminds us that tourism is only one of many industries whose operation may have adverse environmental effects and that the environment has to be protected against these, whether the source is petrochemicals, logging, mining, or tourism. In Oahu, Hawaii, it can be argued that the worst environmental effects of development (including "eyesores") are not to be found in Waikiki, but on the island's southwest coast, a region dominated mainly by military installations and manufacturing centers, such as Pearl Harbor, Pearl City, and Aeia. The second question reminds us that the protection of environmental resources should be seen as good tourism business since tourism-induced environmental deterioration—for example, air pollution, water pollution, and traffic congestion—usually lessen the appeal of destinations so affected. One would think, therefore, that tourism developers would be preoccupied with conservation if only as a matter of economic survival. However, developers will often have alternative profit-making opportunities available to them, so that short-term gain and a movement of capital to other projects—tourism or otherwise—may be an alternative to investing in environmental protection. And there are tourist destinations that remain economically viable despite environmental degradation: Blackpool, in northwest England, attracts almost seven million visitors annually to its Pleasure Beach alone, despite heavy water and beach pollution. Unlike Blackpool's traditional holidaymakers, who took their annual two-week vacation in the town, most of today's visitors are "weekenders" who come to the Pleasure Beach's amusement centers and theaters for concentrated doses of excitement and entertainment.

Environmental Stress Analysis

The concept of *environmental stress* was employed by the OECD in its Tourism and Environment Program of the early 1980s. It was there defined as: "The strain imposed on people and their enjoyment of amenities, or on the resources, the impact of which can be objectively measured or may be subjectively experienced in the light of defined values" (Pearce, 1989, pp. 229–232). Environmental stress analysis tries to identify various stressor factors, trace their effects, and propose remedial measures. There is no interest in the identification of positive or beneficial effects of tourism on the physical environment.

The OECD's Tourism and Environment Program involved a survey of 17 case studies and 11 national reports of tourism's environmental impacts. Results of the survey suggested that environmental destruction was most commonly associated with tourism situations characterized by rapid destination development, pronounced seasonal peaks in tourist activity, inadequate planning and controls, and technical or financial inability to provide adequate infrastructure. It was also observed that environmental deterioration does not always lead to the demise of the area as a tourist destination. Such a decline seemed most likely to occur in single-attraction destinations such as lakeside resorts. In other places, advertising, publicity, and the creation of new attractions succeeded in attracting new tourists with different tastes and expectations (Pearce, 1989).

Working along lines similar to the OECD, the Environment Committee of the WTO has devised a set of indicators for measuring environmental sensitivity to tourism-induced changes. These are designed to ensure that tourism forms and practices are sustainable by alerting planners and managers to the potential for problems before they arise. They include *core indicators* whose use is applicable in all destinations, and *ecosystem specific indicators* specially designed for particular destinations or ecosystems (Table 7.1).

Tourism and Environment in Conflict: Some Examples

Boracay—Beyond Hope?

Boracay is a small Philippines island whose tourism development has been examined by Smith (1992). Its residents have traditionally been small-scale rice farmers and fishers, and at one time copra was produced for cash, though this is no longer done. Fishing was adversely affected by the practice of dynamiting, which resulted in the destruction of most of the island's coral reefs. Lack of wage employment

Table 7.1 Indicators of Environmental Sensitivity

Core Indicators

Indicator	Specific Measures
1. Site Protection	1. Category of site protection
2. Stress	2. Tourist numbers visiting site (per annum peak month)
3. Use Intensity	3. Intensity of use—peak period (persons/hectares)
4. Social Impact	4. Ratio of locals to tourists (peak period)
5. Developing Control	5. Existence of environmental review procedure or formal controls over development of site and use densities
6. Waste Management	6. Percentage of sewage from site receiving treatment (additional indicators may include structural limits of other infrastructural capacity on site—e.g., water supply, garbage)
7. Planning Process	7. Existence of organized regional plan for tourist destination region (including tourism component)
8. Critical Ecosystems	8. Number of rare endangered species
9. Consumer Satisfaction	9. Level of satisfaction by visitors (questionnaire-based)
10. Local Satisfaction	10. Level of satisfaction by locals (questionnaire-based)

Ecosystem Specific Indicators

Ecosystem	Sample Indicators
1. Coastal zones	• degradation (% of beach degraded, eroded) • use intensity (persons per meter of accessible beach) • shore/marine fauna (number of key species sightings) • water quality (fecal coliform and heavy metals counts)
2. Mountain regions	• erosion (% of surface eroded) • biodiversity (key species counts) • access to key sites (hours waits)
3. Cultural sites (traditional communities)	• potential social stress (ratio average income of tourists/locals) • in seasonal sites (% of vendors open year round) • antagonism (reported incidents between locals/tourists)
4. Small islands	• currency leakage (% loss from total tourism revenues) • ownership (% foreign/nonlocal ownership of tourism establishments) • water availability (costs, remaining supply) • use intensity measures (at scale of entire island as well as for impacted sites)

Source: WTO News Service, May–June 1996.

opportunities encouraged out-migration, especially on the part of young Boracayans, and led to a weakening of formerly strong family ties. The government hoped to arrest the process of economic decline and stagnation by developing tourism, and declared the island a Tourist Preserve in 1978. Responsibility for development was given to the Philippines Tourism Authority (PTA), which helped to establish a Cottage Owner's Association whose membership was restricted to Filipino cottage owners. No tourism development was to be permitted closer than 30 meters from the sea, and power vehicles were to be barred except for a few government service trucks.

The island became popular with middle-class, family-oriented tourists in the early 1980s. Most of them were expatriate Americans and Europeans working in the Philippines and other parts of Southeast Asia, and who were attracted by the pristine beach, friendly inhabitants, and relatively low costs of food and accommodation. From 1985 onward, Boracay began to attract long-term budget travelers—mainly young single men and women—referred to as *backpackers* by the Boracayans. As the island became increasingly popular with these new kinds of tourists, the numbers of tourists of the earlier type began to decline. The PTA commissioned an American engineering firm to prepare a resort plan for Boracay, which was completed in 1984. *The Helber Plan,* as it was called, envisioned a maximum nightly visitor count of between 3,750 and 4,200 persons, requiring between 1,700 and 1,900 accommodation units, and a daily employee count of between 2,400 and 2,600 persons. The plan also proposed five activity zones for the island:

- *Tourist Village Zone*—Along the West beach, this would have economy-class accommodations.
- *Integrated Resort Zone*—In the northern part of the island, this would have two or three resort hotels, an 18-hole golf course, a horse stable complex, and other high-quality amenities.
- *Traditional Barangays Areas*—These would contain employee accommodations.
- *Community Facility Zone*—Besides farm lands, this would contain a market place, schools, and recreational facilities.
- *Open Space Reserves*—In these areas no new building would be allowed, although existing structures could remain.

Political turmoil following the overthrow of President Marcos diverted attention away from Boracay, and the Helber Plan was not implemented. But the number of tourists continued to grow as word spread about the island's beauty, friendly people, and low costs. Responding to increased demand, unauthorized cottages and beachfront stands were constructed, while some visitors entered into "partnerships" with Filipinos, in this way circumventing regulations prohibiting outright sale of land to foreigners. This uncontrolled expansion of "alternative" tourism produced a number of negative environmental impacts. Visitor demand for flush toilets caused serious pollution problems along White Sands Beach, where the water table is only about four feet beneath the surface. The removal of vegetation to build hillside cottages with ocean views caused soil erosion, while garbage accumulated along the roadside, to be scattered by winds or dogs (Smith, 1992). An effort to halt environmental deterioration was made in 1996 when the Philippines Department of Tourism formed a joint task force with the Canadian Urban Institute to develope a program of sustainable tourism for the island. Unfortunately, this initiative did not come in time to prevent the closure of White Sands beach the following year, when the Philippines Department of Environment and Natural Resources declared the ocean unsafe for bathers because of high coliform levels. The future of tourism on Boracay is now uncertain and the task force has encountered opposition and resistance from some local stakeholders who ignore or defy development regulations and restrictions (Trousdale, 1999).

Nepal—Degradation and Conservation

This small Himalayan kingdom faces some of the most serious environmental problems of any nation on earth. Between 1960 and 1990 its population doubled from 9 million to 18 million, and since firewood is used for nearly all cooking and heating needs, this increase has had a devastating effect on the country's forests. Among the factors exacerbating the situation are the illegal export of timber to neighboring India and vote buying by politicians who offer stands of trees to constituents. In the 1950s forests covered about 60% of the country, but now they cover only about 17%. The consequences of forest depletion are extremely grave: the worsening of an endemic problem of soil erosion, making Nepal the most eroded country in the world; and the endangering of some of the country's 800 species of birds (10% of the world's total) and over 600 species of butterflies.

Over 270,000 tourists visited Nepal in 1991, some 70,000 of whom were trekkers. It is estimated that approximately 100,000 trekkers now visit Nepal annually, most heading for the Annapurna region in the western part of the country. This area of magnificent scenery provides habitats for the endangered snow leopard, musk deer, and blue sheep, as well as for rhododendron and over 100 varieties of orchids. Environmental pressures from trekking tourism are intensified due to its seasonal nature and concentration patterns: more than 60% of the trekkers arrive during the period October through April, and the majority concentrate in three particular areas of the region. Each trekker consumes more firewood per day through meals, hot baths, and so on, than the average Nepali does in a week. This, together with increased demand for timber for lodge and tea shop construction, has worsened the longstanding problems of deforestation and soil erosion. Sanitation and waste disposal facilities along the main trekking routes are inadequate, and the trailsides have become depositories for human excrement, toilet paper, cans, bottles, and other garbage.

In 1986 the Annapurna Conservation Area Project (ACAP) was established in an effort to halt and reverse the process of environmental degradation in the region. Emphasizing local involvement, gradual implementation, and the needs of many users of the region (tourism, forestry, farming), the project has addressed some of the more obvious environmental problems. Alternative energy sources, such as micro-hydroelectricity from small local streams, and solar heating have been used. More fuel-efficient technologies such as back-boiler water heaters have been introduced as replacements for the traditional, open-hearth system. Reforestation programs involving the creation of tree nurseries have been developed, as well as training programs in forest management and conservation education. The project shows considerable promise and has already achieved some very positive results. However, much will depend on how willing the government will be to control the number of trekkers visiting the region. Since much of the funding for the conservation project comes from tourism revenues, this will require a very fine balancing act (Gurung and De Coursey, 1994; Weaver, 1998)

Mykonos—Architectural Pollution?

Mykonos is a Greek island of the Cyclades group in the Aegean Sea. Before World War II it attracted tourists who were mainly interested in cultural attractions, especially the archaeological site on the neighboring island of Delos. On Mykonos itself the attractions were primarily the island's tranquil ambience and its folk architecture. Mykonos benefited from the boom in European international tourism beginning in the 1960s, the number of arrivals—measured in hotel bookings alone—rising from around 5,000 in 1965 to 23,000 in 1970 and to 60,000 in 1990. To this last figure may be added another 10,000 or so visitors staying in other kinds of accommodations, as well as day visitors from the cruise ships that call daily during the main tourist season from May to September.

Overcrowding at Platis Yalos and Agios Stephanos—the two most popular beaches on the island—has apparently taken much of the pleasure out of the residents' customary evening promenade and visits to outdoor cafes. The longstanding water shortage has become a serious problem and underground water reserves have been polluted by hotel sewage. New-found wealth from tourism has changed the appearance of Mykonos. New buildings for tourists are replete with large windows, large balconies, elaborate iron doors, and marble staircases. These features reflect the architectural style of many tourist accommodations in Athens, rather than the traditional Cycladic style with its simple forms, small windows, and narrow wooden balconies. Attempts to regulate and control building in Mykonos have sparked controversy in the community. Most residents believe the island would be less attractive for tourists if changes in architectural styles continue, but not all are willing to accept public building restrictions. Interest in preserving Mykonos' traditional character is most pronounced among educated residents and newcomers who have settled on the island. Younger people and those who own their own homes are the ones most strongly against building restrictions, believing that flexibility in this matter is in their own best financial interests, as well as contributing to the public good. Thus far, the modernists appear to be winning the battle (Coccossis and Parpairis, 1995; Loukisias, 1978; Stott, 1996).

British Columbia, Canada—Writing on the Wall?

Although the tourism industry is a major component of British Columbia's (BC's) economy its importance tends to be somewhat obscured because of its fragmentation and low public profile in comparison with the province's traditional economic mainstays like forestry, mining, and fishing. Political thinking often seems to reflect this, as in recent provincial government intervention in the Canada–U.S. "salmon war" which risked alienating large numbers of American tourists. The consequences for BC tourism were not as bad as they might have been, but this has been due mainly to a decline in the value of the Canadian dollar relative to that of the U.S. dollar, rather than to remedial action on the part of provincial politicians. BC's touristic appeal rests mainly on its natural resources—its scenery, mountains, lakes, and rivers—and so the province has been advertised and marketed as "Super Natural British Columbia." Thus far, the negative environmental effects of tourism have not reached the crisis stage witnessed in some other places that offer nature-based tourism. But worrying signs were detected several years ago by Deardon (1983).

Deardon warned that the government and tourism authorities had not learned from the experience of BC's forestry and fishing industries, both of which had perfected the techniques of marketing and harvesting, but had proven to be grossly inadequate in the area of resource conservation. Scenic resources were being degraded by clear-cutting, even in areas traversed by large numbers of tourists, such as the route to Whistler Ski Resort. In the Okanagan Valley, BC Hydro was planning to erect hydro towers and sling cables across McIntyre Bluff near Vaseaux Lake, while aquatic weed infestation was spreading in Okanagan, Skaha, and Osoyoos Lakes.

While there now appears to be a greater recognition of the need to protect tourism resources, especially from the environmental effects of other industries, one is not aware that this is regarded as a matter of the highest importance. In a number of local communities it has been groups of concerned citizens, rather than municipal authorities, who have been most active in trying to safeguard these resources. A recent example was Pitt Meadows' residents' organized opposition to a developer's plan to build resort accommodation at Swan-E-Set golf and country club on the ecologically fragile Pitt Polder. Amid mounting concern over the future of BC's forestry and fishing industries, one can expect tourism to have a higher profile in the future. Hopefully, this will be accompanied by a keener awareness of the need to protect the resources on which this is based.

Back to Nature

Environmental protection and conservation should be considered good business practice for tourism, and this principle is of central importance in *ecotourism*. This term itself has been used in a variety of ways, some of them so broad as to be almost platitudinous—as when, for example, it refers to any kind of tourism that seeks to minimize social, cultural, and environmental disruptions. Elsewhere the term has been restricted in its application to tourism that actually achieves conservation and development objectives (Lindberg, Enriquez, and Sproule, 1996). This, of course, has the unfortunate effect of placing ecotourism beyond serious criticism. Here I use the term in a fairly narrow yet open-ended way to refer to tourism in which the natural environment and its flora and fauna are the main attraction, and where their preservation and enhancement are primary concerns of both promoters and tourists. The question of whether or not preservation, enhancement, or any other site-specific aims actually result is left open for empirical investigation.

Ecotourism, as I have defined it, is part of the tourism mix in nearly all destination countries, but in some it has been given special emphasis or attention. These include quite highly developed countries like Australia and New Zealand (Hall, 1994a), as well as many less developed countries such as Nepal (Gurung and De Coursey, 1994; Weaver, 1998), Kenya (Akama, 1996; Sindiga, 1995, 1996; Weaver, 1998), Thailand (Cohen, 1989; Deardon and Harron, 1994; Weaver, 1998) and Belize (Cater, 1992; Lindberg et al., 1996; Weaver, 1998). Costa Rica in particular has gained worldwide recognition as a major ecotourism destination, and since it is considered by many to offer a viable model for other less developed countries, I shall briefly outline the main features of ecotourism in this Central American country, drawing on the work of Chant (1992), Baez (1996), Weaver (1998), and Campbell (1999).

With a population of under three million, Costa Rica is one of the smallest countries in Latin America. It has enjoyed an enviable reputation for political stability and public safety, and this no doubt adds to its attractiveness for international visitors. Its economy was traditionally dependent on tropical agricultural export crops, mainly coffee, sugar, and bananas, and it depended on imports for almost one-third of all goods consumed domestically. A drop in world prices for its agricultural exports, and an external debt crisis in the 1970s and 1980s, provided much of the impetus for the development of the country's tourism industry. International arrivals increased from 155,000 in 1970 to 792,000 in 1995, while revenues rose from $21 million to $661 million during the same period, and tourism is now the country's main source of foreign exchange earnings.

Costa Rica is not particularly well-endowed with tourism resources: although it has beaches, volcanoes, and vegetational variety, it does not have the archaeological resources possessed by other countries in the region; and unlike neighboring Mexico or Guatemala, there are no major indigenous communities that could be active in cultural tourism. Nonetheless, its tourism industry is diverse, with segments promoting beach tourism, cruise ship tourism, business and convention tourism, as well as ecotourism. And despite Costa Rica's popular image as an important eco-tourism destination, this form of tourism is only a small part of the country's over-all tourism inventory and is found mainly in a number of public and private re-serves. Tourists already staying in the coastal resorts make up a large proportion of the visitors to these reserves (Weaver, 1998).

Costa Rica has 25 national parks with conditions ranging from tropical rainforest to alpine. The parks are usually well-managed, access to them is carefully regulated, and the results of ecotourism for the environment have been positive on the whole. Steps have been taken to prevent unplanned coastal tourism and to conserve the natural beauty of the country's 646 KM of beaches. A 1977 law created a 200-meter-wide marine land zone, subdivided into "public zones" where development is usu-ally prohibited, and "restricted zones" where it is subject to government regulation.

A major attraction is the Monteverde Cloud Forest Reserve, located in the north-western part of the country and extending down both sides of the Cordillera de Tilaran mountain range. Apart from spectacular scenery, it has six major ecological zones and an amazingly diverse range of flora and fauna: 2,500 plant species, 400 species of birds, 120 species of reptiles and amphibians, 100 species of mammals, and several thousand species of insects. The reserve was funded by dairy-farming American Quakers, who still dominate in ownership of tourist accommodations in this area, although locals have been encouraged to produce traditional crafts for sale to tourists at an on-site cooperative. Between 1974 and 1992 the annual num-ber of tourists visiting the reserve rose from 471 to 49,552, and the reserve contrib-utes about 18% of Costa Rica's total tourism revenues.

While ecotourism appears to have succeeded reasonably well in Costa Rica, it has not been without problems. It still depends to a considerable extent on day trips by tourists who are taking more conventional holidays in the country's coastal re-sorts. In the northeastern part of the country, Tortuguero National Park was created as a protected area for the green sea turtle, which used the beach for nesting. Villag-ers had to abandon their practice of harvesting turtle eggs and lumber from the area. Their subsistence agriculture declined as a cash economy developed around tourism. Lacking the capital to invest in tourism themselves, most villagers became involved in casual employment—working as childminders, food preparers, roof thatchers, and so on for the few permanent residents engaged in tourism or scien-tific research. At Monteverde and some other ecotourism areas land values have increased sharply, as have the costs of food; and in some small rural communities tourism development has proceeded in an ad hoc, haphazard fashion, with little or no governmental assistance or control. Ecotourism in some parks is being threat-ened by illegal activities such as gold mining, which the government officially op-poses, but recognizes the "squatters' rights" claimed by the miners.

It seems likely that Costa Rica's popularity as an ecotourism destination will grow as concern among tourists over environmental issues becomes more wide-spread, and as this form of tourism is promoted energetically by tour operators in Western societies. In that event, the authorities will have to be vigilant and tough minded in protecting its precious environmental resources from human impacts. Unfortunately, their record thus far is hardly encouraging, being marked by lack of proper planning and adequate funding for ecotourism, as well as a tendency to view increases in visitor arrivals as evidence of a successful tourism policy.

Keeping Things in Perspective

The effects of tourism on the physical environment can vary considerably between different destinations, and arriving at an accurate balance sheet of positive and negative effects is no easy matter. While we should be cautious about making broad generalizations and subjective assessments, it is probably fair to say that of all the criticisms leveled against tourism, those citing its harmful environmental effects are the most telling and serious. Industry leaders have become increasingly sensitive to such criticisms and many have been engaged in campaigns to promote sustainable forms of tourism and to construct an environmentally friendly image for the industry. The WTO has been at the forefront of such efforts by encouraging research on tourism's environmental effects, organizing a program to ensure clean beaches, producing manuals and guides for national parks development and sustainable tourism, and spearheading a number of other initiatives. In 1998 the WTO, in collaboration with the United Nations Environment Program (UNEP), held a major conference on sustainable tourism in small islands, which are particularly susceptible to environmental damage from tourism development. The delegates concluded that more economic and technical support should be forthcoming from international bodies, and they also urged island authorities to eschew quick gains and instead plan for moderate, sustainable tourism development.

Ecotourism has been heralded as the form of sustainable tourism most likely to succeed in reconciling touristic and environmental interests in a mutually advantageous way. In places like Belize and Costa Rica the results have been promising, and there has been a growth of interest in ecotourism worldwide. Like other forms of tourism, however, ecotourism requires careful planning and regulation, and strict limits on the numbers of visitors have to be enforced. We should also bear in mind that despite the wide publicity ecotourism has received, "gazing on nature" is a *primary* travel objective for only a small minority of tourists at present. Swarbrooke and Horner (1999) suggest that, although there has been a lot written about the "green tourist," the empirical evidence for the existence of this market segment is scanty. They cite British and German surveys showing that tourists consider the environmental quality of the destination to be an important contributor to vacation satisfaction, but suggest that this finding reflects narrow self-interest (in having a nice vacation, this year, in this place) rather than a general concern with environmental issues.

Perhaps we should pray that ecotourism does not become anything larger than a niche market. If most of us become "born again" ecotourists and forsake our favorite haunts, such as Waikiki, Miami Beach, Las Vegas, and the like, the pressures on the world's most fragile ecosystems would quickly become unbearable. Urry (1990) suggests that the growing interest in both visiting and protecting nature is related to major social changes in Western societies. He believes that it is among members of the *service class* that the attachment to the countryside and heritage traditions is most pronounced. According to Urry the service class is made up of persons who (a) do not own significant amounts of capital or land; (b) are engaged in institutions that service capital; (c) enjoy superior work situations and benefits; and (d) follow "careers," entry to which requires educational credentials higher than those required for most other white-collar occupations (1990). In Britain, *The Independent,* a national daily newspaper with a mainly middle-class readership, has produced a *Guide to Real Holidays Abroad* which covers nature-oriented and other more "authentic" and "worthwhile" travel opportunities. These service-class tastes are also expressed in a desire for country houses or, failing that, for houses designed in rustic style in suburban subdivisions with names that evoke rusticity, for example, Village, Manor, Meadows, and Grove.

According to Urry, such contemporary service-class tastes express an opposition to modernism. This takes a number of different forms: for example, distaste for the "shiny barbarism" of mass tourist resorts popular among the working class, or in "alternative constructions" of nature. In these alternative constructions, "nature" includes things like health foods, microbrewed ale, non-Western medicine, natural fibers like cotton or wool, and so on. This particular vision of the countryside involves a "romantic gaze" which emphasizes certain natural scenes, while others (such as farm machinery, farm laborers, telegraph wires, concrete farm buildings, motorways, and derelict land) are filtered out. From Urry's perspective, concern for the countryside and its conservation is mainly a service-class preoccupation. The upper class is safe and secure in its rural estates and hideaways and has no cause to feel anxious. The working class, meanwhile, continues to treat the countryside as a temporary playground—a nice place for farmers, or a pleasant place to have a picnic in, but a bit too quiet and dull to get seriously attached to.

Chapter 8
No Escape From Politics

Government Involvement in Tourism

National and International Organizations

Governments are involved in tourism in a variety of ways, most notably through their respective National Tourism Administrations (NTAs). According to a WTO survey, these were mainly government ministries or sections within government departments (two-thirds of NTAs surveyed); sometimes they are corporations linked to or supervised by the central government (one-third of NTAs surveyed). The WTO survey found considerable variation in the activities of NTAs, but their most common functions were promotion and information; research, statistics and planning; resource inventory and protection; facilities development; manpower development; facilitation of travel; and promoting international cooperation in tourism (Pearce, 1989).

In 1997 some 133 countries and territories were members of the WTO, an intergovernmental organization that deals with global tourism policy and issues. This body also has over 300 affiliated members from both the public and private sectors. Besides acting as a vehicle for gathering and communicating information on tourism, the WTO acts as a coordinating body for tourism projects involving the United Nations Development Program. Its mission is to promote and develop tourism to encourage international peace and understanding, economic development, and international trade. The main functions of the WTO are cooperation for development; tourism education and training; environment, planning and financing; maintaining the quality of tourism services; statistics and market research; and communications and documentation.

The WTO has forged a significant degree of international consensus on a number of major tourism issues, these being expressed in formal agreements such as the Manila Declaration on World Tourism (1980), the Tourism Bill of Rights and Tourist Code (1985), The Hague Declaration on Tourism (1989), and the Global Code of Ethics for Tourism (1999). It has also been active in worldwide campaigns to eliminate sex tourism in Southeast Asia, and to encourage environmental conservation and the development of ecotourism. Besides the WTO, other major international tourism bodies are the Department of Regional Development in the Organization of American States (OAS) and the Travel Committee of the Organization for Economic Cooperation and Development (OECD).

Other Forms of Government Involvement

Besides working through organizations of the kind mentioned here, government influence on the tourism industry is brought to bear in a number of other ways (Pearce, 1989):

- *Through government regulation in tourism-related areas.* These areas include such things as customs and immigration, liquor licensing and shop trading laws, civil aviation, and regulation of conservation.
- *Through government fiscal policies.* Policy areas can include currency exchange rates, foreign investment codes, taxes, grants, and incentives.
- *Through government actions as landowner or resource manager.* Decisions on "nontourism" matters, such as soil conservation or forestry, can often affect tourism development.
- *Through local government policies and regulations.* In connection with such matters as building codes, provision of local infrastructure, and zoning regulations.

Government policies and actions regarding tourism can serve a number of different purposes. According to Pearce there are four main kinds of objectives pursued by governments with respect to tourism:

1. *Economic.* For example, improving the balance of payments, promoting economic diversification, promoting regional development, creating jobs and raising income levels, stimulating other investments, or raising taxes.
2. *Sociocultural.* For example, promoting tourism as part of a general policy on leisure, recreation and social welfare, or minimizing adverse sociocultural effects of tourism.
3. *Environmental.* For example, protecting and conserving the physical environment in the context of tourism development.
4. *Political.* For example, to broaden support for a regime domestically or internationally (1989, pp. 40–41).

Examples of tourism promotion in which generating support for a regime was a consideration are Franco's Spain and Marcos' Philippines. Bowman (1992) looks at the ways in which sympathy for Israel is promoted by Israeli tour guides and suggests that the very presence of tourists creates an atmosphere of normalcy for many Israelis. He also suggests that the Israeli situation shows that host societies, so often portrayed as powerless victims of international tourism, may often have considerable influence in shaping the images visitors form about these societies.

The nature of government involvement in the tourism industry can shift subtly over time, as has happened throughout much of Southeast Asia. This shift has been examined by Wood (1984), who shows that government involvement in tourism in this region has moved through three phases:

- *Phase 1—The government as planner of tourism development.* Government presence is necessary in the early stages of mass tourism development, with the high infrastructural costs of providing international-class airports, luxury hotels, and so on. It is also encouraged by donor agencies, such as the World Bank and the International Monetary Fund (IMF).
- *Phase 2—The government as marketer of cultural meanings.* It is often necessary to define a national identity or cultural heritage in ways responsive to the needs of tourists. In both Malaysia and Indonesia Islam was felt to be unmarketable, so Malaysia marketed beach resort tourism and Indonesia marketed the Hinduism of Bali and the Hindu-Buddhist heritage of Java. These state definitions of tourist attractions are gradually accepted by locals.
- *Phase 3—The government as arbiter of cultural change.* Although governments do not invent cultural change by promoting and sponsoring tourism, they mediate it in two main ways: by becoming involved in redefining *custom* and *authenticity* within the culture (for example, by issuing certificates of competence and authenticity to groups performing for tourists in Bali); and by becoming involved in redefining the culture's relationship to the rest of society (for example, by granting legitimacy to the religion of Toraja in Sulawesi, Indonesia, which was formerly looked down upon by authorities who favored Protestant expansion in this part of the country).

The Government as a Problem

A common complaint among tourism industry leaders is that tourism does not get the kind of government support warranted by the industry's size and economic importance. The industry's lack of "political clout" is attributed, in part, to its highly fragmentary character and the predominance of women and minorities in tourism employment. Matthews and Richter (1981) argue that tourism in the United States suffered from political neglect, despite the magnitude of the industry. They point out that, although the tourism caucus is the largest special interest caucus in the U.S. Congress, both Presidents Carter and Reagan tried to abolish the U.S. Travel Service (USTS) and its successor, the U.S. Travel and Tourism Administration (USTTA). Citing budgetary constraints, the Clinton administration in 1996 closed down the USTTA and also withdrew from the WTO. Increasingly, tourism administrations are being forced to accept reduced levels of government financial support and are entering into partnerships with the private sector.

❖   ✦   ❋   ❖   ❖

Government and Business Partnerships in Tourism

After a period of uncertainty, the U.S. government finally decided not to withdraw from tourism completely, as initially expected. Following the disbanding of the U.S. Travel and Tourism Administration (USTTA), it established the U.S. Tourism Industries as a 13-person section of the International Trade Administration—one of 15 agencies that make up the Department of Commerce. Its responsibilities cover tourism research, tourism policy, and technical assistance for U.S. companies seeking to attract foreign tourists. It also acts as secretariat for the Tourism Policy Council (TPC), which is made up of representatives of the federal agencies. Its role is to assist and advise on tourism trade development issues. At the same time, the U.S. House of Representatives formally approved the establishment of the U.S. National Tourism Organization (USNTO), proposed by the Travel Industry Association (TIA) as a new public-private sector marketing body to replace the USTTA. For the time being, however, it is being funded solely by the industry.

Public-private sector partnership is growing at the local level as well as nationally. The passing of the California Tourism Marketing Act in 1997 resulted in the establishment of the nonprofit, mutual benefit corporation, the California Travel and Tourism Commission (CTTC). This is a public-private sector partnership between the state government and all companies and organizations from tourism or related industries—such as retail outlets, photographic equipment manufacturers, and restaurants—which benefit in some way from tourism. The concept behind the CTTC is to leverage the existing state allocation of funds for tourism marketing—which has been declining over the last few years—with private funds raised by an industrywide assessment. Private sector membership contributions to the CTTC funds, which are self-assessed according to turnover, are expected to result in annual funding of US$7.5 million to supplement the state's US$7.3 million contribution, thereby helping to improve visitor information and facilities, as well as increase promotional and marketing efforts.

Asia's economic and financial crisis has resulted in a squeeze on the budgets of a number of NTAs and NTOs. Countries suffering budget cuts include Australia and Japan. A request to government from the Tourism Authority of Thailand (TAT) for a supplementary budget of 640 million baht (US$16 million) was recently turned down. Nevertheless, there are a number of positive developments in the region's tourism industry. India's Tourism Secretary, Madan Prasad Bezbaruah, says his ministry is currently in the process of drafting a new policy which will involve the private sector in tourism management and promotion in partnership with the government, regional, and local authorities. A Board of Tourism Industry and Trade has already been set up, with representation from all industry associations, and the ministry is now aiming to create a National Tourism Authority—a joint venture between the public and private sectors for tourism management and promotion.

Southern Africa's single largest tourism development, encompassing five Southern African Development Community (SADC) countries, is expected to be created through the planned US$10 billion Okavango Upper Zambezi International Tourism Development Initiative. First discussed more than five years ago, the project aims to establish a Southern African wildlife sanctuary in the wetlands of the Zambezi and Okavango deltas. The development will incorporate game parks in Angola, Namibia, Botswana, Zambia, and Zimbabwe and is expected to cover more than 260,000 square miles of land. The donor community has indicated an interest in helping the SADC states develop the project, which presents a strategic opportunity for public-private sector partnership. The five participating states will finance 10% of the project's infrastructure, with the private sector covering the major 90% share.

WTO News Service, June 1998. Reprinted with permission of the World Tourism Organization.

☀   ╬   ✳   ✦   ☀

Besides the charge of government neglect, industry representatives often point to various government-imposed regulations and restrictions which, they believe, impede the industry's progress. A number of these impediments have been identified by Edgell (1990):

- *Travel allowance restrictions.* Over 100 countries still impose such restrictions, usually by setting a limit on the amount of foreign currency the individual can purchase from a bank and take outside the country or outside a particular currency area. A few countries prohibit the purchase of foreign currency for international travel purposes. These measures serve to protect the domestic tourism industries of the countries imposing the restrictions.
- *Duty-free allowances.* Nearly all countries place limits on the duty-free importation of goods by visitors and returning residents. These have a constraining effect on tourists' shopping and thereby limit international tourism expenditure. European visitors to the United States have relatively low duty-free allowances, while those from Japan have much larger ones.
- *Entry and exit requirements.* These vary widely from one country to another. The United States levies customs and immigration user fees on all visitors except nationals of Canada, Mexico, and the Caribbean. Australia charged a

$5 immigration fee and $20 departure tax until 1988, when pressure from the public and the international airlines resulted in the abolition of the immigration fee and a reduction in the departure tax to $10. Most developing countries impose an exit tax on all departing visitors.

- *Obstacles to companies.* Foreign-owned tourism businesses may be disadvantaged by government economic policy, for example, limitations on market access, restrictions on the remittance of earnings, exchange controls, domestic content laws in advertising, local labor laws, and so on.

Lickorish (1991) has noted a number of obstacles that need to be cleared away by European Economic Community governments in efforts to harmonize policies and practices among member countries. Among the most important of these, he suggests, are:

- *Fiscal measures.* Different countries apply value added tax (VAT) at different rates, and these have the effect of acting as tariffs and distorting competition. In addition, excise duties or international taxes on such things as gasoline and liquor also vary from one country to another.
- *Frontier controls.* Although most frontier controls have been reduced or eliminated, some member countries still apply restrictions on currency exchange or availability. Passport controls have been greatly simplified, but visitors from outside the Community may still have their passports checked when crossing from one member country to another.
- *Transport.* In air transport there continue to be controls aimed at limiting competition and protecting national carriers.
- *Fiscal and financial regulation.* These include regulations restricting investment in such things as land or airlines, variable port and departure taxes, and different subsidies and levies that can affect tourism.

It should be noted, however, that the WTO predicts that the switch to a single currency (the euro) will have a positive impact on European tourism by making prices more transparent and thereby increasing competition. The WTO believes this will make the countries of the euro currency zone the world's most powerful tourism force, outperforming its nearest competitor—the United States—in terms of tourist arrivals, tourism receipts, and outbound trips.

The World's Peace Industry?

The claim that tourism can improve international understanding and contribute to world peace is one regularly made by organizations such as the WTO, OECD, and the World Bank, as well as by industry representatives and some tourism scholars. Actual research on this subject is quite scanty, and the results tend to be mixed and inconclusive. A good deal of the research has focused on attitudes to visitors in tourist destinations. While close contact with tourists (for example, by hotel employees) has sometimes been associated with positive attitudes towards them, this is a long way from demonstrating that international understanding is significantly improved through tourism contacts (Mings, 1988).

The optimistic view of tourism's role in fostering international understanding forms part of the basic philosophical underpinnings of an emerging "Tourism for Peace" movement. It is too early to determine how strong or effective this movement will become, but a major conference in Vancouver in 1988 attracted over 500 participants. The theme of the conference was "Tourism—A Vital Force for Peace." Not all of the participants agreed about tourism's positive contributions to peace so far, but the overwhelming majority felt that tourism certainly had enormous potential for improving international understanding and tolerance. The participants included some notable academics, but most were from the industry itself or from government tourism agencies. Whether this embryonic movement represents heartfelt conviction or a good public relations move by an "unloved industry" remains to be seen.

In a paper prepared just prior to the Vancouver conference, D'Amore (1988) argued that tourism can operate as a form of "track two" diplomacy, spreading information about beliefs, aspirations, perspectives, cultures, and politics of the citizens of one country to those of another. This is different from "track one" diplomacy, which is conducted through official government channels and agencies. By breaking down established patterns of isolation and mistrust, and providing opportunities for people to know and understand each other better, D'Amore suggested that tourism does help improve international relations and is the world's main peace industry.

Unfortunately, the research on this topic has yet to produce firm support for D'Amore's contention. Pizam (1996) examined the results of four studies of this topic conducted between 1990 and 1994, all of which focused on the effects of tourism contacts between people from traditionally hostile or unfriendly countries (Americans and Soviets, Israelis and Egyptians, and Greeks and Turks). The studies compared the attitudes of tourists before and after their visits, and also involved the use of control groups who did not travel. The results showed that only a few of the attitudes of travelers changed as a result of their tourist experiences and that the majority of these changes took a negative direction. Pizam's conclusion, therefore, was that tourist experience by itself does not necessarily change attitudes in a positive direction, or reduce perceived differences between ethnic or national groups. In another study involving a cross-national comparison of college and university students in Australia, Canada, England, Korea, Turkey, and the United States, the researchers concluded that, until further research produces confirming evidence, the tourism-promotes-peace hypothesis "remains simply a platitude" (Var and Ap, 1998, p. 55).

It may be that in trying to assess tourism's role in improving international relations, the concern with attitudinal change through host-tourist contact is misplaced. If tourism does contribute to peace or an improvement in international relations, it seems more likely that the mechanisms are primarily economic. As we know, the process of globalization involves the proliferation of linkages and ties of interdependence between various national economies, so that an economic problem in one part of the world can have repercussions in other parts. The effects of the crisis in Asian financial markets, for example, were felt outside this region; and a country like the United States now has a vested interest in ensuring that the economy of Japan, its former enemy, remains strong and healthy. International tourism is not the only economic activity that promotes these global linkages and ties of economic interdependence, but it is certainly an important contributor in this respect. So if there is any improvement in international understanding as a result of tourism, it is probably an improvement in our understanding of how national economies are interconnected and interdependent. Any deterioration in relations between Western European countries—where most international tourism activity is concentrated— would not only threaten tourism in the region, but would also threaten the economies of all the nations involved.

Tourism and Political Ideology

Tourism as a form of imperialism or neocolonialism has been one of the pervasive themes in the literature on tourism in developing countries. This theme is summarized in a useful fashion by Mathieson and Wall (1982), who suggest that contemporary relations between rich, powerful, industrial societies and poor, weak, Third World societies resemble those that existed in colonial times. For these authors, North-South tourism may be viewed as a new and subtle form of imperialism or colonial exploitation. Three features in particular form the basis of their analogy between international tourism and colonialism: first, the host country's political and economic priorities and organization have been geared to satisfying the needs of tourists; second, tourism development may be accompanied by a one-way transfer of wealth from the destination area to the tourist-generating areas; and third, nonlocals may be employed in professional and managerial positions, while the owners may be absentees. Mathieson and Wall nevertheless acknowledge that the similarities between the two are not exact: the encouragement of the growth of the tourism industry by locals is not typical of colonial beginnings (tourism is invited or negotiated, while colonialism is imposed); foreign manipulation and control of local politicians is unlikely to be as strong or as influential in tourism as it is in outright colonial domination; and detailed and reliable analysis of the economics of North-South tourism are somewhat scarce, so that the full nature and extent of economic exploitation is not known.

Until quite recently, the adoption of tourism by Third World governments often presented ideological problems of a kind not encountered in industrial capitalist societies. The association of tourism with neocolonialism was one of these problem areas; its association with luxury and wastefulness was another; and its association with servility (towards tourists) was yet another. These concerns were especially important for countries that had recently emerged from a colonial past, or saw them-selves struggling against present-day imperialism—particularly when the govern-ments in question embraced state socialism in one form or another. For them, North-South tourism could easily be interpreted as a manifestation of international capitalism's domination over the world's hinterlands.

Because of these ideological problems, several Third World countries were sus-picious of, or lukewarm towards, tourism development. Tourism was at first consid-ered to be incompatible with Ghana's brand of African socialism during the Nkrumah period between 1957 and 1966, and this was one of the reasons why it was neglected in national development plans at that time. In Tanzania, a similar situation existed, and even when the government decided to develop tourism, it met with determined opposition from young ideologues. In 1973 a public debate on the ideological cor-rectness of tourism was initiated by the Youth League of the Tanzanian African Na-tional Union (TANU), the ruling party. Youth League members were highly critical of Tanzanian tourism and questioned a number of its features: its ability to generate foreign exchange; its capacity to create employment and stimulate improvement in social services; and its ability to promote international understanding. They further insisted that tourism stood unmasked as part of the international imperialist strat-egy against socialism (Shivji, 1973).

Economic considerations—especially the need to earn foreign exchange—have driven many Third World countries into tourism development, and ideological res-ervations appear to have been placed on the back burner. In 1986 the Sandinista government of Nicaragua gave control of the Montelimar estate of the deposed dic-tator, Antonio Somoza, to the Nicaraguan Tourism Ministry. It was authorized to build an upscale resort on the estate, provided that no government funds would be required. The ministry succeeded in obtaining a $10 million loan from Italian in-vestors in 1988. Sandinista militants protested, claiming that the project was elitist and counterrevolutionary. President Daniel Ortega's response? "We need the money." Naturally, the United States is the ultimate target market for this project. More and more countries are joining the tourism bandwagon for the same basic reason: Ko-rea is making an effort, as is North Vietnam, and even Iraq is trying to attract tour-ists (personally, I would sooner spend a cold, wet November hiking through Glen Dreary—at least for the time being).

One of the latest developing countries to embrace tourism is Cuba. The cir-cumstances under which tourism development occurred and the difficulties of rec-onciling it with revolutionary socialist ideology are discussed by Hall (1992). From the beginning of the present century to the Castro-led revolution in 1959, Cuba had been an important tourist destination for North Americans. The revolutionary gov-ernment rejected tourism as an agency of imperialism, but this view began to change in the 1980s. Foreign exchange was in short supply, and economic growth slowed down as a result of a series of poor sugar harvests and falling world prices for this commodity, as well as for other important Cuban exports like tobacco and nickel. The crisis led to the suspension of repayment of debts to the West in 1986; and Cuba also began to lose the economic and ideological support that had come from the Soviet Union and other Eastern Bloc countries. In 1987 the government decided to give tourism development the highest priority, but insisted that it be qualitatively different from the hedonistic tourism typical of the prerevolutionary period. As a result, Cuba is now engaged in the development of several kinds of tourism, the most important being:

- *Coastal and Water-Related Tourism*—Cuba has just under 6,000 KM of coast-line, and its 289 recognized beaches constitute the largest number of any Caribbean country. It is also capitalizing on its reputation (fostered by the famous writer, Ernest Hemingway) as an outstanding center of sport fishing, both in its coastal waters and its rivers and lakes.
- *Heritage Tourism*—The major attraction here is the old colonial district of Havana, but other historic sites exist in the country's smaller cities and towns. One such city—Trinidad—dates back to 1514 and was designated a UN World Heritage Site in 1988.
- *Ecotourism*—The country has numerous wildlife parks, marine reserves, and a botanical garden that is home to 380 species of birds and 8,000 species of flora. In the interior, tourism facilities have been made available for such activities as trekking, horse riding, camping, and caving.
- *Health Tourism*—For some time, wealthy Latin Americans have visited Cuba to avail themselves of the country's relatively inexpensive, high-quality health-care. Tourism authorities are building on this base by developing a number of healthcare resorts featuring modern sanitoria and hotel complexes.
- *Conference and Business Tourism*—This has centered mainly on catering to visitors attending conventions at Havana's International Conference Center. In 1990 a new hotel—the Biocaribe—was built in Havana primarily to serve visiting professionals and scientists.

The most serious problem facing Cuban tourism is the U.S. ban on travel to that country—a ban that is likely to be lifted only after Castro has gone. Meanwhile, it effectively locks Cuba out of a large and lucrative segment of the market for international leisure travel. The U.S. trade embargo on Cuba has also adversely affected the country's ability to gain access to the important market for cruise ship tourism. Nonetheless, Cuba's tourism has grown rapidly, rising from 238,000 arrivals in 1985 to 1.1 million in 1997. Long-term prospects for success seem good, with companies like Club Med establishing themselves in the popular Varadero beach area.

Tourism and Political Instability

This is one of the most important topics in the politics of tourism, and one which is now receiving a good deal of research attention (Hall, 1994b; Pizam and Mansfield, 1996). Political stability is not always a sign of a democratic political system: in the former USSR and some African countries, authoritarian systems succeeded in maintaining high levels of political stability over long periods; in a country like Italy, on the other hand, frequent political crises and changes of government occurred within more open political systems. As the example of Italy suggests, there are also different degrees and kinds of instability: in some cases it may be mild and nonviolent in nature, or even semi-institutionalized and managed within the system itself; in others, it may be manifested in violence directed against the system, or against those who control and support it. More broadly, political instability may assume regional or global proportions, when normal rules and procedures governing international relations are either malfunctioning, or have been abandoned in favor of war. How do these kinds of situations affect tourism? Let us consider a number of forms and examples of political instability and note their consequences.

Military Coups

Military coups have been a serious problem for many developing countries, particularly in Africa. In The Gambia the only successful coup took place in 1994, although an unsuccessful attempt had occurred some 13 years earlier. In the year following the unsuccessful attempt, international arrivals dropped by about 25%, but recovered fairly quickly thereafter. In the year after the successful attempt, arrivals dropped by almost 58% when many European tourists heeded their governments' warnings against visiting The Gambia. However, two years after the successful coup, The Gambia's international arrivals had nearly reached their precoup level. Ghana, on the other hand, was plagued by a series of plots, attempted coups, and successful coups during the 1970s and 1980s, and has only been able to develop its tourism industry during the more recent period of political stability. In Fiji, ethnic conflict between Indians—who mainly controlled the country's tourism industry—and indigenous Fijians resulted in a coup in May of 1987. Although the tourists were in no great danger, the effects of the coup were immediate and dramatic. Tourist arrivals from the United States, Australia, and New Zealand dropped by about 75%, while those from Japan fell by about 50%. Again, government warnings in the tourist-generating countries appear to have had a major impact on people's decisions to cancel their travel plans. The devaluation of the Fijian dollar, and drastic price cuts by the local tourism industry, contributed to an increase in arrivals from Australia and New Zealand. However, a second coup took place in September of 1987, leading to a 30% drop in arrivals. It took until 1990 for arrivals to once again reach their 1986 mark, and since that time Fiji has been struggling to reestablish consumer confidence. Its efforts have been hampered by lingering fears about long-term political instability, and also by the attempts of rival destinations such as Bali (Indonesia) and Queensland (Australia) to profit from Fiji's troubles (Hall, 1994b).

In Thailand military coups, rather than elections, have long been the most common method of changing governments. Typically, these have been bloodless affairs which did not receive much publicity outside the country, and had little impact on

Thailand's tourism industry. In May 1992, however, the military coup was a violent one and included the shooting of civilian demonstrators. Ugly scenes of violence were captured on television for audiences around the world. The immediate effect of this was a sharp reduction in arrivals, and financial losses estimated at between $400 million and $1.2 billion. Hall suggests that a long-term effect of the 1992 coup has been a change in the way tourists now perceive Thailand. They now consider it to be much less safe and stable than they had formerly imagined. The main problem for Thailand, Hall argues, is the restoration of the country's positive destination image—one that is already threatened by sex tourism and an AIDS epidemic (Hall, 1994).

Wars

Whether civil or international, wars have had some of the most adverse effects on tourism, and this has been true throughout the long history of travel. Prior to the civil war, Yugoslavia was one of the most attractive and promising tourist areas in Europe. Today, the various countries that once comprised Yugoslavia have been left with a massive task of rebuilding a shattered tourism industry, its infrastructure, and its image. In Sri Lanka, the longstanding conflict between the Sinhalese—the key players in Sri Lanka's tourism industry—and the minority Tamils has also had serious consequences. As in Fiji, tourists were hardly affected by the conflict, but the industry itself was almost wiped out because of negative reactions in major tourist-generating countries.

The civil war between Turkish and Greek Cypriots, which led to the partition of Cyprus, had important consequences for the island's tourism industry. In the southern (Greek) part of Cyprus, loss of territory and tourism resources prompted a major reconstruction and expansion of coastal and mountain tourism. In the northern (Turkish) part, new territory was gained that included some well-established resorts, but several countries imposed an economic boycott of this area due to its continued occupation by the Turkish army (Mansfield and Kliot, 1996). The Gulf War in 1991 not only deterred most tourists from visiting Middle Eastern countries, but also raised fears of terrorist attacks on airports used by American travelers.

Terrorism and Independence Movements

In some instances tourism and tourists have been singled out as targets in terrorist attacks. These attacks may be attempts to undermine the credibility of the government by showing its inability to provide adequate protection for tourists. Or they may be designed to destabilize a country by weakening its economy and causing discontent among the unemployed or underprivileged. These objectives appear to have been paramount in Islamic fundamentalist attacks on tourists in Egypt since 1992, although another reason may have been to protect Islam from the "corrupting influences" of Western culture—of which tourists are often the most visible carriers.

In several places, including Corsica and the Caribbean, Club Med resorts have been targets of violent attacks by nationalist and separatist groups (Blednick, 1988).

The conflict between Protestants and Catholics in Northern Ireland did not involve the deliberate targeting of tourists in that country, but seriously affected tourism nonetheless. Between 1967 and 1976—a period marked by numerous sectarian attacks and killings—the number of tourists visiting Northern Ireland dropped dramatically from over one million to only 423,000 (Wall, 1996). In England, however, Irish Republican Army (IRA) bombings often focused on areas popular with tourists, and heavy security measures had to be put in place at several tourist sites, as well as at major airports. During the 1980s the British government had to mount a determined campaign to restore tourist confidence.

While many groups seeking independence or political autonomy use terror and violent intimidation to further their ends, others have adopted a strategy of peaceful persuasion and propaganda. Where tourism is a vital part of a country's economy, this strategy may be directed especially towards tourists. Although one aim here may be to weaken the economy and the government, another is to enlist the support of tourists in the cause. With their many linkages to other countries, some tourists might then spread the message and generate worldwide sympathy for the independence movement. Both aims appear to have been important for Hawaiian rights activists quite recently. Early in 1994 a Hawaiian family was ordered to remove a small concession stand from Waikiki beach, since no vending is allowed on Hawaiian beaches. The Ohana Council—one of several Hawaiian sovereignty groups active in the islands—responded by printing leaflets outlining its position on sovereignty, on tourism as a perpetuation of the illegal occupation of their lands, and on the special rights of native Hawaiians to work on the beaches. These were passed out to tourists in Waikiki, with the polite request that they go home, as well as with a traditional *Aloha* (the term can mean *love, fond welcome,* or *fond good-bye*). This gentle, low-key campaign did not have widespread support from other Hawaiian sovereignty groups, but its focus on tourists clearly worried the state government. The tendency of local advocacy groups to exploit Hawaii's dependence on tourism led Governor John Waihee, himself a native Hawaiian, to complain bitterly. This official reaction is understandable, but perhaps the Governor should count himself lucky that these gentle Hawaiians did not turn really nasty, and adopt some of the tactics employed by independence groups in other parts of the world.

Politics and Tourism in Ghana

There are few countries where politics and tourism are so closely intertwined as they have been in Ghana, a country with a wealth of raw resources for tourism. A brief look at the situation there will show how tourism's fortunes have been shaped by political circumstances, and also illustrate some of the themes and issues discussed in the previous sections.

Ghana's total population is just over 16 million, 70% of whom live in the southern half of the country. There are over 100 different ethnic groups, none of which constitutes more than 15% of the population. In the south, the major ethnic groups are the Akan, Ewe, and Ga, while the Mole-Dagbani, Gurma, and Grusi are the largest in the north. For linguistic and ethnic homogeneity, Ghana ranks 27th in the world, with 29% homogeneity (by contrast, Korea ranks 135th, with 100% homogeneity). The country's official language, however, is English. About 62% of the population professes Christianity (mainly in Protestant forms), and 16% is Muslim. Some 21% follow traditional animist religions.

The coastal area has a long history of contact with Europe, beginning in the fifteenth century with the arrival of the Portuguese. Merchants and missionaries from various nations including France, Sweden, Denmark, Holland, and Britain have been active in what is now Ghana, but Britain established firm control over the coastal area in the early part of the nineteenth century. The interior Ashanti region was subdued only at the end of the nineteenth century, and the British colony of the Gold Coast was then established. In 1957 the colony gained independence and became Ghana, with Kwame Nkrumah as its charismatic first President. After nine years of relative stability, Nkrumah was overthrown in a military coup while he was absent on a visit to Hanoi. From then on, the country became one of the most politically unstable countries in Africa.

Ghana's major tourism assets include over 300 miles of coastline, with excellent sandy beaches and picturesque lagoons; guaranteed sunshine throughout most of the year, and especially during the winter months; a coastal region rich in history, with tangible reminders in the form of numerous well-preserved forts and castles dating from the slave-trade era, three of which have been designated World Heritage sites by the UN; interior regions containing a variety of interesting ethnic cultures and lifestyles; Lake Volta, which is one of the world's largest man-made lakes; and game and wildlife reserves that, though not as large or as interesting as those of East Africa, far surpass those of The Gambia. Despite these and other natural advantages, Ghana seemed neither willing nor able to promote international tourism in a sustained and systematic way until quite recently.

During the 1960s tourism was not encouraged by the Nkrumah government, which viewed it as another form of imperialism or neocolonialism. However, at that time Ghana and its leader occupied a prominent place in the Pan-African movement, and the country was a magnet for many African Americans. These visitors were on roots-seeking journeys and most identified strongly with Ghana as the first of the newly independent African nations, its exciting efforts in nation building, as well as its attempt to develop and practice *African socialism*. After the heady days of the Nkrumah period ended in 1966, Ghana slipped from prominence on the world's stage, and relatively few tourists bothered to visit this interesting country.

In the period of political turmoil and economic decline following the collapse of the Nkrumah regime, international tourism in Ghana was virtually nonexistent.

Of the 36,000 international arrivals recorded for 1984, more than half involved returning Ghanaians. Since then, arrivals have increased substantially, rising to 85,000 in 1985 and 329,000 in 1997.

Ideological opposition to tourism during the Nkrumah period (1957–1966) meant that a good deal of valuable time was lost which could have been spent on developing and implementing a national tourism policy. Moreover, this was a period of relative affluence and stability in Ghana—one in which internal economic conditions were more conducive to tourism development than they were to be later. With few exceptions, successive governments failed to take tourism seriously as part of their overall plans for national economic development. Besides their ideological skepticism or ignorance about tourism as a development tool, Ghana's politicians felt they had more pressing political and economic problems to worry about.

Adu-Febiri (1990a) attributes Ghana's slow pace of tourism development to two fundamental factors: one of these was the country's low rate of capital accumulation, making it difficult to develop tourism along conventional lines with international standard accommodations and other tourism facilities; and the other was the "collectivistic ethic" which obliged wealthier Ghanaians to assist poorer relatives, making it difficult for them to fully embrace the Western entrepreneurial and managerial styles required in conventional tourism. Adu-Febiri believes political factors were of secondary importance, having the effect of discouraging foreign investment in the tourism industry.

While Adu-Febiri's thesis is interesting and the primary factors he analyzes are of importance, it seems more likely that tourism development in Ghana was retarded by the country's volatile political climate. There have been eight major changes in government since independence in 1957, five of them resulting from military coups. Numerous attempted and aborted coups have also taken place, besides reported plots to remove particular governments. During the 1980s the number of suspected plots and coup attempts averaged approximately four per year. Ghana thus has the highest *total military involvement score* (TMIS) in Africa. The TMIS is a quantitative index that assigns countries five points for a successful coup, three for an unsuccessful one, and one point for a reported plot (Teye, 1988).

Political instability of this magnitude had a number of adverse consequences for Ghanaian tourism: first, it discouraged potential visitors by making Ghana seem a highly dangerous and unpredictable part of the world; second, the governments of many foreign countries issued warnings to their citizens who might be contemplating travel to Ghana; third, as Adu-Febiri acknowledges, it discouraged potential investors from participating in the country's development projects; and fourth, it rendered virtually impossible the continuous, systematic planning and implementation of a national tourism policy. At the same time, the various regimes often differed greatly in their relations with Western societies: some were friendly, others neutral, and others—like the first Rawlings' regime—stridently hostile to the United States and a number of Western European countries.

Given the fragility and illegitimacy of many of these Ghanaian regimes, their fears of subversion and counterrevolution were understandable. This fear sometimes resulted in situations that were not without their comic aspects. In 1986, for example, the government staged an international tourism fair and conference—Intertourism '86—in Accra, the nation's capital. This was designed to showcase the country's tourism potential for overseas lenders, investors, and tour operators. Ghana would show that it had plenty to offer, and that it was now a safe place in which to visit or to do business. It would also emphasize the fact that Ghanaians were the friendliest people in Africa—that when they said, *"Akwaaba!"* (Welcome!), it came from the bottom of their hearts. However, the nervous government was afraid that its party would be spoiled by subversives disguised as Intertourism visitors, so Kotoko International Airport in Accra was placed under tight security. Visitors were greeted by noisy, rifle-toting, aggressively nasty soldiers and police as they entered the airport arrivals area and tried to get out of the terminal building. The impression generated was hardly what the government had hoped for and Intertourism produced few positive results for Ghana's tourism industry.

There have been numerous government plans to develop tourism in Ghana. In 1972 the Obuam Committee prepared an evaluation of the country's tourism resources, and a 1973 government white paper on tourism made recommendations regarding foreign participation and investment policy. Other studies and proposals followed, several of which were financed by international development agencies. The most significant of the early studies led to the Tourism Master Plan of 1974, which was intended to guide developments between 1975 and 1990. It was prepared by a group of Danish tourism experts, with financial assistance from the Danish International Development Agency. Among its recommendations were the primary development of coastal tourism, the creation of island resorts in Lake Volta, the development of game parks, and the institution of local and overseas training programs for workers in the industry. It projected a massive expansion of tourism: 357,000 visitors were expected by 1990, as well as the creation of 35,700 new jobs and foreign exchange earnings of $57 million. No serious attempts were made to implement the Tourism Master Plan, and the same can be said of the other plans prepared during the 1980s. Tourism was eventually identified as a key sector for development in the 1985 Investment Code; but, inexplicably, it was omitted from the National Five-Year Development Plan in 1987. The fruitless trail of plans and projects led around in a circle, due mainly to political uncertainty and lack of capital investment resources.

Political and economic conditions also made it difficult for Ghana to develop an effective and efficient national tourism organization to coordinate, synthesize, and implement the various plans. Two years after independence, the Ghana Tourist Board (GTB) was established, only to be replaced in 1964 by the State Tourist Corporation (STC). In 1968 the National Tourist Corporation (NTC) was created as the central advisory board with responsibility for formulating tourism policy and for promoting tourism development. In 1970 the Ghana Tourist Corporation (GTC) was created, but this was replaced a short time later by the Ghana Tourist Control Board (GTCB). These short-lived national tourism organizations muddled along with weak mandates and inadequate resources. Tourism, as we know, is a highly fragmented industry even in developed industrial societies. In a developing country like Ghana, where public sector initiative is crucial for the coordination and implementation of tourism policy and planning, the chaotic situation just outlined proved to be a major handicap.

The GTB was reestablished in 1973 and was especially active in the promotion of domestic tourism during the 1980s. While such tourism was seen to have considerable merit in itself, it was also a matter of making a virtue out of necessity. Discussions with the executive director and members of the board during that period made it clear that, given favorable circumstances, their energies would have been directed primarily towards the international tourism market. Lack of government support made this unrealistic. Even at Intertourism '86, whose focus was to be on international tourism, the GTB bowed to external pressure and included exhibits and seminars relating to domestic tourism. Quite apart from the fact that few ordinary Ghanaians have sufficient discretionary income to spend on leisure travel, the very notion of travelling for pleasure is, as noted in chapter 3, not yet well-developed in Ghana. Nonetheless, the GTB has been quite successful in organizing domestic tourism events such as "Meet Me There" excursions to the beaches and to Lake Volta.

Ghana's tourism attractions have been something of an unknown quantity as far as the main European and North American tourist-generating areas are concerned. Very little promotional literature was produced for these markets by the GTB, Ghana Airways, and Ghanaian tour operators. Most of what was produced had an amateurish appearance and did not display the country's attractions to best advantage. Little effort was made to target the African American market segment in the United States, despite the existence of a large number of African American newspapers, magazines, and societies, and a growing interest in foreign travel by African Americans. Compared with The Gambia, which has a well-defined destination image, Ghana's attractions were not presented in a coherent way. In trying to show that Ghana had "a bit of everything," the country's image appeared somewhat fuzzy and fragmented. Consequently, it tended to lack the distinctiveness that might have set it apart from other West African countries, such as The Gambia, Senegal, or the Ivory Coast.

Tourism reception and handling facilities were also neglected. Obtaining visas for a visit to Ghana was usually a time-consuming business. In countries like Canada, for example, lack of provincial consular offices meant that people planning a trip to Ghana had to send their passports to the Ghana High Commission in Ottawa several weeks before the planned departure date. Arrival at Kotoka International airport in Accra was typically a harrowing and sometimes frightening experience, with long lineups, intimidating immigration and customs personnel, and an army of hustlers posing as accredited airport officials. Lengthy customs searches were carried out on all arriving passengers, and since there was no electronic screening equipment in place, this process was repeated at departure, with the added thrill of a body search by security officers in a tiny, screened-in cubicle. And this was during "the good times." During periods of political crisis, of which there were many, the experience could be even worse, with armed soldiers waving guns and barking orders at jet-lagged visitors. Visitors were also required to report to the Ministry of the Interior within 24 hours of arrival, and to relinquish their passports to the Chief Immigration Officer two days prior to departure, in order to obtain the necessary "exit permits."

The results of years of government neglect were also apparent in a lack of skilled tourism manpower, poor entrepreneurial attitudes, outdated office systems and equipment, and the absence of a competitive marketing strategy by local tour operators. In the accommodation sector of the tourism industry there was a shortage of hotels suitably located and designed to cater to leisure travelers. The few hotels that were merely adequate in these respects were all in Accra, with nothing comparable existing in other parts of the country. Much the same was true of restaurants and bars. In dealing with international visitors, service in most hotels and restaurants was usually friendly, albeit in a somewhat casual and offhand way, and was much less efficient or professional than in The Gambia. The most striking exceptions were to be found in Accra's Chinese restaurants, where Ghanaian waiters were unfailingly courteous, provided prompt and efficient service, and kept a watchful eye on the diners so as to keep things moving along without long delays.

Most of the problems outlined here were identified in a hard-hitting report by a Tourism Task Force appointed by the government to prepare a medium-term, national tourism development plan (1992). Since then there have been signs that Ghana has moved from the stage of talking about tourism to actually doing something to develop it. Promotional and marketing campaigns are now under way in Europe and the United States. The coastal area of Ghana's Central Region, which has some of the best beaches and most interesting sites, is being developed with UN Development Project assistance. A major activity here is the restoration and renovation of the coastal forts and castles and the creation of some tourist accommodations within them. This is part of a WTO-UNESCO "Slave Route" project, which is designed to appeal particularly to African American tourists.

Accra is also warming to international visitors and what is happening here is a key to understanding the recent general upsurge of tourism activity in Ghana. It cannot be said that this new vigor has been entirely due to the compelling logic of the Tourism Task Force, or to the benefits of recent political stability. These things have certainly helped, but accident and expediency may have helped just as much. In 1991 the Ministerial Conference of the Non-Aligned Movement (NAM) was held in Accra. In preparation for this important and prestigious political event, which would bring about 5,000 delegates, support staff members and media representatives to the capital, some of the city's older and larger hotels were rehabilitated. New hotels were built with foreign partners, such as Golden Tulip/KLM of Holland and Novotel of France, and so was a new 1,600 seat conference center. These significant new tourism resources came into being only because the government had secured a

major "political plum" in hosting the NAM conference. They have provided the cata-
lyst for Ghana's serious entry into the international tourism market. The superior
accommodations and facilities left behind after the NAM conference had to be utilized somehow—and the obvious way of finding users was to go out and attract
international tourists.

Is it not more than a little ironic, then, that initial interest in Ghana as a tourist
destination was linked to that country's unique *political* character, that its subsequent touristic nosedive was mainly due to *political* problems of various kinds, and
that its recent tourism revival was stimulated by a major *political* gathering?

But Should We Go There?

Earlier we considered the possibility that tourism contacts can be a positive force in
promoting international understanding. This issue is also part of the debate on the
appropriateness or otherwise of visiting countries whose regimes are offensive. It is
often suggested that contacts with foreign visitors are welcomed by many people in
such countries, and that they are especially valued as lifelines by younger residents
with democratic aspirations. Just how influential these contacts may be is unknown
at present. It would be most interesting, however, to have a detailed political analysis of the unintended influence of Western tourists on events leading to perestroika,
glasnost, and the eventual collapse of the Soviet Union. From what has been said
already, it would appear that most tourists are concerned with political situations in
countries they plan to visit only when there is a suggestion of personal danger.
Perhaps they deliberately put political considerations aside when deciding where to
travel, or prefer to remain blissfully ignorant about the politics of the countries
they visit. No doubt there are exceptions, as in the case of young North American
tourists who visited and stayed on in Nicaragua during the Sandinistas' struggle for
control of the country. Inspired by Sandinista aims, some became camp followers
and attendants; and, because of their preferred footwear, were referred to mockingly
in the Western media as *Sandalistas*. And it is probably the case that some Western
visitors to the former Soviet Union were interested in seeing communism firsthand, an interest that may also be important for some visitors to Fidel Castro's
Cuba. But, in general, we find that tourists have been quite happy to visit dictator-
ships like Franco's Spain, to take holidays in Bali, Indonesia, despite that country's
authoritarian regime, and to return to places where elected governments have been
overthrown by military conspirators.

One of the clearest examples of apolitical tourist behavior is afforded by the
post–Tiananmen Square situation in China. The brutal and globally televised sup-
pression of prodemocracy supporters in the spring of 1989 posed little or no threat
to tourists. But it generated widespread revulsion in the West and raised troubling
moral questions about the appropriateness of visiting a country with such a regime.
In 1988, 1.8 million foreign tourists visited China, this number dropping to 1.4
million in 1989, largely as a result of the Tiananmen Square massacre. By 1992,

however, the number had increased to 4 million, and by 1998 it had soared to 24 million. What we see, then, is that China's tourism suffered only a temporary set-back due to Tiananmen Square, and that it has gone on to make an amazing recovery from this event. This example, as well as others where tourism has been seriously but only temporarily impaired by political events, raises an important question that has hardly been touched in the literature to date: namely, how tourism boycotts might become effective levers against autocratic regimes in countries heavily dependent on tourism. Given the apolitical nature of most tourist decisions, the apparently short "tourist memory," and the effectiveness of destination recovery campaigns, the answer is probably that tourist boycotts are not likely to work. Even the U.S. boycott of travel to Cuba has not succeeded in toppling Castro or in undermining his regime. At the level of the individual tourist, however, the moral problem remains.

Chapter 9
Trouble in Paradise

Introduction

In this chapter I present the first of two case studies of tourism in contrasting destinations. These studies provide concrete examples and illustrations of many of the problems and issues raised in previous chapters. My initial study is of Maui County, Hawaii, where tourism was initially welcomed as a substitute for the declining sugar and pineapple industries. However, in recent years there has been organized opposition to tourism development in Maui, as the county approaches the limits of its carrying capacity. I outline some of the public controversies that have surrounded tourism development during the 1990s, showing how they have unfolded and identifying the key areas of contention.

General Background

The Hawaiian islands were first settled by Polynesian voyagers over a period lasting approximately 300 years, probably from about 400 A.D. to 800 A.D. The first wave of settlers may have come from the Marquesas, with subsequent migrations having their origins in Tahiti. The first white visitors appeared in 1778 with the arrival of Captain Cook's expedition. Merchants, missionaries, and whalers followed soon afterwards. The islands became a unified kingdom in the latter part of the eighteenth century, following a successful campaign by King Kamehameha the Great of the Big Island of Hawaii. During the nineteenth century the islands grew in commercial importance, particularly the major trading center of Honolulu on the island of Oahu. By the 1840s the town of Lahaina, on Maui's west coast, was the most important whaling port in the Pacific. Today, Lahaina has come full circle. It is now a tourist town that has successfully packaged its whaling past for tourist consumption, most notably through its whaling museum and as a popular base for whale-watching cruises. In the mid-nineteenth century, reforms permitted the private ownership and sale of land. As the whaling industry declined, several American merchants acquired large tracts of land that were developed as sugar and pineapple plantations. Indentured plantation laborers were imported from China, Japan, and other parts of the world, and Hawaii's population began to acquire the ethnic heterogeneity that is now one of its chief characteristics. American landowners and merchants became increasingly powerful, and their machinations led to the overthrow of the

Hawaiian monarchy in 1898 and the annexation of Hawaii by the United States shortly thereafter. Hawaii was a U.S. protectorate until 1959, when it attained statehood. In 1992 Hawaii's resident population was 1.1 million, of whom only 8% were native Hawaiians. The main "unmixed" ethnic groups are Caucasian (23%); Japanese (19%); Filipino (10%); and Chinese (4%). There is a good deal of intermarriage between members of these groups, however, and a further 36% of Hawaii's population is classified as *ethnically mixed.*

Hawaiian Tourism

Sugar and pineapple have been surpassed in economic importance by tourism and defense spending. Thousands of U.S. service personnel were stationed in Hawaii during World War II and were instrumental in spreading the word about the islands' attractions. Hollywood films also played an important part in drawing attention to Hawaii and helped shape its destination image as a Pacific paradise complete with lush scenery, miles of beautiful beaches, swaying hula dancers and, above all, its warm "Aloha spirit" (Farrell, 1982). With the coming of the jumbo jet age in the 1970s, Honolulu could be reached in less than six hours from major West Coast cities like Los Angeles, San Francisco, and Seattle. In 1959, when Hawaii attained statehood, the number of arrivals was 243,000. By 1990 this had soared to 6.9 million, falling to 6.1 million in 1993 in the aftermath of the Gulf War, but climbing again to 6.6 million in 1995. In 1994 visitor-related expenditures were estimated at $11 billion, total sales or output at $19.5 billion, state and county revenues at $1.1 billion, and jobs (direct, indirect, and induced) at 245,000.

In a purely technical sense, Hawaii is primarily a domestic tourist destination inasmuch as the vast majority of visitors are from other parts of the United States. In 1994 the main tourist-supplying countries for Hawaii were the mainland United States (3.4 million), Japan (1.6 million), and Canada (312,000). However, the economic importance of Japanese visitors for Hawaii can hardly be overstated. In 1994 their average expenditure per visitor day was $340, compared with $134 for visitors from the U.S. mainland. No comparable figure is available for Canadians, although it is generally assumed to be much lower than that for Americans. This is because Canadian visitors are more likely to stay in condos rather than hotels, and generally operate with somewhat smaller holiday budgets than their American counterparts. Many Hawaiians appear to be involved in a "love-hate" relationship with the Japanese at present. Well aware of Japanese visitors' high-spending habits, they are anxious to cultivate this particular group and cater to their tastes; but, at the same time, there is mounting concern over increasing Japanese investment in and ownership of the local tourism industry. Ironically, Hawaii's success in attracting Japanese tourists may prove to be part of the problem facing the industry over the next few years. In a recent survey conducted in Japan on behalf of the Hawaii Visitors Bureau, it was found that a frequently given reason for not wanting to visit Hawaii was "too many Japanese!"

Tourism in Maui

Maui County consists of the islands of Maui, Molokai, Lanai, and Kaho'olawe, the latter island being uninhabited. In 1831 the county's population was estimated at 42,742, declining to 14,904 by 1878. With the growth of commercial sugar and pineapple production, the population steadily increased, reaching 56,146 by 1930. The dwindling fortunes of these industries led to another population decline, so that by 1960 it had fallen to 42,855—lower than it had been 40 years earlier. With the growth of Maui's tourism industry, which took off during the late 1960s, the county registered the highest rates of population growth of all counties in the state. In 1994 it had 113,030 residents, over 90% of whom lived on the island of Maui itself. Native Hawaiians constituted 2% of the population, the largest unmixed ethnic groups being Caucasian (21%), Japanese (17%), and Filipino (16%). The ethnically mixed group accounted for 41% of the county's population and included over 24,000 persons who were part-Hawaiian.

Tourism is concentrated primarily along the relatively dry west and south coastal areas of Maui island. A number of planned resorts of exceptional quality have been developed here by some of Maui's large landowners. The first of these was at Ka'anapali, on sugar cane and cattle-grazing land belonging to AMFAC (American Factors), Hawaii's largest business conglomerate. The Ka'anapali resort established a standard that other large developers sought to emulate. North of Ka'anapali is the Kapalua resort, a project of the Kapalua Land Company, a subsidiary of Maui Land and Pineapple. Kapalua resort is widely regarded as one of the finest of its kind in the world. In south Maui, a luxury resort-residential complex has been developed at Wailea, on 1,500 acres owned by Alexander and Baldwin, a major landowner traditionally involved in sugar and pineapple cultivation. This was a collaborative venture between Alexander and Baldwin and Northwestern Mutual Life Insurance Company. A fourth major resort has also been completed at Makena, just east of Wailea, on a 1,000-acre property owned by a Japanese company—Seibu Group Enterprises. On the island of Lanai, two luxury resorts have been built by Castle & Cooke through its subsidiary, Dole Foods (of canned pineapple fame); and on Molokai, Kukui Molokai (a subsidiary of Tokyo Kosan) has expanded and upgraded the old Kalui Koi resort, which it purchased from the Louisiana Land and Exploration Company.

Where large tracts of land are controlled by single landowners, it has been possible to develop carefully planned, integrated resorts of the kind mentioned in the previous paragraph (Farrell, 1982). But not all tourism developments in Maui have been of this kind. A notable departure from the Ka'anapali model has occurred at Kihei, near Wailea. Here a large number of small landowners were involved in over 100 separate projects, most of which were carried out independently of each other. Kihei did have a master plan for resort development, but this was largely ignored in the opportunistic scramble to maximize project size and ocean access. Many of those directly involved in the development of Kihei had political connections at state or county levels. One study has shown that, among those who had a financial interest in Kihei as investors, corporate officers, members of partnerships, lawyers, consultants, and so on, no fewer than 88 were government officials during or prior to their involvement in Kihei projects (Cooper and Daws, 1990). The result was a mishmash of condominium complexes of varying quality, interspersed with gas stations, small shopping malls, and ABC convenience stores. Despite its inauspicious beginnings and unplanned character, Kihei is a thriving resort and is especially popular with Canadian visitors.

Between 1964 and 1994 tourist arrivals jumped from 304,437 to 2.3 million. While capitalizing on aspects of Hawaii's familiar image as tropical paradise, Maui's tourism industry has also tried to emphasize the county's cultural attractions and to highlight traditional Hawaiian music and dance. The value of high-volume resorts such as Kihei and Napili is well-recognized, but industry leaders would prefer to market Maui as a more relaxed and uncongested island than Oahu, one that will appeal especially to more affluent and discriminating travelers.

Tourism and Public Controversy

Throughout the 1970s and most of the 1980s tourism development in Maui proceeded without much local opposition. The few protesting voices heard were mainly those of people recently arrived from the mainland who had been attracted by Maui's relaxed ambience and unspoiled charm. Since they were not particularly wealthy, had shallow local roots and few political connections, their protests could easily be ignored by county authorities who were decidedly prodevelopment. Moreover, unlike project developments on the islands of Oahu and Kauai, those on Maui did not result in the evictions of entire communities with no proper relocation plans. And residents of Maui island had neither the community cohesiveness nor environmental conservatism of those on Molokai, where there was a large native Hawaiian community (Cooper and Daws, 1990).

Today, transplanted mainlanders are still prominent among those opposed to tourism and tourism-related development, but many are now actively involved in local community associations and environmentalist groups that provide much of the organizational basis for public opposition. And a pattern has recently emerged whereby various interest groups form temporary alliances and coalitions to collectively oppose particular developments. The battles are often played out in public meetings organized by the rival groups, in public hearings conducted by the County Council or its special committees and commissions, in court sessions, in reports and letters in *The Maui News* (the county's daily newspaper), and occasionally in public demonstrations. These controversies are often protracted and highly divisive, splitting the communities most concerned with the developments at issue.

We shall now look at some of the more heated controversies that have surrounded tourism-related projects in recent Maui history. Together, they underscore some of the key issues surfacing at this particular stage in Maui's tourism development: concern over environmental impacts; resentment over Japanese control of resources; fear of "Waikikianization," that is, the massive development of high-volume tourist resorts; complaints about inadequate infrastructure; allegations of overdependence on tourism for job creation; resentment over the power of large landowners; and concern over a too rapid transition from plantation agriculture to tourism. Interestingly enough, while all these problems are openly and publicly debated, most tourists can spend two weeks in Maui without ever becoming aware of them. They clearly do not affect the affluent readers of *Condé Nast Traveler* magazine, who have voted Maui "Best Island in the World" for the past six years.

Pukalani—The Sports Shinko Affair

This controversy erupted in the small upcountry town of Pukalani, located at an elevation of about 1,800 feet on the lower, northwestern slopes of Mount Haleakala, a 10,000-foot dormant volcano that dominates the landscape of Maui island. Once inhabited almost entirely by workers at the nearby sugar plantation, by 1990 the town's population of 5,879 included many residents who were retirees from the U.S. mainland, or who commuted to work at the nearby commercial and administrative centers of Wailuku and Kahului. Superficially, the controversy, which began in 1990, had all the appearance of a "storm in a teacup"—a purely localized affair of little consequence to anyone outside the town. As it unfolded, however, it became clear that it touched on issues of much broader public concern: fear of Japanese influence; fear of tourism spreading outside the coastal area and into the upcountry districts; and resentment against the undue influence of mainland *haoles* (whites) or *malihini* (newcomers) in local political affairs. And so it was covered closely and extensively in *The Maui News,* and was also the subject of occasional reports in the state's two main newspapers, *The Honolulu Advertiser* and *The Honolulu Star-Bulletin.*

The problem began when directors of the Pukalani Community Association (PCA) discovered that a parcel of land adjacent to the Golf and Country Club had for years been zoned for hotel and apartment construction. Although Sports Shinko, the Japanese owners of the Golf and Country Club and the land in question, had not formulated any plan for developing the property, the PCA directors tried a preemptive strike by asking county authorities to "down zone" the property. If successful, this strategy would have limited development on the property to single-family residences. The aim was to forestall any future development of a golf tourism resort for Japanese visitors. For a time it appeared as if the directors, who claimed to be speaking on behalf of all residents, were going to be successful. Very soon, however, Sports Shinko managed to rouse the "silent majority" into action and, after a series of heated meetings and hearings, the longstanding zoning arrangements were upheld. In the process, the PCA was transformed from a largely Caucasian group of about 100, to a multiethnic organization with over 300 members. The PCA directors, almost all of whom were Caucasians, were ousted after refusing to accept the decision of the new majority (alleging foul play, the signing up of nonresidents, Sports Shinko manipulation, and other "dirty tricks"). For a time thereafter, two rival PCA's vied for legitimacy with local residents and the county authorities. In the end, however, the old guard had to accept defeat and, with it, a more realistic understanding of its place in the community. The divisiveness and rancor generated by the controversy has not been entirely forgotten. Sports Shinko has not yet developed the property in question (Wyllie, 1998b).

Hana—The Last Hawaiian Place

The small community of Hana is located on Maui's east coast well away from the main tourist resorts. Because of its substantial native Hawaiian population and tranquil ambience, it is often referred to as "the last Hawaiian place." Developments here are of great interest to many residents of the state, for whom Hana represents the old Hawaii that has been lost elsewhere on the islands. Following the closure of the Hana sugar mill in 1945 a large tract of sugar land was sold to Paul Fagan, a wealthy San Francisco businessman. It was he who developed a cattle ranch on the lands and built a small inn as a retreat for wealthy visitors from the mainland. In 1968 the ranch and inn were sold to a Delaware lumber company, then to the Rosewood Corporation in 1984, and eventually to Keola Hana Maui—a consortium headed by a group of Japanese investors. Over time, the original inn had been transformed into the luxurious, 97-room Hotel Hana Maui, whose clientele consisted mainly of the "rich and famous."

Like the previous owners, Keola found the hotel to be an unprofitable operation. Its plan to change this involved the construction of an 18-hole golf course on Keola-owned land a few miles south of the hotel. The project was to be financed by the sale of private and corporate golf club memberships to Japanese buyers. When the plan was made public early in 1993, it caused a furor in Hana and opinions in the community were sharply divided. As the largest employer in the area, Keola was supported by most of its employees and their families, many of whom were native Hawaiians. Opposition was led mainly by local residents who were not directly dependent on the company, including many *malihini* who had settled in Hana as writers, artists, or retirees, or who wintered there on a regular basis. For Keola supporters, the issue was primarily that of job security and stemming the exodus of younger people who had found it difficult to find employment. For those opposed to the project, environmental and cultural impacts were of paramount concern. A number of Maui's environmentalist and other watchdog organizations threw their weight against the project. Their support was welcomed by Hana's own opposition group, but other local residents viewed them as "interfering outsiders" who should keep out of the controversy. Both sides acknowledged Hana's special character and expressed a desire to retain it. But they differed fundamentally on the question of how this was to be achieved.

After almost a year of public controversy, the County Council finally approved the golf course proposal. However, no fewer than 21 conditions of approval were stipulated—the most stringent set of requirements ever attached to any golf course project in Hawaii up to that time. Many of the conditions were designed to satisfy local objections, while others, for example, a 1,500-foot buffer zone around the golf course, reflected Council's exasperation with Keola's devious negotiating tactics. Although the conditions were reluctantly accepted by Keola, they made the project much less practicable and attractive for them. To date no work has been done on the project. In 1995 Keola reached a preliminary agreement to sell its Hana assets to a New York investment firm, but this deal collapsed after a year and a half of fruitless negotiations. Eventually, in June of 1999, Keola's Hana assets were sold to Meridian Financial Resources, a private financial investment firm whose head office is in Batavia, Illinois. The two general partners in the enterprise are Chicago businessmen, one of whom had supervised the construction of additional accommodations when Rosewood owned the property. Initial plans emphasize the creation of a sophisticated health spa, and the new owners have been noncommittal on the possibility of golf course development.

In some ways the outcome of the Hana controversy has been encouraging for those who want to preserve "the last Hawaiian place," as well as for others who are concerned about unchecked tourism development in Maui. But this may prove to be only a temporary victory. Unless the ranch and hotel operations become more profitable, or viable alternatives to them can be found, Hana's future as a community will remain uncertain (Wyllie, 1998a).

Lanai—A New Kind of Pineapple

The island of Lanai lies about 10 miles west of Maui across the Auau Channel. Castle & Cooke owns 98% of Lanai and the island has been a major center of pineapple production by Dole Foods—a Castle & Cooke subsidiary. Long known as the *Pineapple Isle,* the name is now obsolete. Because of declining profitability, pineapple production has been phased out. Tourism has replaced the old plantation economy and the plantation lifestyle of Lanai's residents is being rapidly transformed as a result.

In making the switch from pineapples to tourism, Castle & Cooke chose to target the upper reaches of the tourist market by building two luxurious resorts. The Lodge at Koele, opened in January 1990, lies in the interior of the island at an elevation of 1,500 feet and is designed in the manner of an English baronial estate. The Manele Bay Hotel, opened in April 1991, is a superbly designed beach resort on the island's southern shore. Advertising for both resorts emphasizes luxury, impeccable facilities and service, and privacy. The island is now being referred to in the promotional literature as *Hawaii's Private Isle.*

Although Castle & Cooke has created two outstanding resorts, made commendable efforts to employ locals in the new industry, and built affordable housing for its employees, the transition from pineapples to tourism has, perhaps inevitably, created problems. Some observers have suggested that the company, in its position as island owner, did not feel obliged to consult widely with local residents. The paternalistic approach developed in the plantation system, however benevolent in intention, was being continued in the company's approach to economic and social change on the island. In a "company island," it was suggested, misgivings and opposition to new developments were necessarily muted and people could not freely say what they felt about the changes. Relations between company representatives and the County Council have often been problematic: the former sometimes expressed frustration over having to seek permission to develop its "private island" and over delays in securing Council approval of its plans; and the latter often seemed intent on demonstrating its independence and its ability to make even Castle & Cooke toe the line. It did not help that Castle & Cooke's chairman, David Murdock, was a fairly classic example of the direct, blunt-speaking, "rags-to-riches" capitalist who had little time for doubters and critics, and who genuinely felt that the company was a positive and beneficial force in Lanai.

The following vignette conveys something of Murdock's personal philosophy and style, as well as the doubts and reservations of some Lanaians about changes on the island.

❋   +   ✳   ╬   ❋

A New Kind of Pineapple

Lanai took another step into its future and away from its plantation past with the official opening Friday of the luxurious 250-room Manele Bay Hotel. David Murdock, chief executive officer of Castle & Cooke Inc., and Gov. John Waihee cut the red ribbon while about 150 invited guests looked on.

Earlier in the day the talk was not about red ribbon but about red tape. At the blessing and dedication of a 123-unit multifamily housing project for hotel employees, Murdock complained about the time it takes to get zoning permits. "Two days is enough, two weeks is forever," he said. Murdock also suggested that "Hawaii holds itself back, holds its people back from getting housing . . . by its antiquated laws." Murdock said he has "improved without exception the quality of life on the island" and that the island is "far better than when we found it." In describing Lanai back then, he said it was "overgrown; other than pineapple it was a mess."

Maui County Council Member Goro Hokama, a resident of Lanai, took exception to Murdock's comments. "Quality of life does not mean only material," Hokama said. The emotional and social impact of change also need to be considered, he said. "It bothers me when people take lightly the phrase 'quality of life' because it cheapens the quality of life." Hokama also complained of the lack of input the county had in the housing project, which was a joint venture of Castle & Cooke and the state Housing Finance Development Corp. "(The county) has to maintain the infrastructure," but "we have no control on what is dedicated to us to maintain," he said. Hokama also vented concern about the economic future of Lanai. "In 1955, in the original discussion of the development of this island, one major point was we can't remain a one-industry island . . . but we have remained a one-industry island."

For 60 years the sole industry on the island was pineapple. As resorts on the island come on line, the plantation will phase out despite some residents' assertions the company promised to keep the plantation operational to give residents a choice of employment. According to Murdock, the phase out may occur sooner than the 1992 date originally announced. "(Castle & Cooke Inc. is) losing lots of money in Hawaii pineapple—about $23 million a year. We will phase out as we have jobs. We are running pineapple for the benefit of the people who don't have jobs, not for the benefit of Castle & Cooke," Murdock said. The cannery on Oahu also will shut down, but the plantation on Oahu will continue to operate, he added.

Although Castle & Cooke no longer intends to sell Dole Co., its agricultural subsidiary, "we would consider selling a part interest in the hotels," Murdock said. Besides the Manele Bay Hotel, the company owns a companion five-star resort near Lanai City. "We are the hospitality island. I want to make us known as the hospitality island around the world," Murdock said. Much to the dismay of some Lanai residents, Murdock also has described Lanai as a *private island*—a term used in hotel brochures. "It is a private island—sorry if it makes them irked," he said. Castle & Cooke owns 98% of the island and all its major developments.

Murdock insisted that the vast majority of Lanai residents support the changes. He said there are only 5 to 15 residents who have commented against it, but their concerns have been publicized "because the press likes the negative side of things." In response to comments that a two-tiered society of haves and have-nots is being developed on the island, Murdock said he "didn't know what the haves are and what those that have not are." He then added that, because of infrastructure, shipping and the lack of carpenters and plumbers on the island, the marketable houses to be built around the hotels and their respective 18-hole golf courses cannot be constructed for less than $1 million each. About 1,100 luxury single-family and multifamily units are planned. "If someone can afford (one), I guess you'd say they would be the haves," he said. But, he added, the have-nots are merely those who have not arrived at their potential. Reflecting on his own success, Murdock said that with a ninth grade education and a pick and shovel in hand, he did not spend his money on movies but concentrated on business. "We all have the same opportunities," he said, encouraging people to change their status "as they are willing to improve upon their intellectual quota." He also said "this island can't be any different than anywhere else in the world where you have those that live in a $1 million house and those that live in a $65,000 house." "Yes, we will be importing the haves because that's the only way to sustain an economy," he said.

Of the new employee houses, which range from 537 square feet for a one-bedroom unit to 969 square feet for a three-bedroom unit, Murdock said they are of such quality that "I could spend some time in any one of them." Rates for the units will range roughly from $500 to $800 per month. At the Manele Bay Hotel, the least expensive room measures 500 square feet (550 square feet with lanai) and runs $295 per night. The suite dubbed "Murdock's suite" by employees is one of the 13 butler suites available at $1,200 per night. Affordable housing on Lanai has cost Castle & Cooke $50 million, including $28.53 million in contributions and subsidies, Murdock said. "Nowhere in the entire islands has a developer spent as much money on low-income housing," he said.

In addition, Castle & Cooke has spent $5 million on a new water system in Lanai City and will provide $6 million for a Lanai institute for business and culture in order to "change the thought process of the island" and create entrepreneurs, Murdock said. He said he gave the figures "not to brag, but to stifle criticism." "We are not going to make a dollar for at least 10 years and we have spent hundreds of millions of dollars on this island," Murdock said. The resorts reportedly have cost about $260 million to construct.

Murdock said he loves the island and "our people." "Yes, they need a certain amount of protection and shelter," he said. Despite claims by some residents that he has left a trail of broken promises, Murdock stated, "I keep my word 100% plus and never deviate." "Your dreams are my dreams. Please make some of my dreams our dreams."

Prior to cutting the ribbon of the Manele Bay Hotel, Gov. Waihee stated that "while change can be painful, it can be beneficial." He expressed his gratitude to Murdock and Castle & Cooke in grappling "with the state and the community to bring about change."

Constance Agliam, a Lanai resident and Manele Bay Hotel employee, took the microphone to tell the audience that Lanai is ready to move beyond being "the little house on the prairie."

The Rev. John Richardson then blessed the hotel, after which Waihee and Murdock snipped the ribbon.

Sylvia Spalding, Lanai's Plantation Past Fades With Opening of Hotel, *The Maui News,* April 14, 1991. Reprinted with the permission of Sylvia Spalding.

☀   ╬   ✳   ✦   ☀

Much of the friction between Castle & Cooke and the Council has resulted from company efforts to expand its resort facilities. Although golf courses were not part of the company's original resort plans, Council eventually gave permission for them to be built first at Koele and then at Manele Bay. For the construction of the Koele golf course, the company was permitted to tap into the island's only aquifer for a period ending in November 1994. In approving the Manele Bay course, however, Council issued an ordinance against using the aquifer, and the company was advised that approval for this course was being given on the understanding that Castle & Cooke should find alternative water sources. It was subsequently found that the company was ignoring the ordinance, arguing that it believed the restriction applied only to potable water and not brackish water. Potable water floats above the brackish water, and it was this deep-lying water the company claimed to be tapping.

In early 1993, Mayor Lingle allowed the company to violate the ordinance temporarily until the golf course was completed. She said she was persuaded that it was necessary to do so because Lanai's economy was at stake, and a golf course was needed for the resort to be competitive. The company also sought permission to expand the Manele Bay resort by building 325 luxury homes and 100 condominium units. This request ran into stiff opposition from the County Planning Commission, which expressed concern about the likely effects of such a project on the island's water supply. In March 1994, the County Planning Commission heard testimony at a public hearing in Lanai City, but took no action. About 200 people were in attendance, most of them wearing green baseball caps—a sign of their support for company plans. Of 21 people who testified, 18 spoke in favor and three asked that development be postponed until a water use model had been devised by the State Commission on Water Resource Management and the U.S. Geological Survey. The lawyer representing the company claimed that developments at Manele Bay would add between $1.6 and $2.6 million a year to the county's property tax base after four years, adding that "what will benefit the company also will benefit the county." In June 1994, the State Land Use Commission rejected the Manele Bay development proposal, but then agreed to reconsider the matter after David Murdock indicated that massive layoffs were inevitable if the project did not go ahead. In August the luxury housing development at Manele Bay was finally approved. Approval had earlier been given for a similar housing development at the Koele resort.

Castle & Cooke's battles have not only been with county and state authorities. A citizens' group called *Lanaians for Sensible Growth* (LSG) has opposed the company every step of the way, but without much success. While acknowledging the need for tourism as an alternative to pineapple production, LSG has argued for much slower growth and has been particularly vigilant in monitoring the company's water use practices. One of its leaders, Ron McOmber, was especially active in this respect and regularly challenged the company's figures on the amount of water it claimed to be using for golf course irrigation. In June 1993, Castle & Cooke banned McOmber from various sections of its property near the two golf courses. Another LSG leader is Jon Matsuoka, a native of Lanai and a professor of Social Work at the University of Hawaii in Honolulu. Matsuoka has been involved in assessing the social impacts of economic changes in Lanai, documenting increasing rates of crime, juvenile delinquency, drug and alcohol use, and so on, and demanding that Castle & Cooke take responsibility for alleviating these problems.

The Great Runway Debate

No tourism-related issue has been so protracted or widely debated as that concerning the runway at Kahului airport, Maui's main entry point for visitors. Because of this, it is worth considering in somewhat greater detail than the previous cases. In 1988 the State Department of Transportation (DOT) produced a plan to lengthen the runways at the main airports on Maui, Kauai, and Hawaii to make it possible for wide-body jets, such as Boeing 747s, to use them. It was argued that such aircraft—fully loaded with fuel and passengers—need a runway of at least 10,000 feet for takeoff. The runway at Kahului airport is 7,000 feet, and the plan provided for its extension to 10,500 feet. The larger aircraft could then fly directly between Maui and important tourist-generating areas, such as the U.S. mainland and Canada. The DOT view was that this runway extension would help relieve congestion at Honolulu airport on Oahu—at that time the only airport on the islands with a runway long enough for wide-body jets to take off. It was also felt that it would benefit travelers by reducing travel time and inconvenience involved in making touchdowns or flight transfers at Honolulu.

The DOT plan was hotly contested by Maui County Council and was widely debated in the community at large. Opponents of runway extension expressed fears that it would result in sharply increased arrivals, causing more traffic congestion and unbearable strain on the local infrastructure. Concerns were also expressed about the "internationalization" of the airport that would surely follow runway extension and open up Maui to drug trafficking and the introduction of alien animal and plant species. Some opponents mentioned the dangers of terrorism at international airports, while others argued that further tourism was unnecessary at present, there being no unemployment problem in Maui. More general criticisms were that tourism had already produced an economy relegating locals to the bottom of the ladder, and had destroyed the true spirit of *Aloha* by making it into a commodity.

Supporters of runway extension argued that internationalization was not part of the plan; besides, this lay within federal, rather than state, jurisdiction. Hotel industry spokesmen suggested that a longer runway could not generate an increase in visitors beyond the capacity of existing accommodations to absorb them. It was also argued that the extended runway would make it easier for Maui's agricultural producers to gain access to mainland markets and that work on runway extension and associated airport improvements would provide needed jobs for local construction workers. Supporters, including Governor John Waihee, raised the issue of airport safety, enlisting the support of the Airline Pilots' Association and warning of the state's legal liability in the event of a major accident at Kahului airport.

In August 1990, the County Council—by a vote of six to three—approved an amendment to the County General Plan (which sets out general guidelines for development in the county) restricting the length of the runway at Kahului airport to 7,000 feet. The newly elected mayor, Linda Crockett Lingle, one of only two Republicans in an otherwise Democratic Council, was opposed to the restrictive language. However, in the following month she allowed the amended General Plan to become law without her signature. A few weeks later, the state cut $105 million from funds earmarked for a new airport access road and nearby beach park improvements. Runway extension opponents viewed this as the state's way of showing its displeasure over Council's amendment to the County General Plan. In any event, Council felt it had successfully blocked the plan for a longer runway. The state, meanwhile, began work on an Environmental Impact Study (EIS) to assess the probable effects of runway extension.

In April 1991, Mayor Lingle revived the issue in her annual State of the County address. A supporter of extension from the beginning, she speculated that opposition to the plan might have softened in light of economic recession and layoffs of hotel employees and construction workers. She indicated that she had consulted with state officials about dropping the restrictive language from the County General Plan, but said she would not push for this unless the state promised to return the capital improvement funds it had cut previously. Council member Bagoyo, who was an opponent of runway extension, agreed with the mayor's assessment, although he personally remained opposed to the plan. He particularly noted the "mobs of construction workers who have turned out at recent Council meetings to voice support for various projects." Council took no immediate action, despite mounting pressure from construction workers and local building contractors. The state EIS would not be completed until the summer of 1992.

In her State of the County address in April 1992, the mayor again expressed her view that the runway should be extended because of safety considerations and continued sluggishness in Maui's visitor industry. She insisted that she did not intend to act as a "lone ranger" and promised she would support extension only if Maui's residents showed they were in favor and if airport improvement funds were returned by the state. This speech was the first occasion on which a call was made for some test of general public opinion on the matter. Until this time it had been gauged in various Council hearings at which members of the public could testify. On these occasions, opponents of runway extension invariably outnumbered proponents. Speakers—especially those opposed to extension—often claimed to be reflecting the views of the majority of Maui's residents and not simply those of special interest groups. Smokey Burgess, a Kihei condominium owner, spoke against extension, saying that "the will of the people is not in doubt." And firebrand Council member Wayne Nishiki berated the state government for "wasting its money on an Environmental Impact Study for a project which is opposed by the majority of county residents. You people are going to extend the runway despite the fact that the majority doesn't want it."

The various interest groups now began to coordinate their plans and strategies, and two major coalitions were formed. One of these, the *Maui No Ka Oi* (Maui is the Best) Coalition, embraced environmentalist groups such as the Sierra Club and Maui Tomorrow, members of women's groups, flower-growers, and small business operators. Led by a part-Hawaiian activist, Dana Hall, it opposed runway extension. The other was the *Pueo* Coalition, an alliance of various farming, business, tourism, and labor groups, led by another part-Hawaiian, Jimmy Rust. Rust is a former bulldozer operator who now works for the Operating Engineers Labor Stabilization Fund—an organization serving the interests of heavy equipment operators. Rust lent the name of his family's totem—the *pueo,* or Hawaiian owl—to this coalition supporting runway extension, although the coalition's name also stands for *People United for Economic Opportunity*. Each coalition tried to stress its Hawaiian or local roots. For example, at the start of one public hearing, members of *Maui No Ka Oi* made a traditional Hawaiian offering of fruit to Council members; and at the same meeting, Jimmy Rust's group delivered an appropriate riposte by donating cans of food for Maui's unemployed.

In August 1992, following completion of the state EIS, which suggested that no serious environmental impacts were likely to follow a runway extension to 9,600 feet (900 feet shorter than the original DOT proposal) and with a deepening recession affecting the tourism and construction sectors, the County Council held another public hearing. Its purpose was to get public input on a request from the DOT that the language banning runway extension be removed from the County General Plan. This turned out to be a marathon event which produced 10 hours of public testimony. It ended with exhausted Council members unanimously voting to refer the DOT request to the County Planning Commission. Many saw this as "buck-passing" by the Council, some of whose members would be candidates in the upcoming County Council elections. The County Planning Commission wasted no time in tossing the ball back to Council, and voted eight to one in favor of recommending that Council remove the restrictive language from the County General Plan. Anticipating no further difficulties, the DOT formally requested Council to reclassify 210 acres of land from agricultural to urban designation, to permit extension of the runway.

In October of 1992, however, the extension supporters suffered a setback. A lawsuit was filed by Isaac Hall, the lawyer husband of Dana Hall, and two other lawyers representing the Sierra Club and a number of individuals and organizations belonging to the *Maui No Ka Oi* Coalition. This lawsuit challenged the adequacy of the state EIS, alleging that it did not meet standards set by state and federal environmental protection laws. It was argued that the state EIS focused only on the immediate and proximate effects of runway extension and failed to assess likely long-term and wider environmental impacts. The suit asked that no work be done on the runway until another, more adequate EIS could be undertaken. According to Jimmy Rust, this move was a delaying tactic and was not entirely unexpected. Nonetheless, he was disgusted and suggested that:

> Isaac Hall and his Sierra Club friends want to control the future
> for Maui's working people. They are milking unsuspecting main-
> landers to fund their legal maneuvering. . . . The thousands of
> families represented by the *Pueo* Coalition are sick at heart that
> there are people like Isaac Hall and other Sierra Club attorneys
> who don't give a rip if Maui people have jobs or are at risk of losing
> their homes. . . . We are fed up with people who openly oppose
> diversified agriculture, who openly oppose new clean high-tech
> industry, who openly oppose the visitor industry. (Perry, 1992a)

A few days later *The Maui News* published results of a survey undertaken on its behalf by SMS, a Honolulu-based company. A random sample of 400 adults was surveyed by telephone, and the results, which were highly encouraging for extension supporters, showed that over 54% were in favor of runway extension, while 35% were opposed. While *Pueo* Coalition members were delighted with the results, leaders of the rival *Maui No Ka Oi* Coalition tried to make the best of it. Dana Hall said the results showed that there was an "uninformed majority" influenced by a highly successful *Pueo* Coalition public relations campaign that reduced complex issues to simplistic slogans, such as "We need jobs." She said she was not distressed by the results, because she believed most people were unaware of the adverse effects of runway extension and internationalization (Perry, 1992b). The somewhat patronizing tone of Hall's remarks did not sit well with many members of the "uninformed majority," who took it as a sign that Hall and *Maui No Ka Oi* would never accept runway extension, no matter what the majority of Mauians felt or what the findings of the next EIS might be.

It was not until March 1993 that a judgment was made on the lawsuit. The judge ruled that federal standards had not been met by the state EIS, but would not indicate how the state had failed to comply. He did, however, observe that failure to meet federal standards was itself a violation of a 1981 court order requiring the state to treat airport expansion projects as a whole, and not as smaller, discrete, items that would not require environmental impact studies. Meanwhile, the DOT's request for reclassification of 210 acres from agricultural to urban designation was considered in a series of public hearings organized by the Maui Land Use Commission. These hearings were postponed after the court stipulated an agreement between the DOT and runway extension opponents. The agreement prohibited all work on the proposed runway extension until completion of a new EIS to be conducted jointly by federal and state authorities.

It took about four years to complete the new EIS, during which time the two coalitions slipped out of public view, its leaders surfacing occasionally to fire off the odd verbal shot. Early in 1997, they began to marshal their forces once more in anticipation of the long-awaited EIS. By the time a final draft had been issued in October of 1997, the familiar battle lines had been redrawn and the old field marshals were back on their steeds, although there were some new faces among their lieutenants. Weighing in at more than 20 pounds, the five-volume EIS is probably the most comprehensive one Hawaii had ever seen. Both sides in the battle claim to have carefully read and digested its contents, which give no indication that serious environmental effects will come from runway extension. It documented risks and dangers, proposed mitigating actions, and was officially accepted as adequate by state Governor Cayetano.

By this time most people in Maui appeared to have tired of the issue, and it was generally expected that runway extension would finally take place. With victory apparently in sight, Maui's tourism industry representatives were buoyed by the prospect of expanding their small share of the lucrative Japanese market. They looked

forward to duplicating the experience of their neighbors on the Big Island of Hawaii, where runway extension at Kailua-Kona airport had led to the introduction of
regular, direct flights from Japan. But in 1998 Isaac Hall again filed a lawsuit on
behalf of runway extension opponents, arguing that procedural irregularities and
errors of omission rendered the new EIS deficient as a matter of law and fact.

Both sides now dug in for another long and rancorous battle, which was not
resolved until February 2000, when Governor Cayetano announced that the state
was cancelling plans for runway extension on Maui and Kauai. Among the main
reason given for this decision was a sharp drop in airport revenues from duty-free
concessions at Honolulu International Airport, due primarily to the recent decline
in the number of Japanese visitors to the state. For runway extension to proceed,
the reduction in revenues would have to be compensated for by charging higher
landing fees, thereby increasing the costs of air travel to Hawaii. Another reason
given was the development of new, wide-body aircraft capable of operating efficiently
and safely with smaller runways such as that at Kahului airport. A practical demonstration of this came only a fortnight after the Governor's announcement when a
United Airlines Boeing 777 made its first Maui flight from San Francisco. Carrying
348 passengers it landed safely at Kahului and took off again with a full complement
of passengers and four 3,000-pound containers of fresh pineapple (Perry, 2000). If
such flights become a regular occurrence, Maui tourism may continue to grow without runway extension and despite the opposition of *Maui No Ka Oi* and other
antidevelopment groups.

During the controversy in Maui, people seemed to take special care to avoid
mentioning the Japanese factor in the equation. Extension supporters did not want
to alarm people who were already worried about Waikikianization, while opponents
did not want to be accused of racism or of Japanese bashing. Yet the Japanese factor
was never far below the surface during the public debate. When people expressed
fears about the internationalization of the airport, they certainly were not thinking
about the possible impacts of increased traffic from Canada.

Conclusion

Tourism development in Maui has obviously reached a stage at which questions
concerning its carrying capacity and the limits to growth will increasingly be raised
and publicly debated. Social, cultural, and environmental policy issues are being
thrashed out in public forums, although most visitors are unaware of this. Despite
heated public controversy surrounding tourism, relations between local residents
and tourists are a long way from Doxey's antagonistic stage. Opposition and hostility
towards tourism is directed at local authorities, developers, and industry leaders, and
only rarely towards tourists. The recent and current situations in Maui point to a
need for tourism researchers to pay more attention to the dynamics of relationships
between various segments and groupings *within* host populations, and how these are
affected by tourism development. As the Maui case shows, attitudes towards tourism

may differ widely between different sections of the population, and unlikely alliances may be formed around tourism-related issues. It is laudable to advocate "community-sensitive" tourism and to encourage input from residents on tourism planning and policy. In relatively homogeneous communities, these ideas may be implemented in a fairly smooth fashion. However, in heterogeneous communities where people are sharply divided on the issues, it takes more than an elaborate process of public consultation and debate to settle the differences. Indeed, it sometimes appears that public consultation and review processes provide arenas and opportunities for individuals and groups to harden their positions rather than to find compromises. I will return to this problem in my final chapter.

Chapter 10

Slim Pickings
on the Smiling Coast

Introduction

My second case study deals with The Gambia, where tourism development origi-
nated with trips organized by Scandinavian tour operators and later became a major
and integral part of national economic development policy. This case highlights the
difficulties of making tourism work in a small, poor country with few economic
alternatives. We see that tourism here is beset by a number of serious problems,
over which The Gambia has little control (Campbell, 1990; Dieke, 1993; Esh and
Rosenblum, 1975; Farver, 1984; Harrell-Bond, 1978; Thompson, O'Hare, and Evans,
1995; Wagner, 1981). Nonetheless, this small West African country is likely to remain heavily dependent on tourism as the mainstay of its struggling economy.

General Background

The Gambia is one of the smallest countries in Africa, covering an area of only
11,295 sq. km. In 1992 it had a population of just under one million, most of whom
live in rural areas, and there are three main ethnic groups: Mandinka (42%), Fula
(18%), and Wolof (16%). The official language is English and Islam is the main
religion. Located on the continent's west coast, The Gambia is intersected by the
Gambia River, which runs from east to west and empties into the Atlantic Ocean at
Banjul, the country's capital. The landscape is mainly savannah, with mangrove
swamps along the river banks. About 20% of The Gambia consists of saline marshes.
The country forms an enclave surrounded on three sides by the larger nation of
Senegal, which was formerly a French colony. The Gambia's climate is tropical,
with a rainy season from June through October.

   The banks of the Gambia River have been inhabited since at least 2000 B.C. and
the area was known to Carthaginian sailors of the fifth century B.C. Between the
eighth and sixteenth centuries most of the Senegambian area formed part of the
empires of Ghana, Mali, and Songhai. In 1455 Henry the Navigator's expedition
reached the Gambia River, and the Portuguese established trading and missionary
settlements along the river's banks. The British arrived at the beginning of the seventeenth century, dislodging the Portuguese from James Island and making it their
principal base, while the French built a trading station at nearby Albreda on the
north bank of the river. The British and French struggled for control of the area,

and in 1765 Senegambia became a British Crown Colony with its headquarters at St. Louis. The French meanwhile retained their station at Albreda and established themselves in various parts of Senegal. With the abolition of the slave trade in 1807, James Island was used as a base for checking the now illicit trade. Between 1821 and 1888, The Gambia was administered from Sierra Leone, after which it was given a separate administration. It was not until 1904 that the boundaries of The Gambia and the French colony of Senegal were finally defined. In 1965 it gained independence from Britain and became a republic in 1970.

The Gambia is one of the world's poorest countries. Its gross national product (GNP) per capita is only $367, its economy is undiversified, and it has high rural-urban migration. It ranks low on the UN human development index, which measures life expectancy, infant mortality, literacy, and general living standards. The economy has traditionally depended almost entirely on the cultivation and export of groundnuts in the form of nuts, oil, and cattle cake. Fluctuations in world prices for groundnuts and other agricultural products present a continuing problem, along with regular periods of drought and low rainfall. However, agriculture, forestry, and fishing remain the dominant sectors of the economy, providing employment for about 80% of the population and contributing approximately 60% of GNP, whereas the industrial sector contributes only about 3%. The country is also heavily dependent on overseas suppliers for food, fuel, and manufactured products.

The Gambia's basic economic problems, then, are a shortage of foreign exchange and a national debt crisis. General economic policy is concerned with trying to diversify and broaden the productive base of the economy and foster economic growth and development. Two macroeconomic reforms have been introduced: the 1985 Economic Recovery Program, orchestrated by the International Monetary Fund (IMF), and the 1990 Program for Sustained Development. These measures stress the importance of market forces in promoting economic development and the government's role in providing general economic and political frameworks for the operation of these forces. They signal a clear shift towards a private sector–led economy while retaining the fabric of a mixed economy. They also show the government's acknowledgment of the importance of tourism as a means of promoting economic diversification and generating income and employment.

Tourism Development

Initiation and Growth

Organized tourism to The Gambia appears to have begun in 1966, when the Swedish tour organizer Vingressor Club 33 brought 300 charter tourists for a two-week package holiday. At that time only three hotels were in operation, all owned by expatriate Lebanese. Vingressor remained the sole foreign tour agent for Gambian vacations until 1971, when Spies of Denmark and Wings of Great Britain also began organizing and selling Gambian vacations. Resor, another Swedish company, became active in The Gambia in 1973.

Although tourism was under way in The Gambia during the 1960s, development was largely unplanned until 1972. In that year the government, with UN Development Project assistance and IMF financing, initiated the Tourism and Infrastructure Project, usually referred to as the Bufaloto Plan. This plan involved physical and environmental planning studies for the development of tourism in the Bufaloto coastal area and was to cover the period 1975 to 1980. The plan designated a number of coastal resort sites and also the sites of two new towns to be located outside the resort areas. Each resort site was to be equipped with a bengdula (meeting place), where souvenirs and handicrafts could be sold; these, it was hoped, would discourage commercial squatting and selling on the beaches themselves. A school, sponsored by the UN, was to be established to show local craftsmen how to mass produce items for the tourist market. Subsequent five-year development plans have elaborated upon and refined these goals, so that tourism policies were integrated into the overall national development strategy.

The 1988 Development Act was designed to provide incentives to investors and to speed up the approval process, making it possible for an investor to go into business within 90 days of application. Incentives were also provided if the proposed investment guaranteed contributions to certain national development objectives: the achievement of net foreign exchange earnings or savings; the generation of domestic value added; the promotion of employment and training for Gambians; the maximum utilization of local resources and services; the formation of a national productive capital; and the spatial decentralization of development projects.

Among the incentives offered to investors whose plans supported these objectives were fiscal exemptions and tax relief, for example, total or partial exemption of customs duties on capital equipment; preferential treatment in the allocation of land in tourism development areas; and the provision of infrastructural services. Tourism lands are leased at below market value for an initial period of 21 years, and the lease is open for renewal. These and other measures worked reasonably well, with substantial investments being made by Vingressor of Sweden and Copthorne Hotels of Britain. A number of joint ventures between foreign investors and Gambians have also been undertaken. The Gambia now has more than 25 tourist hotels, most of which are geared primarily to the needs of charter tourists.

Tourism has thus come to occupy a significant place in the Gambian economy. By the late 1980s it was contributing 12% to the GNP and yielded net foreign exchange earnings of $25 million. Tourism provided, directly and indirectly, approximately 7,000 jobs for Gambians. The Gambian government has estimated that about 3,000 people are engaged in informal sector activities, for example, taxi services, handicrafts, prostitution, and other "befriending" activities (Thompson et al., 1995).

The number of tourist arrivals rose steadily during the 1970s, but demand was adversely affected by the international oil crisis of 1979 and then by an abortive coup attempt in 1981. The industry was just recovering from these setbacks when the government imposed a 6% sales tax on international tourist packages and a 10% sales tax on domestic bookings. Both of these measures had a deadening effect on international tourist demand, but by 1993 the industry had again begun to show signs of recovery (Table 10.1).

Destination Image

What is it that attracts charter tourists to The Gambia? Apart from the reasonable prices and convenient flying time (just over five hours from London), it is presented as an attractive alternative to the increasingly congested and shopworn Mediterranean or Caribbean resorts. The promotional literature presents The Gambia as *The Smiling Coast,* whose attractions are described in the following way:

> The Smiling People. Gambian people are renowned in West Africa for their friendliness. They give a smiling welcome to holiday-makers unforced by commercialism and represent one of the nation's chief tourist assets. The "smiling coast" applies to the Gambians as much as to the sunshine.
>
> The Climate. Of course, the weather helps. It's generally agreed that The Gambia has the most agreeable climate in West Africa. It is subtropical and has a long dry season from November to June— glorious uninterrupted sun and blue skies with temperatures in the 80s. Even the hottest day is softened by a light breeze.
>
> The Beaches. The golden beaches that stretch for miles along the Atlantic seaboard combine with the sun to make The Gambia a magnet for winter chilled northerners. Here cocoanut palms form

Table 10.1 International Arrivals: The Gambia, 1986–1997

Year	Arrivals (thousands)
1986	74.0
1987	97.0
1988	102.0
1989	85.0
1990	100.0
1992	66.0
1993	64.0
1994	78.0
1995	45.0
1996	77.0
1997	80.0

SOURCE: World Tourism Organization Statistics Service.

sun dappled groves on the edge of the sands. And here too are to be found some of the most attractive and modern hotels in Africa.

Good Food. You'll enjoy the variety and excellence of the food. Some of the hotels can rival the best Mediterranean establishments and add their own specialties from the region. Gambian food is both distinctive and delicious. In the shops and market places are luscious fruits, vegetables, and fine fresh fish and meat.

(Ministry of Information and Tourism Brochure)

You needn't go as far as the Caribbean in search of winter sun. The Gambia is much closer to home. Between November and May this little country on the coast of West Africa has the perfect climate with day after day of cloudless skies and tropical sunshine virtually guaranteed. What's more there are some 30 miles of uncrowded silver sands washed by the blue waters of the Atlantic.

The Gambia, a British colony until 1965, is the smallest nation in Africa. This narrow sliver of land, never more than 30 miles wide, follows the course of the Gambia River into the heart of Senegal. You won't find an abundance of big game in The Gambia, but hippos, crocodiles, and dolphins can be seen in the river and the country has an unrivalled variety of colorful and exotic birds. A simple, unsophisticated country, you'll return with fond memories of a people, warm and musical, secure in a way of life that has changed relatively little over the centuries. The Gambia is a land of smiles and friendliness, spontaneous, but not forced or commercialized. *"Nanga Def"* (How are you) say to any Gambian as you start a conversation, and see how he reciprocates, is willing to help with a genuine warmth.

(The Gambia Hotel Association Brochure)

As always, the reality is somewhat different from the image, and the beaches, while neither golden nor silver, are very good. The Gambians do appear to be generally friendly towards and curious about visitors, and the place is certainly much less commercialized than most Mediterranean resorts.

Charter Tourism From the Inside

What do the charter tourists actually do in The Gambia? In the following vignette, which is based on my observations as a charter tourist in 1993, we take an insider's look at the tourists' subculture. In some respects the tourists resembled the common, negative stereotypes, but they were not the helpless dummies one would anticipate from Smith's description (see chapter 1). Had he been with us, Paul Theroux would probably have found them sadly wanting, although in some ways they might have surprised him. They were generally well-behaved and, with a few startling exceptions, interacted pleasantly with their hosts. It was also interesting to observe how they behaved in relation to each other, forming little subgroups, creating their own micro-society of strangers, and occasionally quarrelling with each other. It goes without saying that the tourists' subculture, the world in which they move during their holiday, stands in sharp contrast to the world of ordinary Gambians. We see how some of these Gambians—bummerboys in Banjul and children in Albreda—try to squeeze a living out of their visitors.

☀   ✦   ✳   ⁻ᵢ⁻   ☀

Charter Tourists in The Gambia

Arrival

It was 23 years since I had visited Banjul and at that time it was called *Bathurst.* Apart from that, nothing much seems to have changed. Bright sunshine and that familiar West African smell of hot, damp vegetation. The airport looks pretty much as I remembered it: the walk from the aircraft across the tarmac, the terminal buildings with their thatched roofs, the Gambian airport workers calling out greetings and asking passengers for English newspapers, and the general air of friendly confusion. This I found a little surprising. I had expected The Gambia's tourism experience would have shown in a slicker airport operation, but the arrival scene is reminiscent of Kotoka International in Accra, Ghana, but without the angst and hustling. There are, of course, the "formalities." Three separate queues form at immigration—Nationals, Citizens of ECOWAS (Economic Organization of West African States), and Others. People switch from one queue to another, depending on how quickly the lines are moving, but it all seems to work out somehow.

Although we were advised that entry would be denied unless we could produce health certificates showing we had had the necessary shots, these are not asked for. We stand under a covered shed outside the terminal while baggage is brought in several trucks and arranged in rows in the yard just beyond. Passengers are allowed to retrieve their baggage in small groups. Then the customs inspection—four tables set up in the yard, bags hoisted on the tables, everything opened up and much rummaging around, but no confiscations as far as I can see. The inspections become more perfunctory as time goes on. Unleashed into the yard near the end of this procedure, I am waved through. The inspectors have now lost interest. The bags are placed on small pickup trucks destined for the hotels, while the tourists pile into buses marked with the names of their respective tour operators. I find the Magictours bus easily.

My fellow tourists are a mixed bunch: younger couples with small children; middle-aged couples; pairs of women and pairs of men; a few single women, but I seem to be the only male traveling alone. There is lots of excited chatting, with English regional accents—mainly Lancashire and Yorkshire—predominating, but there is a Welsh voice also: "I think we 'ave enough power now—keep the tach goin'" (as the driver revs his engine). The Magictours representative is with us on the ride into Banjul—a young woman named Billie from Manchester who sounds like Daphne Moon on the "Frasier" television show. She gives us a quick rundown on The Gambia. Beware of hustlers but give to genuine charities, naming a few. Take time to speak to the Gambians—says they love to chat. Watch out for young men outside the hotels who say they want to be your "friend"—they are hustlers, she says, although they won't mug you. This is like any other place—nice people and people who want to cheat you. Remember, it's a poor country, so people do see you as being very rich. Best thing is, don't do anything here that you wouldn't do at home.

The passengers are dropped off at various points along the coastal strip until we reach our hotel. Set in nice gardens, it looks quite good. Once inside, however, it appears somewhat dingy and in need of renovation, but still not bad. North American hotels spoil you, I think, despite fashionable criticism of them as characterless glass-and-concrete blocks. Our baggage is left in the foyer for porters to bring to the rooms. Even if you only have one bag, as I did, they won't let you carry it yourself. My bag is brought to my room by two porters. They are very inquisitive about my traveling alone. Since I don't have any Gambian money (dalasis) yet, I can't tip them. They go off, somewhat disappointed, but still fairly cheerful. No doubt it's happened to them before.

First Impressions

There is a "welcome meeting" this morning, with Billie orienting us to The Gambia, the hotel, and the local attractions. However, some tourists have already decided that they don't like this particular hotel and she tells them she is working on this and that changes of accommodation should be possible. For some of these tourists the hotel is not quite up to expected standards—the furniture in the rooms is dark, heavy and, in some cases, a bit lopsided. For others, however, a sore point is the fact that the swimming pool is not in operation. It is being completely retiled. She takes us out to inspect progress on the pool and gets an assurance that it will be ready for use in two days. This seems to me to be highly optimistic, especially since the workers have not completed the removal of existing tiles, and the ground around the pool has been dug up and will need repaving.

Mr. and Mrs. Colley, who are here with their two teenage sons and a teenage daughter, are discussing the situation at poolside with Mr. and Mrs.

Sharp, who have come with their two children, ages 10 and 8. The Sharps are bitterly disappointed and say they really think they would prefer to move to another hotel with a decent swimming pool. "It's not that we mind so much, but the kids, y'know—they have to be kept amused somehow." The Colleys are much less concerned. "But the beach is right outside the hotel, Joanne. What's wrong with that? They won't come to any harm in the sea." The debate swings back and forth in an inconclusive fashion and they all wander off to the coffee shop to continue the discussion. I'd like to have gone with them to hear the rest of their discussion, but decide against it.

I have a good look at the restaurant this morning and confirm my impressions of the previous evening. It's certainly the most attractive part of the hotel. The menu lists fairly standard tourist offerings, with a couple of Gambian dishes included. Four courses, generous helpings, and a good dessert trolley. Fatima, the Gambian manageress who runs the show, is very impressive. I later learn that she was trained in Belgium and has worked in restaurants in that country, as well as in Switzerland and Italy. And the waiters—all Gambian males—give prompt, friendly service. The tourists dine at their own tables—couples, family groups, and the occasional single woman—all keeping to themselves for the most part. The Sharps and their children share a table with Mr. and Mrs. Colley and their daughter. The Colley boys, however, eat at a separate table at the far end of the restaurant—an assertion of teenage independence, no doubt. One young couple from the south of England (probably on honeymoon?) chat with Fatima, who has come to ask them if they are enjoying the meal. The young woman asks Fatima if she is married and is told she is not. When the waiter appears after the main course, the young woman asks if they have gooseberries (she pronounces it *goozbris*) "down here." The waiter is puzzled and doesn't know. She describes them for him: "They're like little green berries with fur on them." The waiter is now certain they don't have them. Snippets of conversation float from nearby tables: "Dad, you can have all the chips you want when we get home." "When we were in Malta last year, they take advantage of you when they know you're on your own."

Parting of the Ways

The swimming pool is still a long way from being ready. At about 10:30 A.M. I go to the Magictours desk to chat with Billie. She is dealing with a group of tourists who have decided to move to another hotel. They have had three room changes already and have had enough. Mr. and Mrs. Colley are hovering nearby and are clearly anxious to talk with Billie. When she is free they approach her about their friends, the Sharps. Billie knows all about this anyway. The Sharps had left earlier that morning for another hotel, without telling the Colleys of their decision. The Sharps and Colleys have been friends for 18 years in Manchester. But, as Sally Colley said, "You think you know people, don't you?" (to me, as an interested and possibly sympathetic bystander). "We knew they weren't too chuffed with this place, what with the pool and all, but as I said to Alf (Mr. Colley), 'It's only for a couple of weeks, after all.' And we didn't come all this way just for a swimming pool. Of course, her argument is that her kids'll get bored without the pool. But there's that lovely beach just outside there. What's wrong with that? Our own kids are quite happy with that, although of course they are a bit older. But you'd think they would have said. Just took off, like. The laugh is, it was their idea to come with us. We didn't ask them. Said they'd like to come along when we said we were going to The Gambia. I don't know what to make of them." Alf says little, but shakes his head from time to time as his wife tells the story. He too is shaken and disappointed.

The Colleys go off and I learn later that they spread the word of the Sharps' odd behavior to other tourists. Billie tells me that "It's a shame when this sort of thing happens. But you'd be surprised what goes on when people go on holiday. I keep my family and friends entertained for weeks when I go back home, with stories like this one. It's an interesting life, I'll tell you. Even married couples fall out after a couple of days. I think it's one thing to get along at home, but it's another matter when you're away. Some of them don't see all that much of each other at home, I suppose, being out at work and that. Then they have to put up with each other for a fortnight and begin to get on each other's nerves. Then the sparks start flying. You have to be a marriage counselor sometimes! But mostly people get on fine."

I take Billie's advice and hire a "hotel guide" for a walk into town. They stand on the hotel steps, identifiable by their red shirts and identification tags. They are not paid by the hotels, but are authorized to work from them. They rely on the tourists to pay them what seems appropriate, but there is an unofficial tariff in operation. Ibrahim is about 28 years old and is from Banjul. He is a soccer enthusiast. He says he is a Liverpool fan but that his favorite player is "Gazza" (Paul Gascoigne), who was at that time playing for Lazio of Rome. He tells me he has a Scottish friend named John who plays for Glasgow Rangers. John was here on holiday last year and now sends him soccer shirts and equipment. By the time we return to the hotel, Ibrahim has asked me to send him a track suit—Adidas, preferably. I mumble something about seeing what I can do. Ibrahim has also worked out an itinerary for us for the remainder of my stay. I tell him I don't like to make plans, preferring to take each day as it comes. He is disappointed and not a little puzzled by this. These young Gambians all seem to be soccer crazy. Another guide told me his name was Roy, but that his real name was Abdul. He took the name Roy when his friends told him how much he resembled Bryan Roy, a well-known Dutch soccer player.

Soul Brothers

On the beach outside the hotel I am approached by two bummerboys—young men who act as freelance guides and companions for tourists. Ali is fairly quiet, expresses curiosity about Canada, and tells me I am the first person he has met from that country. "We don't get many people from the far east in The Gambia," he says. His companion Abdul is more aggressive, asks if I have any cigarettes, and questions me closely about my job, my family, and so on. He tells me he has been to Essex in England, which was "OK," but that he would really like to come to Canada and could I help? After about an hour of his insistent questioning and bragging, I tell him he is beginning to bother me. He explains angrily that he is only being friendly and suggests my problem is that I don't understand how friendly Africans are. I tell him I do know and that I worked in Ghana for many years. This slows him down, but he recovers quickly. "Ah, you see, but we Gambians are much friendlier than Ghanaians." Since he is glaring malevolently at me as he says this, I decide to let him have the point.

The pool is still not operational. The Colleys seem to have adopted Jan, a middle-aged lady traveling on her own. They sit together on the beach. Ron and Ada from Wiltshire are there also, a little way off. And so are most of the others, including George and Betty Tompkins and Betty's mother, who are from Birmingham. By midafternoon they have all moved back into the hotel grounds and sit at tables watching the progress being made on the pool. This, and the departure of the Sharps, provides a good topic for conversation and most are now on first-name terms. Isolation patterns are breaking down and some "clumping" is now in evidence.

This is also noticeable in the evening. Lots of leaning over to call to or converse with people at other tables. Jan dines with the Colleys. Plans for excursions are outlined. One sour note is a "scene" involving African American tourists and the waiters—the first of three such encounters I saw during my stay at the hotel. The African Americans are on three-country trips to West Africa (Senegal, their main base; a three-day excursion from Senegal into The Gambia; and then on to Ghana). They spend two nights in hotels such as this one, seem to have all kinds of problems finding acceptable food, and give the distinct impression that they would rather be back home in the States. This evening one group of African Americans appears to find nothing suitable on the fairly extensive menu. They seem to have the mistaken impression that they are in an IHOP restaurant somewhere in Los Angeles or Chicago. When an item is identified as being possibly edible, detailed questions are asked about its provenance and the plans for its preparation. Items not on the menu are called for and special dressings for salads are specified. The ordering process is prolonged and tense. The waiter is not sure he can deliver the goods, or even what some of them are. The diners are visibly annoyed at the waiter's inability to recognize some of the dishes requested. The waiter returns with the wrong dish and the senior man in the party leaps to his feet and berates him. The English tourists say nothing, but look coldly towards the African Americans, who seem completely oblivious to others around them. Eventually, after much loud grumbling and several false starts, the African Americans start their meal. But we haven't heard the last of them. The waiter is summoned loudly and frequently to attend to this or that need—iced water, bread, rolls, and so on.

I am quite surprised by this but write it off as an exceptional occurrence. After the third such incident involving other groups of African Americans, I ask Fatima about it. She tells me that what I saw was not unusual. "When we know they're coming, we get all worked up about it. They can be a headache. They complain about everything. They complained to me once that we were racist because, according to them, we treated the British better than we treated them. But I said our waiters might prefer serving the British because it takes five minutes to get their orders, whereas with you it takes twenty." I asked her why there seemed to be this difference in behavior between British and African American tourists. "When the British first started coming to The Gambia they could be difficult too—nothing like as bad as the African Americans, but they hadn't been around very much. Now they are mostly fairly experienced travelers and are quite easy to deal with. But the African Americans we get haven't traveled very much and often don't know how to behave properly, that The Gambia isn't America. Besides, they're lost people." I asked her what she meant. "Well, they don't belong back in America and they don't belong here. So they have a big problem and they bring this problem with them. This is another reason why they give us a bad time here—they look like us but they want to show us that they are different from us, better than us."

George's South Gambia Adventure

The beach is fairly quiet this morning and the few bummerboys hanging about seem pretty subdued. The beach is regularly patrolled by Gambian police and there seem to be more of them than usual today. Suddenly there is an altercation down the beach about a hundred yards from where I sit. An older youth is pushing a much younger one, who retaliates by aiming a kick at his tormentor. The older and much larger one attacks ferociously, sending the other to the sand with a series of well-aimed blows. The police rush to the scene and, with some difficulty, succeed in breaking things up. The youths are sent off. It begins to rain and we are soon treated to a spectacular tropical downpour, which lasts until the evening.

There is an air of conviviality among the tourists in the restaurant this evening. Many have been on excursions that day and are swapping stories about them. Alf Colley delights others with his humorous description of the Gambian wrestling bouts they went to in the early evening and raises a few laughs with his comparisons between them and the wrestlers seen on British television. George Tompkins, a natural comedian, tells the others of the trip he, his wife, and mother-in-law had just completed. This was the "South Gambia Adventure," in which tourists are conveyed in converted army vehicles over some rough country. They couldn't see a lot, because of the torrential rain, but had "a great time"—although George's mother-in-law looked skeptical and said, "Never again!" Some others in the restaurant had also been on the trip and added their bits to George's descriptions, laughing in recollection of how they must have seemed to the locals— soaked and bedraggled Brits tumbling out of trucks in remote little villages. George told of the stop at a village where the people had set up a small crafts stall in anticipation of the tourists' arrival. "There was this bloke in our lorry. He had a right plummy (upper-class) accent, you know. But give him his due, he were a right good sport—'fact they all were in our lorry, not like some of the other lorries where there were some right miserable gits. Anyway, this bloke has a look at their stuff and asks about these shirts. 'How much for these, my good man?' he says—a right toff he was. The Gambian tells him two hundred dalasis. 'Two hundred dalasis!' says he, 'you must be out of your mind, my dear chap. I'll give you ten.' Well they argued back and forth and his wife was pulling at his sleeve, begging him to leave off. 'No,' says he, 'they are worth no more than fifteen dalasis—at the very most. So that will be my final offer.' Well blow me if he didn't get two shirts for fifteen dalasis! And his wife then gets them to do some alterations on them for nothing! And here's this American woman who just paid ten times more for one shirt and was going around saying what a great deal she got!" George also told of how the food had not arrived for them at one of the prearranged stops on the trip. The tour guide had to go by canoe to fetch it and George and another tourist (by now they were all into the spirit of the thing) volunteered to go along with him. Unfortunately, George slipped out of the canoe and fell headlong into the water. "Well, we were all so bloody wet by that time that it didn't matter. But then I remembered about them crocodiles and I nearly pulled the bloody canoe over trying to get in again."

Some of the guests, who had begun their holiday a week before we did, were due to leave for home next morning. They arranged to have their last dinner together. As one of them said, "After all, it's only right, after all we've been through" (referring, presumably, to disappointments concerning their rooms, the unfinished swimming pool, and the like).

A Visit to Juffure

The West African Tours bus picks me and an English couple up at the hotel just after 9 A.M. and takes us a few miles down the road to Oyster Creek, where we get into a small dinghy for the quick dash into midstream to board the *MV J. Antonia*. The other passengers are already on board. We move through a maze of creeks which eventually leads into the Gambia River and the scene reminds me of Humphrey Bogart and Katharine Hepburn near the end of their epic journey in the movie, *The African Queen*. I expect the Gambia River to be big, but am not quite prepared for this—it must be about six or seven miles wide and we have been going upstream for a good hour. About half of the 30-odd passengers are British and the rest are mainly French and Italians. There are only a couple of Americans. I am surprised that there are no African Americans on this "roots" trip, but am told by a guide that they come mostly in the winter months. We arrive at James Island at about 11:45 A.M., being ferried there in relays in a small dinghy. The island is smaller than I expected—about 70 yards long and 60 yards wide—and contains the ruins of the old Portuguese slave-holding fort. An air of peace and tranquillity pervades the place—completely out of character with the dreadful purposes for which James Island was used. The tourists amble around the ruins, taking pictures and listening to the guide's potted history of the place. Then it is back to the boat for lunch and a cold Julbrew—the tasty local beer. Quite a few of the British passengers are amateur ornithologists and carry with them guidebooks on the country's 500 or more bird species.

Back down the river a little way to Albreda, the former French trading station. The jetty is thronged with villagers—about 200 or more, mostly children—awaiting the arrival of the tourists. One man patrols the jetty dressed in a University of Vermont T-shirt, battered khaki bush hat, and ragged shorts. Since he does not look at all like an "authentic" Gambian villager, the tourists don't know quite what to make of him. But he is obviously a man with a mission. He brandishes a long stick and lays about him whenever the children get too close to the boat. Another, dressed in a khaki shirt, blue pants, and a fedora leans elegantly on a black umbrella, a look of thoughtful intelligence on his face. "Bet that's the local schoolmaster," one English tourist comments. As the tourists alight they are seized upon by the children and youths, sometimes two or three clutching each arm—and the strange procession, led by the Gambian tour guide, makes its way towards the village. A young entrepreneur weaves his way through the procession selling candies, "so you have something to give to the children." More potted history at the entrance to the village before going on to Juffure—a 10-minute walk along a forest trail.

We assemble in the *bengdula* before the village chief, a wiry little man in his sixties. The guide tells us about the chief's role and also that this particular chief has two wives, "But he is interested in taking a third, so if any of you ladies are interested, please let him know." Amused titters all round to what is probably a standard line. The guide then asks us to make donations to the village development fund—a large wooden box with a slit on top sits by the chief's side—and most give 25 dalasis (about $5). The tourists then have an opportunity to have their pictures taken sitting next to the chief. Several avail themselves.

Now we move on through the village to the house of the Kinte family—the alleged birthplace of Kunta Kinte and ancestral home of Alex Haley, author of *Roots*. We assemble in a covered enclosure outside the house and an old lady of about 80 years is led out of the house to take her seat among us. This is Binte Kinte, the oldest living member of the Kinte family. The guide tells us how Haley visited Juffure after being tipped off by a Gambian he met while he was on a visit to Ghana. It does not seem terribly convincing, but no one expresses any reservations. The guide tells us that the old lady is a widow, without any means of support (in an African village?) and we are invited to make personal contributions to her welfare. She has before her a large ceramic bowl, and again most tourists give about 25 dalasis. Unless the tourism authorities and other villagers get a share, the old lady must be doing quite nicely. I wonder if Alex Haley also helped to support her? Then more "photo opportunities" and this time there is quite a demand—it takes about 15 minutes before all those who want to have their pictures taken with Binte Kinte get this done.

Next it is back through the village, stopping briefly at a crafts stall. The prices seem a shade higher than in the coastal tourist centers and there are few buyers. As we head towards the jetty, the hustling is in full swing—requests for dalasis, candies, home addresses—the appeals becoming more frantic, the voices more strident with each step forwards towards the *MV J. Antonia*. Many tourists cannot take final photographs because they have two Gambian children clinging desperately to each arm. I love this—it is hustling at its very best! I manage to avoid a mauling by digging my hands deep in my pockets and clamping my arms tightly against my body. (Not very sporting, perhaps, but a fairly effective defense against this form of panhandling.) Some of the older children try to hide their concern as the tourists near the end of the jetty. A boy of about 16 years has been telling his adopted tourist how tough it is to survive and get an education in The Gambia. He now listens with barely concealed impatience as his tourist tells him that The Gambia needs a free system of public education "just like in Britain," and that it is the young people who must tell the government what to do. "If enough people tell the government then, with a bit of luck, your country will follow the same path." Another tourist is telling a young Gambian of his doubts regarding Juffure and Alex Haley: "It's difficult, even with written records, to go back beyond your great-grandfather's generation."

The tourists get back on board, some literally shaking children off their arms. The man with the stick is back on patrol and whacking away merrily. The vendors of masks and other souvenirs have pushed to the front, holding objects aloft and calling out prices that are a fraction of those being asked back at the village. As the boat pushes off, last-minute sales are made at giveaway prices. Masks and other objects whiz overhead towards the boat and tight little bundles of dalasis fly in the opposite direction.

We arrive back—this time to Banjul harbor—at about 4:30 P.M. This has been a most interesting day all round. I wonder what MacCannell would make of all this? Is it "staged authenticity" or "authentic tomfoolery"? And who are the victims—the locals, the tourists, or both? And what about Alex Haley? Could he ever have imagined that his personal search for roots would have helped create such an unlikely tourist trap as Juffure?

Departure

We had our final dinner last evening as a group, the culmination of a process of solidification that had grown steadily after the first few days of the holiday. All pals together, exchanging addresses and promising to write. Most said they enjoyed the holiday, once they got used to things here. It was a bit different from what they had expected and the pool business had been a bit of a pain. The breakfasts too had been skimpy at first (bread rolls and jam are OK if you're one o' them continental Europeans, but not if you're British), but these had changed to "proper breakfasts" (bacon, sausage, eggs, and other high-cholesterol goodies) after tourists complained to the hotel management. But everything was fine in the end. "Anyway," as Sally Colley observed, "I was determined to enjoy this holiday. Can't let things get you down. You just have to get on and make the best of it. I've always found if you take that attitude you can have a good time most places." The old Dunkirk spirit was alive and well.

The bus picks us up and proceeds to the airport, stopping at various hotels along the way where other departing tourists join us. Since I enjoy other people's awkward situations (don't you?), I look forward with relish to one particular stop, where the Sharps will be getting on. I had met them a few days earlier while on a visit to the Abuko Game Reserve. They talked about the hotel they had moved to, invited me to come and have a look, which I did, and they were extremely pleasant. Not a mention of the Colleys or the rift between them. What would happen when the Sharps boarded the bus for the airport? Would they smile and chat with the Colleys as if nothing had happened? Would the Colleys ask how they had been getting along and tell them that the swimming pool, which finally opened for business eight days after our arrival, had turned out to be wonderful after all? The great moment finally arrived and I felt as if I had stumbled in on the closing scene of a particularly gripping episode of "Coronation Street," the long-running British soap opera about working-class life in Manchester. The Sharp family climbed on board and, without glancing right or left, walked up the aisle past the Colleys. Neither side acknowledged the existence of the other. Will they ever patch things up? Will they ever go on holiday together again? What will they tell their friends back in Manchester? (You can write the next episode and let me know).

Departure procedures at the airport turn out to be almost as confusing as those encountered on arrival. Baggage is placed on the tarmac and owners are called over to claim them and, if necessary, open them for security inspection. The departure lounge is too small to accommodate all the passengers waiting for two flights to Britain, so most of us spill outside—some grabbing seats and others having to stand. It's really hot and sticky and the tourists, who looked pretty sharp and cool in the hotel an hour ago, are now beginning to look a little disheveled. The Foreign Exchange Office, which is supposed to be open at this time, remains closed—although the smiling clerks can be seen lounging around inside. Probably under orders to stay closed until the flights depart. Why give pounds away for dalasis if you don't have to? Isn't this the name of the North-South tourism game, anyway? Since the driver and his mate are hovering around hopefully, I put some dalasis aside for last-minute tips. The rest goes on a hefty cheese sandwich and three Julbrews. Believe me, I don't usually drink three beers in succession, but being a tourist in The Gambia can be a very thirsty business indeed.

☀   ⁑   ✳   ✦   ☀

Tourism Problems

Overdependence on Charter Tourism

The overwhelming majority of holiday visitors to The Gambia are package tourists who arrive on charter flights from European countries. The peak period for air charter tourism is November through April, and the country is mainly a winter escape area for Europeans. This gives the country's tourism a pronounced seasonal character, marked by high unemployment in the industry during the low season. In the early years most of the charter tourists were from Scandinavia. Energetic promotion by British tour operators and travel agents has radically changed this picture, and British nationals now account for about 60% of all tourists visiting The Gambia.

Throughout the holiday months passengers arrive from various European countries on package tours organized and sold by several tour operators. From Britain most come on chartered Monarch Airways, Britannia Airways, Air 2000, or Excalibur Airways flights from London or Manchester, having bought holiday packages from companies like Airtours PLC, Cosmos, The Gambia Experience, Hayes and Jarvis, Kuoni, or Portland Holidays. The packages are competitively priced against those for southern European destinations. In 1993 a midrange 14-day package from a British tour operator cost the equivalent of $800. This included London-Banjul-London airfare, airport-hotel-airport transfers, 13 nights hotel accommodation, and half board (that is, breakfast and dinner daily). From continental Europe the main carriers are Sabena (Belgium), Conair (Denmark), Condor (Germany), Maersk Air (Sweden), and Lennox Air (Italy); and the main continental tour operators active in the Gambian market are Aviatours, Hertzel, Neckermann, Kreuzer Reisen, TUI, Jet Reisen (all from Germany), Leonardo Da Vinci (Italy), Jelmoly (Switzerland), Vingressor (Sweden and Norway), and Spies (Denmark).

Heavy reliance on charter tourism means that The Gambia loses a big chunk of the total holiday price to foreign interests. Most tourists prepay before they leave home, use foreign carriers, and stay in hotels that are foreign owned or run by foreign management. It has been estimated that only 23% of the package price actually accrues to The Gambia (Farver, 1984). And because there are few opportunities for tourists to spend outside hotels, the average daily tourist expenditure per capita is estimated at between $8 and $10.

Overdependence on One Country

The danger of dependence on Britain as the major source of tourists was brought home dramatically following the successful military coup in July of 1994. The British government immediately issued a warning to its nationals, advising them not to visit The Gambia because of the unstable political situation. Thousands of Britons heeded this advice, which was subsequently given also by the governments of some other European countries. A high-level Gambian delegation was dispatched to London to try to have the British government change its position, arguing that the advice had been politically motivated, that is, designed to bring about a quick return to civilian government. The British were not happy about the proposed timetable for the restoration of democracy, which was not planned to occur until 1998. Western donors suspended bilateral aid and imposed economic sanctions in November of 1994.

These measures, together with a drastic decline in the number of tourist arrivals in 1995 (only 45,000 compared with 78,000 the previous year) forced the military junta to revise its timetable and schedule elections for 1997. Arrivals from Britain plummeted from 52,232 in 1994 to 14,171 in 1995, while those from Scandinavia dropped from 9,095 to 4,481 during the same period. Only the German tourists, whose government did not issue a travel warning, seemed unperturbed: arrivals from that country dropped only marginally between 1994 and 1995. The Gambia returned to civilian rule in 1997, but the long-term effects of the 1994 coup are difficult to predict. Until that time the country had enjoyed an enviable reputation as one of the most politically stable in the region. It managed to recover reasonably quickly from the unsuccessful coup attempt in 1981, and it may well be able to rebound from the successful 1994 coup. By 1996 arrivals had reached 77,000, some 37,295 of these coming from Britain and 9,340 from Scandinavia. It would appear that, in the absence of any longstanding pattern of successive political upheavals, tourists were able to view the 1981 and 1994 coups as "one-off" situations.

Lack of Regional Development

Whatever benefits The Gambia derives from tourism, there are few signs of these outside the coastal areas. Although the government has repeatedly stated its intention to spread the economic benefits of tourism by developing *upcountry* tourism, this has not yet materialized. Villages like Juffure and Albreda receive river-cruise tourists twice a week in the winter and once a week at other times; and other villages are on the itineraries organized for excursions like the "South Gambia Adventure." At both Albreda and Juffure large signboards indicated that two development projects for local school extensions and renovations were being sponsored by American religious organizations. But there was no physical evidence of any work actually underway at these places. Questions regarding the disposition of tourist contributions at Albreda brought vague and evasive replies. Both Juffure and Albreda appear to be just as poor and undeveloped as other Gambian villages I saw. The sales of crafts and souvenirs at Juffure were minimal, and the gifts secured by the tourist-hustling children amounted to only a few dalasis. Neither represented significant economic contributions. The children obviously receive a schooling in the art of hustling tourists, which may stand them in good stead when they move down to the coastal tourist enclave in a few years time, as many of them surely will.

The Enclave and the Demonstration Effect

The tourist coastal enclave is a magnet for Gambians seeking employment in and around the hotels, as well as for hundreds of young people looking for excitement, adventure, and dalasis through contacts with tourists. This exacerbates the longstanding problem of high rural-urban migration and involves a considerable degree of social dislocation. A few years ago the hordes of bummerboys were posing a serious problem for the tourism industry. Although encounters between these young men and tourists were markedly free from violence, tourists complained that they could not go anywhere outside the hotels without being pursued and accosted by persistent "hangers on." This is still a feature of life in the immediate vicinity of hotels and on the main beaches, but it is not as pronounced as it once was. The hotels tried to alleviate the situation by giving some of these young men quasi-official status as hotel guides. To qualify, one had to produce a certificate of good character from the police and, following an interview by hotel management, undergo a brief period of training. The successful applicant could then operate legitimately from the hotel entrance but was not put on the hotel payroll. The tourist now has a choice: use a hotel guide or run the gauntlet of freelance guides waiting outside the hotel grounds. Going it alone is still almost impossible, and most tourists find this irksome. Indeed, it was mentioned very frequently by those who told me they did not plan to visit The Gambia again. The bummerboys provide an interesting example of the demonstration effect in an extreme form. As we saw in chapter 6, these young people not only hope to improve their material life conditions in The Gambia, but also try to find tourists who will help them to journey overseas.

Organizational Confusion

Improvement of The Gambia's tourism industry will not be easy, since the implementation of a consistent tourism policy has been hampered by the fact that several different governmental agencies are involved. The Ministry of Information and Tourism is responsible for the overall formulation of tourism policy. Within this ministry, the Tourism Division deals with product development and quality control, marketing and overseas activities. Working under the formal authority of the Ministry of Information and Tourism is the Tourism Advisory Board, made up of representatives of both private and public tourism-related bodies. Also under Ministry of Information and Tourism authority is the Tourism Liaison Board, which coordinates tourism development in relation to the allocation of lands in the tourism development areas. Then there is the National Investment Board, whose area of jurisdiction includes government investments in hotels and other facilities. Coordination between all these bodies has proven difficult and overall control by the Ministry of Information and Tourism has been relatively weak. These cumbersome administrative arrangements make systematic tourism planning virtually impossible (Dieke, 1993).

Summary

Although tourism in The Gambia was initiated by Scandinavian tour operators, it rapidly became an important sector of the economy and a major generator of foreign exchange and jobs. With few viable economic alternatives to tourism, The Gambia has come to depend heavily on an industry that is characterized by weak and inefficient organization, a high degree of foreign control, high import content, and wide seasonal fluctuations in tourism employment. The industry is oriented to mass charter tourism, which is organized by foreign companies; and it has come to depend primarily on one country—Britain—as its main supplier of tourists. The benefits of tourism have not carried over into The Gambia's hinterland, whose people remain poor and have few opportunities for economic and social advancement. A consequence of this has been the exodus of young people from the rural areas to the coastal tourism enclave, where there are not enough jobs to go around, but where opportunities exist in the informal tourism sector as unofficial guides, bummerboys, prostitutes, and the like. Despite these and other problems, and with a fairly modest inventory of tourism resources, The Gambia has succeeded in establishing a favorable reputation as a less brassy and commercialized destination than most of its Mediterranean competitors. During the 1960s its appeal was mainly to more adventurous tourists, but now it has become a mainstream destination where charter tourists like the Colleys, Sharps, Hargreaves, and Tompkins can feel comfortable— at least for a couple of weeks. While The Gambia will never reap the kind of rewards from tourism that are expected by the world's leading destinations, the industry seems likely to remain a vital part of the economy in the foreseeable future.

Chapter 11
Changing Direction

Introduction

This book has focused mainly on mass tourism, and I have tried to adopt a balanced approach to the subject. While there is no denying mass tourism's tremendous appeal, it will be clear from much of what has been said already that it is also associated, directly and indirectly, with a number of major social, cultural, and environmental problems. In this final chapter, I look at some of the ways in which these tourism-related problems might be addressed. First, I consider the concept of alternative tourism and some of the doubts and reservations that have been expressed about it. Next, I look at some small-scale alternative forms of tourism to see how these work out in practice. Then I outline some new directions in contemporary tourism, including the community tourism movement, Krippendorf's proposals for humanizing tourism, and Poon's vision of the new tourism which is thought to be emerging. I end with a reminder that the democratization of leisure travel is far from complete, and provide a summary of some of the developments under way in social tourism for less privileged members of society.

Alternative Tourism

Alternatives to mainstream tourism are not new and have been followed by a minority of travelers since the tourism boom began after World War II (Smith and Eadington, 1992). However, the term *alternative tourism* gained currency during the 1970s and 1980s as a generic term covering forms of tourism believed by some to be morally superior to, as well as more sustainable than, organized mass tourism. Although no universally accepted definition of alternative tourism was ever formulated, advocates stressed a number of common themes, for example, sustainability and environmental conservation; small-scale, modest accommodations; genuine and enriching host-tourist encounters; and local control of the industry.

The ECTWT Approach

A comprehensive attempt to define and operationalize the term was undertaken by the Ecumenical Coalition on Third World Tourism (ECTWT) meeting in Chiang Mai, Thailand, in 1984 (Holden, 1984). Alternative tourism was there defined as a process promising a just form of travel that tries to achieve understanding, solidarity, and equality among all participants.

The main objectives of alternative tourism, according to the ECTWT, were:

1. To provide viable options to the exploitative and destructive elements of mass tourism.
2. To ensure that the economic benefits of tourism are equitably shared with the people of the host countries.
3. To build up mutually enriching relationships between visitors and those visited with due regard to the human dignity and rights of both.
4. To ensure that respect for the religious, cultural, social, and physical environment is shown.
5. To support people's struggles for self-determination in relation to tourism policy.
6. To stimulate action-oriented post-travel responses both by the visitors and those visited.
7. To experiment with and develop new models for alternative tourism.
8. To encourage domestic tourism (Holden, 1984, p. 15).

From the ECTWT definition and list of objectives, it is clear that what was envisaged was not simply another kind of tourism for a special market segment. This was to be a form of tourism that opposed prevailing trends and promised a new set of possibilities for the future.

Some Scholarly Reservations

Both the concept and the practice of alternative tourism were examined at two major research conferences held in 1989. In both cases (Zakopane in Poland and Tamransett in Algeria) participants concluded that the concept of *alternative tourism* was too much of a catchall term embracing a wide variety of different touristic forms, each of which might be regarded as an alternative to the others, as well as to mass tourism. At the Zakopane conference it was recommended that the term *alternative forms of tourism* be used instead of *alternative tourism,* while those attending the Tamransett meetings suggested that *responsible tourism* best described the new emphasis in tourism development. In any event, it was noted that forms of tourism do not become "good" or "superior" simply by defining them as such, but have to be examined empirically and evaluated as they actually operate. It was necessary, therefore, to uncover the ideological dimensions of so-called *alternative tourism* and to see if it really could deliver what its advocates promised.

In an essay following the Zakopane conference, Lanfant and Graburn (1992) tried to identify the common features underlying the diverse claims made for alternative tourism. They argued that such features emerge when alternative tourism is seen as an ideological movement promoting the antithesis of conventional, commercial mass tourism. Whatever is considered bad about mass tourism is subjected to semantic inversion, and these features become the defining characteristics of alternative tourism. In other words, alternative tourism becomes the polar opposite of a worst-case version of mass tourism, and has the following characteristics:

- *It is individualized and selective, expressing good taste* (as against organized, gregarious, and plebian mass tourism).
- *Its accommodations are small- or medium-sized, locally owned and well-integrated into the area, and built by local artisans from local materials* (as against large, foreign-owned and -managed, concrete-and-glass hotels in mass tourist enclaves).
- *Its activities emphasize physical well-being, intellectual-aesthetic attitudes, and genuine encounters between hosts and tourists* (as against comfort, "the four S's," and superficial contacts typical of mass tourism).
- *Its planning expresses local wishes and interests* (as against those of external planners, developers, and tourism entrepreneurs who dominate mass tourism).

If we consider these as a set of minimal requirements of alternative tourism, we may be hard put to find places where alternative tourism actually exists. To what degree must a form of tourism possess these characteristics before it can pass the alternative tourism test? Would hill trekking in Nepal be individualized or tasteful enough? Would relations between trekkers and lodge owners be genuine enough? Do all Nepalese villagers have to agree before we can conclude that planning reflects local wishes and interests (Lanfant and Graburn, 1992)?

Butler (1992) has provided what is probably still the most insightful and provocative analysis of alternative tourism. His aim is not to demonstrate that mass tourism needs no alternatives, or that alternatives to it are useless. It is, rather, to carefully scrutinize the notion that alternative tourism can solve the problems of mass tourism. Like Lanfant and Graburn, he warns against accepting an idealized and simplistic contrast between mass and alternative tourism. Comparing alternative and mass tourism, Butler suggests that the former appears less damaging in the short term, but that this advantage may not last. If alternative tourism is not carefully planned, controlled, and regulated, it is likely to create many of the problems associated with mass tourism. Compared with mass tourism, alternative tourism can penetrate further into residents' personal space, for while tourist-host contacts may be fewer, they are likely to be deeper. This can expose the host culture and resources to greater visitation, and may even involve a proportionately greater leakage of expenditure. Butler raises a number of additional questions regarding alternative tourism:

- *Is it disguised class prejudice?* Alternative tourism seems to be designed to appeal to tourists who are affluent, high-spending, long-staying, committed, educated, mature, and probably white. The claim that alternative tourism is morally superior to mass tourism may be another way of saying that those who avoid mass tourism are morally superior to those who participate in it.
- *Does it create too few jobs or generate too little income?* To achieve its objectives, alternative tourism must be limited in scale. This means that the numbers of tourists must be severely restricted. Such restrictions are difficult to enforce in a free-market situation, and local support for this may be far from unanimous. If tourist numbers are restricted, so too will tourist spending and tourism-related jobs. The "purer" the alternative tourism, the fewer the jobs created and the lower the income earned (for example, true wilderness tourists spend little or nothing, because in the wilderness there is little on which to spend money).
- *Don't most people actually enjoy being mass tourists?* Rather than view mass tourists as dolts who are making the best of inferior tourist opportunities and experiences, and who need to be shown the light, advocates of alternative tourism must recognize that mass tourism is highly attractive and pleasurable for many people. They consider as advantages things like prearranged, comfortable accommodations, familiar food, and hosts who speak the tourists' language, especially since most of these things are often obtained at moderate cost. In exchange for these perceived benefits they willingly forego the experience of immersion in host cultures, especially when this promises inconvenience, discomfort, and deprivation.

According to Butler, weaning tourists away from conventional tourism and educating them about the desirability of becoming alternative tourists would be a mammoth, long-term task. If such a task were ever to be successfully accomplished, and most of us decided we wanted alternative forms of tourism, would it be possible to accommodate the new preferences and still have something we could call alternative tourism? How would alternative tourism withstand the process of massification that this would entail? It would seem that alternative tourism is hardly likely to displace mass tourism and may, in fact, require mass tourism for it to be an alternative to.

Butler's conclusion, therefore, is that many of the claims made for alternative tourism are suspect and have been accepted rather uncritically by many people. But he believes that alternative tourism can be useful in *complementing* mass tourism in five main ways: first, by increasing the variety of attractions; second, by providing opportunities for authentic experiences; third, by catering to the needs of special interest tourist groups; fourth, by supplementing the incomes of rural dwellers in marginal or remote areas; and fifth, by providing suitably limited economic development in areas incapable of sustaining major changes.

Tourism Alternatives

In the previous section we considered alternative tourism as a concept and outlined some of its problematic aspects. In this section I look at a number of touristic forms that seem, in certain respects at least, to resemble the kind of tourism implied by the term *alternative tourism.* However, in order to avoid the ambiguities inherent in that term, we can treat these forms simply as examples of alternatives to organized mass tourism. In other words, they are not presented as examples of a new kind of tourism that will eventually sweep away and replace mass tourism throughout the world. Here we simply want to look at how these tourism alternatives work in practice and evaluate their appropriateness for the particular places in which they have developed.

The Mitchell Formula

Some 12 years prior to the ECTWT meeting in Chiang Mai, the government of St. Vincent in the Caribbean developed a plan for small-scale, sustainable tourism. Although it was not referred to as *alternative tourism,* it appeared to meet some of the specifications that were subsequently attached to this term. Formulated in 1972, the plan was the brainchild of St. Vincent Prime Minister Mitchell. Although he set about implementing his plan with great determination, his government fell two years later, and his approach to tourism was abandoned by the new government. While it is not possible to judge how effective Mitchell's formula might have been had he been allowed to implement it fully, one leading tourism researcher believed that it was essentially sound and represented a useful model for other small island states (Britton, 1977).

Mitchell's underlying philosophy was expressed in his "To Hell With Eden" speech to the 1972 meeting of the Caribbean Travel Association, in which he tried to expose the myth of the Caribbean paradise. He argued that paradise had not been lost in the Caribbean, but had never existed in the first place. The problems faced by people living in this area were often different from those confronting people in the cities of North America, but this did not lessen their importance. Therefore, a new and more realistic tourism message was needed. At Mitchell's insistence, the St. Vincent Tourist Board prepared a color brochure and 20-page guidebook containing no pictures of bikini-clad women or smiling waiters with trays of rum punch. Instead, it featured natural scenes and provided information on activities such as excursions with local fishermen, visits to arrowroot farms, visits to the marketing board, trips on country buses, and so on. The Tourist Board staff established contacts with environmentalist organizations like the Sierra Club, with magazines like *Natural History,* and with other groups likely to be interested in St. Vincent's brand of tourism. This marketing approach reflected Mitchell's desire to create an indigenous and integrated tourism industry, one that would ensure greater local participation and control, allow for gradual expansion, and minimize adverse environmental and sociocultural impacts.

In a proposal introduced in 1972, Mitchell set out seven special priorities for tourism development in St. Vincent:

1. *State zoning of land to separate tourism from agriculture and other activities.* A primary concern here was to ensure that tourism's effect on land values would not price land and livelihood out of the reach of local farmers.
2. *Gradual growth of the tourism industry.* This was meant to control inflationary tendencies that might come from tourism investment and soften the environmental and sociocultural impacts.
3. *The indigenization of tourism.* There would be no casinos, luxury resort complexes, or French cuisine. St. Vincent tourism was to be designed for visitors who would appreciate a genuine Caribbean experience rather than a tropical fantasy vacation.
4. *The utilization of locally produced food, furniture, and crafts.* This would strengthen links between tourism and other sectors of the local economy.
5. *The utilization of local architectural designs for tourist accommodations.* There would be no concrete-and-glass high-rise buildings. Apart from satisfying aesthetic requirements, this would also lessen dependence on overseas sources of building materials.
6. *The promotion of joint ventures between foreign investors and local capital, and the limiting of the amount of land outsiders could buy.* The goal here was to reduce the risk of foreign domination of the tourism industry.
7. *The use of an honest marketing strategy.* The aim here was to avoid perpetuating the Eden myth and to focus instead on things natural and authentic.

Reactions to Mitchell's formula were mixed. St. Vincent's only newspaper endorsed it enthusiastically, while most foreign hotel owners expressed skepticism about the viability of tourism that did not depend on the large hotels. Small hotel owners were greatly encouraged by Mitchell's approach, viewing it as an endorsement of and support for their own brand of tourism. Some local shop owners wondered if the new kinds of tourists would have the spending power of those who favored more conventional forms of Caribbean tourism. Support for Mitchell came from the Caribbean Development Bank and the Caribbean Common Market.

Britton, as indicated earlier, was generally impressed with Mitchell's tourism plan, although he noted a number of difficulties that were not satisfactorily resolved. Without adequate market research and funding for promotional campaigns, St. Vincent's tourism authorities had problems in trying to tap potential markets in North America. Visitor arrivals increased by 25% in 1974, but they leveled off during the following three years. Another problem was accessibility: St. Vincent could be reached only indirectly, with flight transfers at either Barbados or St. Lucia. The fall of the Mitchell government in 1974 and subsequent frequent changes of government were also serious impediments. The onset of a worldwide recession at this time also adversely affected the climate for investment in St. Vincent tourism (Britton, 1977).

"Tourism for Discovery" in Senegal

Tourism in Senegal, West Africa, has focused on the coastal area, where there is a Club Med resort and several well-run hotels catering mainly to French and other European sun-lust visitors. Concern over mass tourism's impacts and a desire for greater local involvement led in 1971 to the initiation of the Tourism for Discovery project in the country's Lower Casamance Region. The Agency for Cultural and Technical Cooperation recruited an anthropologist, Christian Saglio, to help plan and develop the project, which involved close collaboration between Senegalese tourism authorities, local residents, and the anthropologist.

The Lower Casamance Region was selected because of its distance from the major tourism resorts; the attractive natural environment with its rivers, lagoons and inlets; and the interesting culture of its inhabitants, the Diola. The aim was to create a form of tourism that would offer a "genuine voyage of discovery," use simple accommodations managed and run by the Diola, and provide opportunities for intimate contact between tourists and hosts. Tourists would participate in the daily activities of Diola villagers and could travel by canoe on fishing trips along the region's many waterways. Meals would be planned around locally available products and traditional cuisine. Responsibility for the daily management and operation of the project would be in local hands, and profits would accrue directly to the villagers.

Saglio experienced some difficulties during the initial stages of the project. A drought in 1972 caused a temporary shortage of labor because many people left the area. Local preconceptions about what the visitors would want led to delays in constructing the accommodations: most villagers had to be persuaded to use traditional architectural forms and would have preferred to use cement blocks and sheet metal roofs and install glass windows, numbered doors, electricity, and even air-conditioning. Rivalries also developed between various village leaders vying for a stake in the project. However, by 1983 nine tourist villages or camps had been built with a total bed capacity of 310.

The camps are run by village cooperatives, which set prices, arrange excursions and other activities, and decide how camp workers will be remunerated. Senegal's Department of Tourism assists in marketing the camps through contacts with European special-interest travel agencies and with youth travel associations. Low investment costs, local control, the injection of cash directly into the local economy, and a minimum of social disruption are probably among the project's most positive aspects. In addition, construction of the camps led to a renewal of local interest and pride in traditional Diola culture. The camp at the village of Enampore, for example, involved the construction of a large, circular building with clay walls and a traditional, two-layer thatch roof. Its central courtyard was encircled by an interior gallery and formed a center for communal activities, such as cotton spinning, cooking, palm fiber plaiting, and so on. Capable of accommodating 50 people, such a house had not been constructed in Enampore for many years, and it required perseverance and the revival of traditional building techniques for its successful completion.

However, the entire project generates only about 0.5% of Senegal's total tourism earnings, and it has created only about 50 part-time jobs for villagers. The cultural gap between the tourists and the Diola remains large. The project is perhaps best viewed as being complementary to mass tourism, for it depends heavily on established international air connections and an official tourism structure for its success. Moreover, a large proportion of visitors to the camps consists of tourists taking a short break from more conventional vacations in one of Senegal's coastal resorts (English, 1986; Saglio, 1979, 1985).

Losmen Tourism in Bali

Alternative forms of tourism are not always the result of government initiatives or organized community planning. Developments have sometimes occurred in a more spontaneous fashion, as in Boracay (see chapter 7), or along routes frequented by "hippie" travelers in the 1960s and young, middle-class budget travelers in the 1970s. In Bali, Indonesia, *losmen* or home-stay tourism developed alongside conventional mass tourism with the discovery of Kuta village and its beach by low-budget young travelers in the 1960s. Although Kuta is only 1 KM from the airport and 7 KM from Denpasar, the Balinese capital, it was not officially targeted for tourism development because authorities felt the beach was unsafe. Initially, visitors made short, overnight stays and were accommodated in Balinese homes, repaying hospitality with gifts rather than cash payments. As the numbers of visitors increased, special pavilions or losmens were built alongside the villagers' houses to accommodate them, and hospitality assumed more commercialized forms. Other centers of losmen tourism sprang up elsewhere in Bali, especially in the Lovina Beach area in the northern part of the island.

Losmen accommodations are modest, most rooms having only a bed and a small lockup cupboard. Usually there is a communal toilet, although the more ambitious losmen owners have installed toilets in each room. While locals are able to reap direct economic benefits from this type of tourism, concerns have been expressed over a number of undesirable side effects. Parents worry about the effects of tourists' presence on the young—especially the latter's emulation of tourist behavior and their desire for money and Western status symbols such as transistor radios, cassette players, and so on. In some places prostitutes have rented rooms near losmens, traffic congestion has become a problem, and local sewage systems have not been improved since the prelosmen period. Kutu is now an urban area with many of the familiar urban problems. But it also enjoys the highest per capita income of all urban areas in Indonesia (Holden, 1984).

Ecotourism in Pond Inlet, Northwest Territories

In 1983 the European Community banned the importation of seal skins, a move that had serious economic repercussions for the Inuit living in the Baffin Region of Canada's Northwest Territories. Until that time, the Inuit had earned income from selling skins, which were a by-product of subsistence seal hunting. As a partial solution to this economic problem, the territorial government immediately developed a policy for ecotourism development that emphasized six priorities:

1. Development must be consistent with the abilities and aspirations of the host communities; it must respect northern cultures, expectations, and lifestyles.
2. Development must be sustainable, with the use of today's resources not compromising their use by future generations; it should be designed to yield maximum possible economic benefits for residents.
3. Tourism should be well-distributed between communities. To facilitate this government support will be given to small- and medium-sized communities.
4. Development will recognize and respect the spirit and intent of all aboriginal land claims.
5. Major tourism initiatives will embody extensive community and industry participation in the planning process.
6. The private sector should take the lead in developing a viable tourism industry. Government provides financial incentives and public infrastructure support. It will also encourage and support the private sector in the marketing arena (Grekin and Milne, 1997).

One of the Inuit communities to embark on ecotourism development was Pond Inlet (pop. 952 in 1991), which lies on Eclipse Sound in northern Baffin Island. With an unemployment rate of more than 50%, many residents were unwilling to rely on government welfare support, and were enthusiastic about participating in tourism. Pond Inlet tourism offers packaged, guided nature tours, most of which are sold through southern tour operators. A municipal Tourism Committee oversees tourism guidelines and standards, and is supposed to hear residents' opinions on tourism-related matters. The Pond Inlet Cooperative acts as the main outfitter for tourists, supplying clothing, equipment, as well as hiring the guides; and there is also a smaller outfitting service provided by a non-Inuit resident of the village. With some 269 visitors in 1988, Pond Inlet was the third most popular tourist destination in the Baffin Region. For most ecotourists, a stay in Pond Inlet is not cheap. There is a free campsite, but the only hotel—a small, 12-room building—cost $200 per night in 1996. Local attitudes towards tourism and tourists are generally positive, although some residents do not welcome "Greenpeace tourists" (that is, tourists concerned with animal rights).

While ecotourism in Pond Inlet has helped soften the blow caused by the European ban on seal skin imports, a number of problems exist for the new industry:

- *Leakages.* Only about 40% of the retail price of a package tour reaches the community. A large proportion of tourism receipts leaks out of the community to pay for externally produced goods and services needed by local tourism-related businesses. There is, therefore, virtually no multiplier effect.

- *Cultural concealment.* Concerned about the possibility that many tourists strongly disapprove of seal hunting, the Inuit guides try to conceal this activity at all costs. This runs counter to the government's emphasis on culturally compatible tourism, and also works against the expressed desires of both hosts and guests for genuine cultural interaction. While some tourists are offended by evidence of seal hunting, many others are interested in witnessing it directly.
- *Lack of cultural education for tourists.* Many Inuit feel that the tourists come only to see the wildlife and not to learn about Inuit culture. Tourists themselves considered the opportunity for cultural interaction one of the least satisfying aspects of their visits. Besides Inuit concern over tourists' misperceptions of seal hunting, another source of the problem lies in their lack of attention to cultural education for tourists.
- *Lack of opportunities for female crafts producers.* While the sale of arts and crafts is important for the local tourism economy, women play a relatively small part in this sector. Inuit women make clothing and wall hangings from cloth and skins, but few of these items are on display in Pond Inlet's craft shop. Some women claimed that their products were rejected by the cooperative's male manager because he professed not to know how to properly price women's work.
- *Ineffective tourism committee.* This committee has not been particularly active, having met only on an irregular and infrequent basis in the past few years (Grekin and Milne, 1997).

Community Tourism

We have seen that opportunities for resident participation in tourism policymaking, planning, and organization have been built into several of the tourism operations just described. Since the 1980s, the emphasis on resident participation has grown, and this has resulted in the growth of a *community tourism* or *community-responsive tourism* movement among scholars, policymakers, and planners. One of the earliest contributors to this movement was the Canadian tourism planner-consultant, Louis D'Amore, whose main interest was in tourism's carrying capacity and the social limits to tourism growth.

Based on his studies in a number of mid-sized British Columbia communities, D'Amore (1983) proposed a set of nine guidelines for "socially sensitive tourism development" in British Columbia. Most, if not all, might be important considerations for community tourism planning in other places as well:

1. *A promotional campaign should be designed and implemented to educate the general public about BC's tourism industry.* Although tourism is one of BC's major revenue earners, little effort has been made to inform residents of

its socioeconomic significance. Such an effort is necessary for two main reasons: success of the industry depends on the participation of the entire public and not simply on that of industry workers; and people need to feel less possessive about their resources.

2. *Local tourism planning should be based on overall development goals and priorities identified by local residents.* The chances of tourism development exceeding local social carrying capacity will be greatly reduced if due attention is paid to residents' needs, aspirations, and priorities. If local people feel they have little or no control, tourism-related problems and resentment against tourism and tourists are bound to increase.

3. *The promotion of local attractions should be subject to resident endorsement.* This factor is vital because it is the residents who will have to cope with the effects of such promotion. Promotion should not be left up to provincial tourism authorities or local chambers of commerce. It should involve a process permitting input from interested citizens and other community organizations.

4. *The integrity and quality of local opportunities for fishing, hunting, and outdoor recreation should be maintained.* These opportunities are highly valued by residents in many BC communities. If they are impaired or diminished as a result of tourism development, local perceptions of the value of tourism will change for the worse. Tourists must be encouraged to behave in a responsible and locally appropriate manner.

5. *The involvement of native people in the tourism industry in BC should proceed only when the band itself considers that its traditions and lifestyle will not be threatened.* West Coast Indian culture is very attractive to visitors and, under certain circumstances, constitutes a valuable tourism resource. However, its use as a tourism resource requires band consent and must be organized in a way that keeps tourists from intruding into band life.

6. *Programs should be encouraged that involve the use of local capital, entrepreneurial ability, and labor in the tourism industry.* These are important for two main reasons: as a means of maintaining a necessary degree of local control over tourism development; and as a means of generating employment and other economic benefits to the community.

7. *Opportunities should be provided to permit broad-based community participation in tourist events and activities.* If residents are involved in organizing and participating in tourist events and activities, it will increase the possibilities for harmonious relations between tourists and locals.

8. *Local communities should adopt themes and events reflecting local history, lifestyles, or geographic setting.* Doing so can lead to a sense of local identity and community pride. It can also afford locals a greater degree of control over tourism in their community.

9. *Before introducing or expanding tourism in a community, attempts should be made to deal with existing local problems relating to growth.* The needs of permanent residents must be addressed before adopting measures that

might exacerbate existing problems, infrastructural strain, inadequate supply of affordable housing, congestion. If these needs are not addressed first,
tourism may well be blamed for all growth problems.

Most of these guidelines seem appropriate for relatively small communities with
active and well-organized citizens' groups that can monitor, criticize, and help direct the course of tourism development. However, even small communities may not
possess the necessary degree of consensus to make resident participation effective.
We saw in chapter 9 that people were sharply divided on tourism issues in small
places like Pukalani and Hana; and that in Maui as a whole residents may sometimes be forced to accept—through perceived economic necessity or lack of political muscle—development schemes that involve fairly high personal and social costs.
In recent years some tourism researchers have become openly skeptical or even
critical about the community tourism movement.

Ryan and Montgomery (1994) explored the attitudes of residents to tourism
development in the small town of Bakewell, in Cheshire, England. They discovered
that, while most residents were favorably disposed towards tourism, their attitudes
were far from uniform, and that about one-fifth were irritated by the level of tourism in the community. The authors also challenged the common assumption by
industry planners that negative attitudes among residents can be changed with proper
tourism education and argue that strongly held perceptions of tourism's negative
personal impacts may often be quite resistant to educational campaigns. Ryan and
Montgomery further note that active involvement in tourism planning may lead
some residents to oppose all further development—something that also seemed to
occur in the Hana situation described earlier. One of the dangers of community-
responsive tourism, they suggest, is that it becomes "tourism promotion aimed at
those who wish to become responsive."

In a short paper, Taylor (1995) expressed support for the ethic of resident participation, but observed that communitarianism is often impeded by the actions of
more powerful players, some of whom may not even be full-time residents of the
community. Joppe (1996) has acknowledged some of the achievements of community tourism development, but pointed out that, even in apparently successful
projects, a number of flaws are evident: initiatives are often taken by government or
external agencies rather than by community groups; funding agencies take steps to
ensure that private business development is promoted and supported; the community's resources are rarely exploited to a degree that permits the community to
become an equal partner in the project; and that resident participation seldom has
an important effect on key decision making. In an interesting analysis of community-based tourism planning in the town of Squamish, British Columbia, Reed (1997)
has shown how power relations in this community altered the outcome of collaborative tourism planning.

Toward a New Tourism?

In a provocative and controversial book, Krippendorf (1987) sets out some proposals for the "humanization of travel." These are not designed to rapidly dismantle the present tourism system, but to help transform it slowly, step by step. Krippendorf believes that while some forms of new, more meaningful travel will be readily adopted by an enlightened or critical minority, the overall humanization of travel will necessarily be a gradual, long-term process. In order to advance this transformation from *hard* to *soft* tourism, he proposes the following measures:

- *Organize a better distribution of tourist flows.* Many tourism-generated problems stem from "the flight of the mass into the mass," that is, the concentration of travel and holidays into a few weeks or weekends, to a small number of places. So long as this continues, the problem of destination carrying capacity will remain. School and work holidays should be staggered, and tourist facilities should be more evenly distributed throughout destination areas.
- *Promote tourism only when it can bring the host population the desired economic benefits.* These will include incomes and jobs that are durable in nature and do not adversely affect other aspects of life. Tourism should be promoted as part of a nationally diversified economic structure, and not as the "single crop" in the economy.
- *Keep control over property in local hands.* Balanced tourism development requires that local authorities retain firm control over land, which is their most important instrument of autonomy.
- *Rely on the local work force and improve job quality.* Use of outside labor should be kept to a minimum, and locals should be trained for entry to management and other skilled jobs in the tourism industry.
- *Emphasize and cultivate what is typically local.* This may involve less luxurious facilities, the adoption of local architectural styles and materials, the use of local food, and so on. The local tourism product will thus have its own unique character and import costs will be reduced.
- *Use the advantages of the new, artificial holiday centers.* So long as tourism is characterized by periodic mass exoduses, small-scale organizational forms, though desirable, will not be able to handle these flows. Therefore, the development of large tourist ghettoes will still be needed. These, in fact, may help insulate host societies from some of the adverse effects of close contact between tourists and local residents.
- *Develop honest and responsible tourism marketing.* Most tourists are "unsure consumers" who rely heavily on tourism producers and retailers for direction. The humanization of tourism requires that these industry representatives adopt a code of business practices that reflects an acceptance of their moral responsibility to their customers and to people in the destination areas.

- *Provide better training for tourism personnel.* It should go beyond the narrow vocational training currently offered and involve a broad "humanistic education." As well as tourism ethics, personnel should be introduced to all the critical elements involved in travel, for example, economic, psychological, sociological, geographical, and ecological.
- *Inform the host population about tourists and tourism problems.* In order to minimize misunderstandings between tourists and locals, information about tourists—their society, culture, travel behavior patterns, reasons for traveling, and so on—should be offered in a planned, systematic way as part of the curriculum in hotel schools and in educational institutions in the host society.

Krippendorf also believes that the transformation from hard to soft tourism will require a number of attitude changes on the part of tourists themselves, who should be encouraged to:

- *Use holidays as a time for self-communion.* Tourists must learn how to use travel as an opportunity for self-discovery. Only if tourists "know themselves" will they come to know people in the host society. To do this, the tourist should, among other things: (a) take off the watch and forget deadlines and agendas; (b) regain the ability to be stimulated and fight against passivity; (c) learn to observe instead of just looking; (d) cherish small things instead of the biggest or most expensive ones; (e) associate with others instead of passing them by; (f) share their experiences with others; and (g) learn and explore instead of simply seeing the sights.
- *Take a critical consumer attitude as tourist.* This involves developing a skeptical approach to the seductive promises of tourism advertising, being nonexploitive in relations with hosts and, if necessary, protesting against activities which run counter to these principles.
- *Apply basic rules for considerate travel.* Among these are (a) travel with humility and a desire to learn about one's hosts; (b) listen and observe, rather than simply hear and see; (c) be aware of others' feelings and avoid giving offence; (d) acquaint oneself with local customs and practices; (e) do not expect special privileges because one is a tourist; (f) don't waste time and money on travel if one simply wants one's holiday to be a "home away from home;" and (g) don't make promises to locals that one can't keep.
- *Exercise moderation in travel.* There is often little need to travel far to find value in the touristic experience—our immediate surroundings may contain many surprising and interesting things hitherto ignored. There is no need to collect different destinations as if they were stamps—repeat visits to the same destination can enable us to develop a deeper relationship with a country and its people.

It may seem churlish to argue with Krippendorf's well-intentioned proposals, although they often have the preaching tone of the "enlightened" tourism missionary trying to convert benighted recreational or diversionary tourists to "more meaningful" touristic experiences. Some of the attitude changes required of Krippendorf's humanized tourists assume that vacations are worthless unless they are educational or otherwise constructive. This ignores the fact that large numbers of tourists want little more than a sunny escape from winter cold, rain, and snow, and that diversionary or recreational tourism can be both enjoyable and harmless. His suggestions that new "artificial" holiday centers should be considered temporary stopgaps until tourism flows are better distributed, and that small-scale organizational forms are "desirable," reflect values that we need not necessarily embrace. Many tourists (including me) actually enjoy artificial centers like Las Vegas or Orlando, are happy in the company of large numbers of others, and—if finances permit—prefer staying in large, luxurious hotels. And some of Krippendorf's proposals would seem to require an "if at all possible" phrase tagged on; for example, the warning against making tourism the "single crop" is sensible, but in smaller, poorer countries like The Gambia the other options may be extremely limited. What is really lacking in Krippendorf's program, however, are details on the "nuts and bolts"—the actual procedures and mechanisms that would be required to implement his proposals, even in the face of public apathy or resistance.

Poon (1993) has argued that the tourism system is already undergoing a major transformation; and while this will not lead to the disappearance of mass tourism, it is quickly creating what she calls *new tourism*. She predicts that this form of tourism will grow faster than mass tourism and will come to represent a large area of tourism activity. According to Poon, new tourism has six distinguishing characteristics:

1. The holiday is flexible and can be purchased at prices that are competitive with mass-produced holidays.
2. Production of travel and tourism-related services are not dominated by scale economies alone. Tailor-made services will be produced while still taking advantage of scale economies where they apply.
3. Production is increasingly driven by the requirements of consumers.
4. The holiday is marketed to individuals with different needs, incomes, time constraints and travel interests. Mass marketing is no longer the dominant paradigm.
5. The holiday is consumed on a large scale by tourists who are more experienced travelers, more educated, more destination-oriented, more independent, more flexible, and more "green."
6. Consumers look at the environment and culture of the destinations they visit as a key part of the holiday experience.

What accounts for the emergence of these characteristics? Poon suggests that there have been several key driving forces at work:

- *New Consumer Values and Behavior.* Products of changing demographics and universally accepted education, the new consumers are more flexible, spontaneous, independent, and unpredictable. As tourists they want to be in control and they are also more environmentally sensitive than their predecessors. The new tourists constitute the primary driving force in the creation of new tourism.
- *New Technology.* This makes it possible to deal with increased amounts of information on services and facilities, as well as with the increasing diversity and individualization in tourist preferences.
- *New Production Practices.* These are more flexible and innovative, making it possible to satisfy formerly unusual demands in a cost-effective manner. Various services—financial, insurance, travel, and so on—are "diagonally linked," again making their costs competitive with those of mass producers.
- *Changing Management Techniques.* These include the integration of production and marketing, mass customization and the fragmentation of brands, and greater emphasis on market research to find out what the consumers want.
- *Changing Frame Conditions.* The conditions within which tourism operates have changed in significant ways. These include increased awareness of the limits to growth; increased consumer protection; greater spread and flexibility of vacation time; and, perhaps most important of all, airline deregulation.

In order to compete successfully in the new tourism situation, destinations will have to adopt strategies that are different from those that have been used hitherto. Unlike Krippendorf's prescriptions, these strategies are not specifically designed to produce a morally superior or more humanized form of tourism. They are, rather, things that simply have to be done in order that destinations and businesses remain competitive in a rapidly changing tourism environment. The most important of these are:

- *Making environmental protection the top priority.* This means conserving the environmental and cultural assets of tourism by controlling capacity and encouraging pride in local culture. It also means using environmental conservation as an economic opportunity, as in ecotourism.
- *Making tourism a lead sector.* This means developing tourism as an industry capable of creating linkages with the rest of the economy and generating or promoting new industries, for example, in fashion, entertainment, health, or environment.
- *Strengthening marketing and distribution channels.* In particular, this means ensuring adequate air access and reorienting national tourism authorities towards product development rather than relying on promotion.

- *Building a dynamic private sector.* This means that, while multinational corporations and foreign investors may play a necessary role in tourism development, long-term sustainability of the tourism industry requires the development of indigenous entrepreneurship.

There can be little doubt that tourism has indeed been changing in many of the ways indicated by Poon. But are the results of these changes dramatic enough to warrant the use of a special, "fanfare" designation like *new tourism*? Perhaps it may be enough to regard them simply as the latest phase in the development of an industry that has been changing rapidly since at least the time of Cook. While the importance of the technological and managerial changes Poon mentions is hardly in question, her assessment of the "new tourists" may need to be treated with some caution. Are they really all that flexible, spontaneous, independent, unpredictable, in control, and environmentally sensitive? Perhaps their behavior is what we should expect of postmodern tourists, who approach tourism as a "game" that can be enjoyed as well in Orlando or Las Vegas as it can in Florence or Belize? Or are they, as cynical neo-Marxists might argue, simply tourism consumers choosing "mass customized" options that are cleverly packaged as "special," "tasteful" or "responsible" by a technologically sophisticated and powerful tourism industry?

Tourism for All?

The rapid and massive expansion of tourism globally has created problems as well as opportunities. Attempts to devise alternatives to mainstream tourism, or to find remedies for the problems associated with it, have not always achieved the desired results. We have seen that alternative forms of tourism do not always fully attain the objectives of their originators, and may actually require mass tourism to sustain them. And the successful application of community tourism principles seems to be possible mainly in very small, homogenous communities with active and interested participants.

Accustomed as we are to hearing and reading about the massive expansion of leisure travel in the second half of this century, it is easy to forget that not all people have been able to enjoy these new opportunities. Most tourists live in the developed, industrial societies, but even in these societies many poorer members have extremely limited opportunities for leisure travel. In some parts of the world attempts have been made to promote and develop so-called *social tourism*—tourism for the underprivileged. Oriented primarily to the provision of domestic tourism opportunities, social tourism is designed to foster a greater understanding and appreciation of one's own country among people who normally find it difficult or impossible to engage in leisure travel. It is conceived as tourism for the social good rather than tourism for economic gain. Economic obstacles to travel are attacked by a number of methods: holiday savings fund schemes; direct assistance in the form of holiday bonuses and allowances; reduced travel fares through cheap charter flights, credit plans, and so on; and cheap accommodations in places like workers' holiday camps, youth hostels, and trailer parks. I conclude by describing a few of these encouraging initiatives in various parts of the world.

In Argentina the government, trade unions, employers, and local authorities cooperate in creating and maintaining holiday centers for workers. These are usually comprehensive *vacation villages* with hotels, bungalows and chalets, swimming pools, restaurants, shops, parks, and sports facilities. Trade unions have been especially active in Argentina's social tourism system, buying hotels in Mar del Plata and Bariloche for use by their members. Colombia has an organization named *Caja de Compensation Familiar* (CAFAM) which offers members tourism and recreational facilities in villages located throughout the country. These villages contain various types of accommodations, swimming pools, recreation centers for children and the elderly; and they offer educational programs which deal with the natural environment, as well as the art and history of the particular areas in which they are located. In Mexico trade unions cooperate with voluntary organizations through the *Fideicomiso para el Turismo Obrero* (FIDETO), whose aim is to promote working-class access to national tourism and leisure facilities.

In Belgium workers contribute to trade unions' holiday savings schemes. At holiday times these contributions are reclaimed, plus accrued interest; and workers receive holiday wages which are double the normal amount. As part of the holiday package workers can obtain cheap rail tickets for themselves and their families, while accommodations are available at special holiday centers and camps. In Switzerland workers purchase holiday savings stamps at a discounted rate, using these to pay for vacation transportation and accommodation. The difference between the discounted and face values of the stamps is made up from the profits of the invested savings and by contributions from trade unions and employers.

In India domestic tourism is extensive and the provision of low-cost tourism facilities has been a major objective of national tourism policy. Relatively cheap internal rail and road transportation is available and modestly priced accommodations such as travelers' lodges, tourist bungalows, and small hotels have been established in several popular tourist centers.

In Canada social tourism is most highly developed in Quebec. In 1977 the province adopted a social tourism policy in collaboration with the International Bureau of Social Tourism (BITS). This policy had four main objectives: (a) broaden popular participation in tourist activities; (b) end unequal access to leisure and recreation stemming from unequal social and economic conditions among the population; (c) control the commercial exploitation of tourism resources; and (d) reverse prevailing tourism trends by promoting leisure travel for healthy living, the enhancement of creativity, discovery of the land and its culture, and increase the appreciation of nature. Implementation of the policy led to the establishment of vacation village networks and the expansion of youth hostels and outdoor recreation centers. With government assistance, a number of voluntary organizations concerned with social tourism formed the Association of Leisure and Recreation (ALR), which cooperates with local authorities in planning new social tourism developments in the province. Other organizations active in this field in Quebec are the Quebec Family Vacation Movement and the Quebec Agricultural Federation, this latter group promoting low-cost farm vacations (Moulin, 1983; Adu-Febiri, 1990b).

Tourism for all is an ideal espoused by the WTO in Article 7 of its Global Code of Ethics for Tourism (see Appendix). Clearly, it is not yet a reality, but the kinds of social tourism developments just outlined have certainly brought that reality closer.

Appendix
The World Tourism Organization Global Code of Ethics for Tourism

Article 1

Tourism's contribution to mutual understanding and respect between peoples and societies:

1. The understanding and promotion of the ethical values common to humanity, with an attitude of tolerance and respect for the diversity of religious, philosophical and moral beliefs, are both the foundation and the consequence of responsible tourism; stakeholders in tourism development and tourists themselves should observe the social and cultural traditions and practices of all peoples, including those of minorities and indigenous peoples and to recognize their worth;
2. Tourism activities should be conducted in harmony with the attributes and traditions of the host regions and countries and in respect for their laws, practices, and customs;
3. The host communities, on the one hand, and local professionals, on the other, should acquaint themselves with and respect the tourists who visit them and find out about their lifestyles, tastes, and expectations; the education and training imparted to professionals contribute to a hospitable welcome;
4. It is the task of the public authorities to provide protection for tourists and visitors and their belongings; they must pay particular attention to the safety of foreign tourists owing to the particular vulnerability they may have; they should facilitate the introduction of specific means of information, prevention, security, insurance, and assistance consistent with their needs; any attacks, assaults, kidnappings, or threats against tourists or workers in the tourism industry, as well as the willful destruction of tourism facilities or of elements of cultural or natural heritage should be severely condemned and punished in accordance with respective national laws;
5. When travelling, tourists and visitors should not commit any criminal act or any act considered criminal by the laws of the country visited and abstain from any conduct felt to be offensive or injurious by the local populations, or

Adopted by the World Tourism Organization, October 1, 1999. Reprinted with permission of the World Tourism Organization.

likely to damage the local environment; they should refrain from all trafficking in illicit drugs, arms, antiques, protected species, and products and substances that are dangerous or prohibited by national regulations;

6. Tourists and visitors have the responsibility to acquaint themselves, even before their departure, with the characteristics of the countries they are preparing to visit; they must be aware of the health and security risks inherent in any travel outside their usual environment and behave in such a way as to minimize these risks.

Article 2

Tourism as a vehicle for individual and collective fulfillment:

1. Tourism, the activity most frequently associated with rest and relaxation, sport and access to culture and nature, should be planned and practiced as a privileged means of individual and collective fulfillment; when practiced with a sufficiently open mind, it is an irreplaceable factor of self-education, mutual tolerance and for learning about the legitimate differences between peoples and cultures and their diversity;

2. Tourism activities should respect the equality of men and women; they should promote human rights and, more particularly, the individual rights of the most vulnerable groups, notably children, the elderly, the handicapped, ethnic minorities, and indigenous peoples;

3. The exploitation of human beings in any form, particularly sexual, especially when applied to children, conflicts with the fundamental aims of tourism and is the negation of tourism; as such, in accordance with international law, it should be energetically combated with the cooperation of all the States concerned and penalized without concession by the national legislation of both the countries visited and the countries of the perpetrators of these acts, even when they are carried out abroad;

4. Travel for purposes of religion, health, education, and cultural or linguistic exchanges are particularly beneficial forms of tourism, which deserve encouragement;

5. The introduction into curricula of education about the value of tourist exchanges, their economic, social, and cultural benefits, and also their risks, should be encouraged.

Article 3

Tourism, a factor of sustainable development:

1. All the stakeholders in tourism development should safeguard the natural environment with a view to achieving sound, continuous, and sustainable

economic growth geared to satisfying equitably the needs and aspirations of present and future generations;

2. All forms of tourism development that are conducive to saving rare and precious resources, in particular water and energy, as well as avoiding so far as possible waste production, should be given priority and encouraged by national, regional, and local public authorities;

3. The staggering in time and space of tourist and visitor flows, particularly those resulting from paid leave and school holidays, and a more even distribution of holidays should be sought so as to reduce the pressure of tourism activity on the environment and enhance its beneficial impact on the tourism industry and the local economy;

4. Tourism infrastructure should be designed and tourism activities programmed in such a way as to protect the natural heritage composed of ecosystems and biodiversity and to preserve endangered species of wildlife; the stakeholders in tourism development, and especially professionals, should agree to the imposition of limitations or constraints on their activities when these are exercised in particularly sensitive areas: desert, polar or high-mountain regions, coastal areas, tropical forests, or wetlands, propitious to the creation of more nature reserves or protected areas;

5. Nature tourism and ecotourism are recognized as being particularly conducive to enriching and enhancing the standing of tourism, provided they respect the natural heritage and local populations and are in keeping with the carrying capacity of the sites.

Article 4

Tourism, a user of the cultural heritage of mankind and a contributor to its enhancement:

1. Tourism resources belong to the common heritage of mankind; the communities in whose territories they are situated have particular rights and obligations to them;

2. Tourism policies and activities should be conducted with respect for the artistic, archaeological, and cultural heritage, which they should protect and pass on to future generations; particular care should be devoted to preserving and upgrading monuments, shrines, and museums as well as archaeological and historic sites which must be widely open to tourist visits; encouragement should be given to public access to privately owned cultural property and monuments, with respect for the rights of their owners;

3. Financial resources derived from visits to cultural sites and monuments should, at least in part, be used for the upkeep, safeguard, development, and embellishment of this heritage;

4. Tourism activity should be planned in such a way as to allow traditional cultural products, crafts, and folklore to survive and flourish, rather than causing them to degenerate and become standardized.

Article 5

Tourism, a beneficial activity for host countries and communities:

1. Local populations should be associated with tourism activities and share equitably in the economic, social, and cultural benefits they generate, and particularly in the creation of direct and indirect jobs resulting from them;
2. Tourism policies should be applied in such a way as to help to raise the standard of living of the populations of the regions visited and meet their needs; the planning and architectural approach to and operation of tourism resorts and accommodation should aim to integrate them, to the extent possible, in the local economic and social fabric; where skills are equal, priority should be given to local manpower;
3. Special attention should be paid to the specific problems of coastal areas and island territories and to vulnerable rural or mountain regions, for which tourism often represents a rare opportunity for development in the face of the decline of traditional economic activities;
4. Tourism professionals, particularly investors, governed by the regulations laid down by the public authorities, should carry out studies of the impact of their development projects on the environment and natural surroundings; they should also deliver, with the greatest transparency and objectivity, information on their future programs and their foreseeable repercussions and foster dialogue on their contents with the populations concerned.

Article 6

Obligations of stakeholders in tourism development:

1. Tourism professionals have an obligation to provide tourists with objective and honest information on their places of destination and on the conditions of travel, hospitality, and stays; they should ensure that the contractual clauses proposed to their customers are readily understandable as to the nature, price, and quality of the services they commit themselves to providing and the financial compensation payable by them in the event of a unilateral breach of contract on their part;
2. Tourism professionals, insofar as it depends on them, should show concern, in cooperation with the public authorities, for the security and safety, accident prevention, health protection, and food safety of those who seek their services; likewise, they should ensure the existence of suitable systems of

insurance and assistance; they should accept the reporting obligations prescribed by national regulations and pay fair compensation in the event of failure to observe their contractual obligations;

3. Tourism professionals, so far as this depends on them, should contribute to the cultural and spiritual fulfillment of tourists and allow them, during their travels, to practice their religions;

4. The public authorities of the generating States and the host countries, in cooperation with the professionals concerned and their associations, should ensure that the necessary mechanisms are in place for the repatriation of tourists in the event of the bankruptcy of the enterprise that organized their travel;

5. Governments have the right—and the duty—especially in a crisis, to inform their nationals of the difficult circumstances, or even the dangers they may encounter on their travels abroad; it is their responsibility however to issue such information without prejudicing in an unjustified or exaggerated manner the tourism industry of the host countries and the interests of their own operators; the contents of travel advisories should therefore be discussed beforehand with the authorities of the host countries and the professionals concerned; recommendations formulated should be strictly proportionate to the gravity of the situations encountered and confined to the geographical areas where the insecurity has arisen; such advisories should be qualified or cancelled as soon as a return to normality permits;

6. The press, and particularly the specialized travel press and the other media, including modern means of electronic communication, should issue honest and balanced information on events and situations that could influence the flow of tourists; they should also provide accurate and reliable information to the consumers of tourism services; the new communication and electronic commerce technologies should also be developed and used for this purpose; as is the case for the media, they should not in any way promote sex tourism.

Article 7

Right to tourism:

1. The prospect of direct and personal access to the discovery and enjoyment of the planet's resources constitutes a right equally open to all the world's inhabitants; the increasingly extensive participation in national and international tourism should be regarded as one of the best possible expressions of the sustained growth of free time, and obstacles should not be placed in its way;

2. The universal right to tourism must be regarded as a corollary of the right to rest and leisure, including reasonable limitation of working hours and periodic holidays with pay, guaranteed by Article 24 of the Universal Declaration of Human Rights and Article 7.d of the International Covenant on Economic, Social, and Cultural Rights;

3. Social tourism, and in particular associative tourism, which facilitates widespread access to leisure, travel, and holidays, should be developed with the support of the public authorities;
4. Family, youth, student, and senior tourism and tourism for people with disabilities, should be encouraged and facilitated.

Article 8

Liberty of tourist movements:

1. Tourists and visitors should benefit, in compliance with international law and national legislation, from the liberty to move within their countries and from one State to another, in accordance with Article 13 of the Universal Declaration of Human Rights; they should have access to places of transit and stay and to tourism and cultural sites without being subject to excessive formalities or discrimination;
2. Tourists and visitors should have access to all available forms of communication, internal or external; they should benefit from prompt and easy access to local administrative, legal, and health services; they should be free to contact the consular representatives of their countries of origin in compliance with the diplomatic conventions in force;
3. Tourists and visitors should benefit from the same rights as the citizens of the country visited concerning the confidentiality of the personal data and information concerning them, especially when these are stored electronically;
4. Administrative procedures relating to border crossings whether they fall within the competence of States or result from international agreements, such as visas or health and customs formalities, should be adapted so far as possible, so as to facilitate to the maximum freedom of travel and widespread access to international tourism; agreements between groups of countries to harmonize and simplify these procedures should be encouraged; specific taxes and levies penalizing the tourism industry and undermining its competitiveness should be gradually phased out or corrected;
5. So far as the economic situation of the countries from which they come permits, travelers should have access to allowances of convertible currencies needed for their travels.

Article 9

Rights of the workers and entrepreneurs in the tourism industry:

1. The fundamental rights of salaried and self-employed workers in the tourism industry and related activities, should be guaranteed under the supervision of the national and local administrations, both of their States of origin and of

the host countries with particular care, given the specific constraints linked in particular to the seasonality of their activity, the global dimension of their industry and the flexibility often required of them by the nature of their work;

2. Salaried and self-employed workers in the tourism industry and related activities have the right and the duty to acquire appropriate initial and continuous training; they should be given adequate social protection; job insecurity should be limited so far as possible; and a specific status, with particular regard to their social welfare, should be offered to seasonal workers in the sector;

3. Any natural or legal person, provided he, she, or it has the necessary abilities and skills, should be entitled to develop a professional activity in the field of tourism under existing national laws; entrepreneurs and investors—especially in the area of small- and medium-sized enterprises—should be entitled to free access to the tourism sector with a minimum of legal or administrative restrictions;

4. Exchanges of experience offered to executives and workers, whether salaried or not, from different countries, contributes to foster the development of the world tourism industry; these movements should be facilitated so far as possible in compliance with the applicable national laws and international conventions;

5. As an irreplaceable factor of solidarity in the development and dynamic growth of international exchanges, multinational enterprises of the tourism industry should not exploit the dominant positions they sometimes occupy; they should avoid becoming the vehicles of cultural and social models artificially imposed on the host communities; in exchange for their freedom to invest and trade which should be fully recognized, they should involve themselves in local development, avoiding, by the excessive repatriation of their profits or their induced imports, a reduction of their contribution to the economies in which they are established;

6. Partnership and the establishment of balanced relations between enterprises of generating and receiving countries contribute to the sustainable development of tourism and an equitable distribution of the benefits of its growth.

Bibliography

Adler, J. (1985). Youth on the road: Reflections on the history of tramping. *Annals of Tourism Research, 12,* 335–354.

Adu-Febiri, F. (1988). *Leisure travel among affluent urban Ghanaians.* Master's thesis. Burnaby, BC: Sociology and Anthropology Department, Simon Fraser University.

Adu-Febiri, F. (1990a). Developing a viable tourist industry in Ghana. *Tourism Recreation Research, 19,* 5–11.

Adu-Febiri, F. (1990b). Prospects for domestic tourism development in Ghana. In R. W. Wyllie (Ed.), *Ghana tourism: Prospects and possibilities.* Accra, Ghana: Akan-Torede.

Akama, J. (1996). Western environmental values and nature-based tourism in Kenya. *Tourism Management, 17,* 567–574.

Amoakohene, O. (1997). *Welcome stranger: Tourism development among the Shuswap people of the south-central interior of British Columbia.* Master's thesis. Burnaby, BC: Sociology and Anthropology Department, Simon Fraser University.

Archer, B. H. (1982). The value of multipliers and their policy implications. *Tourism Management, 3,* 236–241.

Baez, A. (1996). Learning from experience in the Monteverde Cloud Forest, Costa Rica. In M. F. Price (Ed.), *People and tourism in fragile communities.* Chichester, UK: John Wiley and Sons.

Banks, J. D. (Ed.). (1976). *Changing identities in modern Southeast Asia.* The Hague, Netherlands: Mouton.

Barke, M. (1999). Tourism and culture in Spain: A case of minimal conflict? In M. Robinson and P. Boniface (Eds.), *Tourism and cultural conflicts.* Wallingford, UK: CAB International.

Blednick, P. (1988). *Another day in paradise? The real Club Med story.* Toronto, ON: MacMillan.

Bishop, R., and Robinson, L. S. (1998). *Night market: Sexual cultures and the Thai economic miracle.* London, UK: Routledge.

Blundell, V. (1993). Aboriginal empowerment and the souvenir trade in Canada. *Annals of Tourism Research, 20,* 64–87.

Boissevain, J. (1996). Ritual, tourism and cultural commoditization in Malta: Culture by the pound? In T. Selwyn (Ed.), *The tourist image: Myths and myth making in tourism.* Chichester, UK: John Wiley and Sons.

Boorstin, D. (1961). *The image: A guide to pseudo events in America.* New York, NY: Atheneum.

Bouquet, M., and Winter, M. (Eds.). (1987). *Who from their labours rest.* Aldershot, UK: Avebury.

Bowman, G. (1992). The politics of tour guiding: Israeli and Palestinian guides in Israel and the occupied territories. In D. Harrison (Ed.), *Tourism and the less-developed countries.* London, UK: Bellhaven.

Brendon, P. (1991). *Thomas Cook. 150 years of popular tourism.* London, UK: Secker and Warburg.

Briguglio, L., Archer, B., Jafari, J., and Wall, G. (Eds.). (1996). *Sustainable tourism in islands and small states: Issues and policies.* London, UK: Pinter.

Briguglio, L., Butler, R., Harrison, D., and Filho, W. L. (Eds.). (1996). *Sustainable tourism in islands and small states: Case studies.* London, UK: Pinter.

British Tourism Authority (BTA). (1982). *Employment in tourism.* London, UK: Author.

Britton, S. G. (1977). Making tourism more supportive of small state development: The case of St. Vincent. *Annals of Tourism Research, 6,* 268–278.

Brodsky-Porges, E. (1981). The grand tour: Travel as an educational device, 1600–1800. *Annals of Tourism Research, 8,* 171–186.

Bryden, J. M. (1973). *Tourism and development: A case study of the Commonwealth Caribbean.* Cambridge, UK: Cambridge University Press.

Burkart, A. J., and Medlik, S. (1974). *Tourism: Past, present and future.* London, UK: Heinemann.

Butler, R. W. (1980). The concept of a tourist area cycle of evolution. *Canadian Geographer, 24,* 179–201.

Butler, R. W. (1992). Alternative tourism: The thin edge of the wedge? In V. L. Smith and W. R. Eadington (Eds.), *Tourism alternatives.* Philadelphia, PA: University of Pennsylvania Press.

Butler, R. W., and Hinch, T. (Eds.). (1996). *Tourism and indigenous peoples.* London, UK: International Thompson Business Press.

Bystrzanowski, J. (Ed.). (1989). *Tourism as a factor of change: A sociological study.* Vienna, Austria: Center of Research and Documentation in Social Sciences.

Campbell, L. M. (1999). Ecotourism in rural developing communities. *Annals of Tourism Research, 26,* 534–553.

Campbell, T. L. (1990). The Gambian experience. In R. W. Wyllie (Ed.), *Ghana tourism: Prospects and possibilities.* Accra, Ghana: Akan-Torede.

Cater, E. (1992). Profits from paradise. *Geographical Magazine, 64,* 17–18.

Cater, E., and Lowman, G. (Eds.). (1994). *Ecotourism: A sustainable option?* Chichester, UK: John Wiley and Sons.

Chant, S. (1992). Tourism in Latin America: Perspectives from Mexico and Costa Rica. In D. Harrison (Ed.), *Tourism and the less-developed countries.* London, UK: Bellhaven.

Coccossis, H., and Parpairis, A. (1995). Assessing the interaction between heritage, environment and tourism: Mykonos. In H. Coccossis and P. Nukamp (Eds.), *Sustainable tourism development*. Aldershot, UK: Avebury.

Cohen, E. (1972). Towards a sociology of international tourism, *Social Research, 39*, 164–182.

Cohen, E. (1979). A phenomenology of tourist experiences. *Sociology, 13*, 179–201.

Cohen, E. (1982). Thai girls and *farang* men: The edge of ambiguity. *Annals of Tourism Research, 9*, 403–428.

Cohen, E. (1984). The sociology of tourism: Approaches, issues and findings. *Annual Review of Sociology, 10*, 373–390.

Cohen, E. (1986). Lovelorn *farangs:* The correspondence between foreign men and Thai girls. *Anthropological Quarterly, 59*, 115–127.

Cohen, E. (1988a). Tourism and AIDS in Thailand. *Annals of Tourism Research, 15*, 467–486.

Cohen, E. (1988b). Authenticity and commoditization in tourism. *Annals of Tourism Research, 15*, 371–386.

Cohen, E. (1989). "Primitive and remote": Hill tribe trekking in Thailand. *Annals of Tourism Research, 16*, 30–61.

Craig-Smith, S., and French, C. (1994). *Learning to live with tourism*. Melbourne, Australia: Longman.

Crang, P. (1997). Performing the tourist product. In C. Rojek and J. Urry (Eds.), *Touring cultures: Transformations of travel and theory*. London, UK: Routledge.

Crick, M. (1995). The anthropologist as tourist: An identity in question. In M. Lanfant, J. B. Allcock, and E. M. Bruner (Eds.), *International tourism: Identity and change*. London, UK: Sage.

Cross, G. (1990). *A social history of leisure since 1600*. State College, PA: Venture Publishing, Inc.

Dahles, H., and Bras, K. (1999). Entrepreneurs in romance: Tourism in Indonesia. *Annals of Tourism Research, 26*, 267–293.

D'Amore, L. J. (1983). Guidelines to planning in harmony with host communities. In P. E. Murphy (Ed.), *Tourism in Canada: Selected issues and options*. Victoria, BC: University of Victoria.

D'Amore, L. J. (1988). Tourism—The world's peace industry. *Journal of Travel Research, 27*(1), 35–40.

Dann, G. M. S. (1998). "There's no business like old business": Tourism, the nostalgia industry of the future. In W. F. Theobald (Ed.), *Global tourism* (2nd ed.). Boston, MA: Butterworth-Heinemann.

Dann, G. M. S., and Cohen, E. (1991). Sociology and tourism. *Annals of Tourism Research, 18*, 155–169.

Davidson, T. L. (1998). What are travel and tourism: Are they really an industry? In W. F. Theobald (Ed.), *Global tourism* (2nd ed.). Boston, MA: Butterworth-Heinemann.

Deardon, P. (1983). Tourism and the resource base. In P. E. Murphy (Ed.), *Tourism in Canada: Selected issues and options*. Victoria, BC: University of Victoria.

Deardon, P., and Harron, S. (1994). Alternative tourism and adaptive change. *Annals of Tourism Research, 21,* 81–102.

de Kadt, E. (Ed.). (1979). *Tourism—Passport to development? Perspectives on the social and cultural effects of tourism in developing countries.* New York, NY: Oxford University Press.

Dieke, P. (1993). Tourism and development policy in the Gambia. *Annals of Tourism Research, 21,* 277–289.

Doxey, G. V. (1976). A causation theory of visitor-resident irritants. In *The impact of tourism: Proceedings of the 6th annual conference of the Travel Research Association.* San Diego, CA: Travel Research Association.

Eadington, W. R., and Redman, M. (1991). Economics and tourism. *Annals of Tourism Research, 11,* 41–56.

The Economist. (January 10, 1998). Survey of travel and tourism.

Edgell, D. K. (1990). *International tourism policy.* New York, NY: Van Nostrand Reinhold.

English, E. P. (1986). *The great escape? An examination of north-south tourism.* Ottawa, ON: The North-South Institute.

Esh, T., and Rosenblum, I. (1975). *Tourism in the Gambia: Trick or treat?* Upsalla, Sweden: The Scandinavian Institute of African Studies.

Esman, M. R. (1984). Tourism as ethnic preservation: The Cajuns of Louisiana. *Annals of Tourism Research, 11,* 452–457.

Farrell, B. H. (1982). *Hawaii, the legend that sells.* Honolulu, HI: University Press of Hawaii.

Farver, J. M. (1984). Tourism and employment in the Gambia. *Annals of Tourism Research, 11,* 249–265.

Feifer, M. (1985). *Going places.* London, UK: MacMillan.

Foster, G. M. (1986). South seas cruise: A case study of a short-lived society. *Annals of Tourism Research, 13,* 215–238.

Gee, C. Y., Makens, J. C., and Choy, D. L. G. (1989). *Travel industry* (2nd ed.). New York, NY: Van Nostrand Reinhold.

Gorman, B. (1979). Seven days, five countries: The making of a group. *Urban Life, 7,* 469–491.

Graburn, N. H. H. (1983). Tourism and prostitution. *Annals of Tourism Research, 10,* 437–442.

Graburn, N. H. H. (1984). The evolution of tourist arts. *Annals of Tourism Research, 11,* 393–419.

Greenwood, D. (1989). Culture by the pound: Anthropological perspectives on tourism as cultural commoditization. In V. L. Smith (Ed.), *Hosts and guests: The anthropology of tourism* (2nd ed.). Philadelphia, PA: University of Pennsylvania Press.

Grekin, J., and Milne, S. (1996). Towards sustainable tourism development: The case of Pond Inlet, N. W. T. In R. W. Butler and T. Hinch (Eds.), *Tourism and indigenous peoples*. London, UK: International Thompson Business Press.

Gurung, C. P., and De Coursey, M. (1994). The Annapurna conservation area project: A pioneering example of sustainable tourism? In E. Cater and G. Lowman (Eds.), *Ecotourism: A sustainable option?* Chichester, UK: John Wiley and Sons.

Hall, C. M. (1992). Sex tourism in Southeast Asia. In D. Harrison (Ed.), *Tourism and the less-developed countries*. London, UK: Bellhaven.

Hall, C. M. (Ed.). (1994). *Tourism and politics: Policy, power and place*. New York, NY: John Wiley and Sons.

Hall, C. M. (1994). Ecotourism in Australia, New Zealand and the South Pacific: Appropriate tourism or a new form of ecological imperialism? In E. Cater and G. Lowman (Eds.), *Ecotourism: A sustainable option?* Chichester, UK: John Wiley and Sons.

Hall, D. R. (1992). Tourism development in Cuba. In D. Harrison (Ed.), *Tourism and the less-developed countries*. London, UK: Bellhaven.

Harrell-Bond, B. E. (1978). *A window on the outside world: Tourism and development in the Gambia* (American Universities Field Staff Reports No. 19). Hanover, NH: American Universities Field Staff.

Harrison, D. (Ed.). (1992a). *Tourism and the less-developed countries*. London, UK: Bellhaven.

Harrison, D. (1992b). Tradition, modernity and tourism in Swaziland. In D. Harrison (Ed.), *Tourism and the less-developed countries*. London, UK: Bellhaven.

Harrison, D. (1996). Sustainability and tourism: Reflections from a muddy pool. In L. Briguglio, B. Archer, J. Jafari, and G. Wall (Eds.), *Sustainable tourism in islands and small states: Issues and policies*. London, UK: Pinter.

Hewison, R. (1987). *The heritage industry: Britain in a climate of decline*. London, UK: Methuen.

Hewison, R. (1996). Cultural policy and the heritage business. *The European Journal of Cultural Policy, 3*, 1–13.

Holden, P. (1984). *Alternative tourism: Report on the workshop on alternative tourism with a focus on Asia*. Bangkok, Thailand: Ecumenical Coalition on Third World Tourism.

Holloway, J. C. (1981). The guided tour: A sociological approach. *Annals of Tourism Research, 8*, 377–402.

Holstein, W. J. (1999). Rage on the runway. *US News Online*, March 15.

International Union of Official Travel Organizations. (1975). *The impact of international tourism on the economic development of the developing countries*. Geneva, Switzerland: Author.

Jafari, J. (1986). On domestic tourism. *Annals of Tourism Research, 24*, 491–496.

Jafari, J. (1989). An English language literature review. In J. Bystrzanowski (Ed.), *Tourism as a factor of change: A sociological study*. Vienna, Austria: Center of Research and Documentation in Social Sciences.

Johnson, P., and Thomas, P. (Eds.). (1992). *Choice and demand in tourism*. London, UK: Mansell.

Joppe, M. (1996). Sustainable community tourism revisited. *Tourism Management, 17,* 475–479.

Jules-Rosette, B. (1984). *The messages of tourist art: An African semiotic system in comparative perspective*. New York, NY: Plenum.

Karch, C. A., and Dann, G. H. S. (1981). Close encounters of the third world. *Human Relations, 34,* 249–268.

Kelly, J. R., and Godbey, G. (1992). *Sociology of leisure*. State College, PA: Venture Publishing, Inc.

Kinnaird, V., and Hall, D. (Eds.). (1994). *Tourism: A gender analysis*. Chichester, UK: John Wiley and Sons.

Kruhse-MountBurton, S. (1995). Sex tourism and traditional Australian male identity. In M. Lanfant, J. B. Allcock, and E. M. Bruner (Eds.), *International tourism: Identity and change*. London, UK: Sage.

Krippendorf, J. (1987). *The holidaymakers*. London, UK: Heinemann.

Lanfant, M. (1995). Internationalization and the challenge to identity. In M. Lanfant, J. B. Allcock, and E. M. Bruner (Eds.), *International tourism: Identity and change*. London, UK: Sage.

Lanfant, M., Allcock, J. B., and Bruner, E. M. (Eds.). (1995). *International tourism: Identity and change*. London, UK: Sage.

Lanfant, M., and Graburn, N. H. H. (1992). International tourism reconsidered: The principle of the alternative. In V. L. Smith and W. R. Eadington (Eds.), *Tourism alternatives*. Philadelphia, PA: University of Pennsylvania Press.

Laws, E., Faulkner, B., and Moscardo, G. (Eds.). (1998). *Embracing and managing change in tourism*. London, UK: Routledge.

Leheny, D. (1995). A political economy of Asian sex tourism. *Annals of Tourism Research, 22,* 367–384.

Leiper, N. (1990). Partial industrialization of tourist systems. *Annals of Tourism Research, 17,* 600–605.

Leiper, N. (1993). Industrial entropy in tourism systems. *Annals of Tourism Research, 20,* 221–226.

Lickorish, L. J. (1991). European tourism since 1972. In S. Medlik (Ed.), *Managing tourism*. Oxford, UK: Butterworth-Heinemann.

Lickorish, L. J., and Jenkins, C. L. (1997). *An introduction to tourism*. Oxford, UK: Butterworth-Heinemann.

Lindberg, K., Enriquez, J., and Sproule, K. (1996). Ecotourism questioned: Case studies from Belize. *Annals of Tourism Research, 23,* 543–562.

Liu, J. C., and Var, T. (1986). Resident attitudes toward tourism impacts in Hawaii. *Annals of Tourism Research, 13,* 280–287.

Loukisias, P. J. (1978). Tourism and environment in conflict: The case of the Greek island of Myconos. *Studies in Third World Societies, 6,* 105–132.

Lowyck, E., Van Langenhove, L., and Bollaert, L. (1992). Typologies of tourist roles. In P. Johnson and B. Thomas (Eds.), *Choice and demand in tourism.* London, UK: Mansell.

MacCannell, D. (1976). *The tourist: A new theory of the leisure class.* New York, NY: Schocken.

MacDonald, M. (1987). Chasing culture and tradition in Brittany. In M. Bouquet and M. Winter (Eds.), *Who from their labours rest.* Aldershot, UK: Avebury.

Mansfield, Y., and Kliot, N. (1996). The tourism industry in the partitioned island of Cyprus. In A. Pizam and Y. Mansfield (Eds.), *Tourism, crime and international security issues.* Chichester, UK: John Wiley and Sons.

Mathieson, A., and Wall, G. (1982). *Tourism: Economic, physical and social impacts.* London, UK: Longman.

Matthews, H. G., and Richter, L. K. (1991). Political science and tourism. *Annals of Tourism Research, 18,* 120–135.

McIntosh, R. W., and Gouldner, C. R. (1990). *Tourism: Principles, practices, philosophies.* New York, NY: John Wiley and Sons.

McKean, P. F. (1976). Tourism, culture change and culture conservation in Bali. In J. D. Banks (Ed.), *Changing identities in modern Southeast Asia.* The Hague, Netherlands: Mouton.

McKean, P. F. (1989). Towards a theoretical analysis of tourism: Economic dualism and cultural involution in Bali. In V. L. Smith (Ed.), *Hosts and guests: The anthropology of tourism* (2nd ed.). Philadelphia, PA: University of Pennsylvania Press.

Medlik, S. (Ed.). (1991). *Managing tourism.* Oxford, UK: Butterworth-Heinemann.

Meisch, L. A. (1995). Gringas and Otavelenos: Changing tourist relations. *Annals of Tourism Research, 22,* 441–462.

Mings, R. C. (1988). Assessing the contribution of tourism to international understanding. *Journal of Travel Research, 27,* 33–38.

Mitchell, L. S., and Murphy, P. E. (1991). Geography and tourism. *Annals of Tourism Research, 18,* 57–70.

Morgan, N., and Pritchard, A. (Eds.). (1998). *Tourism promotion and power: Creating images, creating identities.* Chichester, UK: John Wiley and Sons.

Moulin, C. L. (1983). Social tourism: Development and prospects. In P. E. Murphy (Ed.), *Tourism in Canada: Selected issues and options.* Victoria, BC: University of Victoria.

Murphy, P. E. (Ed.). (1983). *Tourism in Canada: Selected issues and options.* Victoria, BC: University of Victoria.

Nash, D. (1981). Tourism as an anthropological subject. *Current Anthropology, 22,* 461–481.

Nash, D. (1997). *The anthropology of tourism.* Tarrytown, NY: Elsevier.

Nash, D., and Smith, V. L. (1991). Anthropology and tourism. *Annals of Tourism Research, 18,* 12–25.

Oppermann, M. (1999). Sex tourism. *Annals of Tourism Research, 26,* 251–256.

Pearce, D. (1989). *Tourist development* (2nd ed.). Harlow, UK: Longman.

Perry, B. (1992a). Runway backers: Lawsuit a delay tactic. *The Maui News,* October 9.

Perry, B. (1992b). Longer runway gets support of all segments. *The Maui News,* October 11.

Perry, B. (2000). Latest generation Boeing aircraft makes maiden Maui flight. *The Maui News,* February 17.

Picard, M. (1995). Cultural heritage and tourist capital: Cultural tourism in Bali. In M. Lanfant, J. B. Allcock, and E. M. Bruner (Eds.), *International tourism: Identity and change.* London, UK: Sage.

Pizam, A. (1996). Does tourism promote peace and understanding between unfriendly nations? In A. Pizam and Y. Mansfield (Eds.), *Tourism, crime and international security issues.* Chichester, UK: John Wiley and Sons.

Pizam, A., and Mansfield, Y. (Eds.). (1996). *Tourism, crime and international security issues.* Chichester, UK: John Wiley and Sons.

Poon, A. (1993). *Tourism, technology and competitive strategies.* Wallingford, UK: CAB International.

Price, M. F. (Ed.). (1996). *People and tourism in fragile communities.* Chichester, UK: John Wiley and Sons.

Pruitt, D., and LaFont, S. (1995). For love and money: Romance tourism in Jamaica. *Annals of Tourism Research, 22,* 422–440.

Reed, M. (1997). Power relations and community-based tourism planning. *Annals of Tourism Research, 24,* 566–591.

Reisinger, Y., and Turner, L. (1997). Cross-cultural differences in tourism: Indonesian tourists in Australia. *Tourism Management 18,* 139–149.

Riley, P. (1988). Road culture of international long-term budget travelers. *Annals of Tourism Research, 15,* 313–328.

Ritzer, G., and Liska, A. (1997). McDisneyization and post-tourism. In C. Rojek and J. Urry (Eds.), *Touring cultures: Transformations of travel and theory.* London, UK: Routledge.

Robinson, M., and Boniface, P. (Eds.). (1999). *Tourism and cultural conflicts.* Wallingford, UK: CAB International.

Rojek, C. (1993). *Ways of escape: Modern transformations in leisure and travel.* Basingstoke, UK: MacMillan.

Rojek, C., and Urry, J. (Eds.). (1997). *Touring cultures: Transformations of travel and theory.* London, UK: Routledge.

Ryan, C., and Montgomery, D. (1994). The attitudes of Bakewell residents to tourism and issues in community-responsive tourism. *Tourism Management, 15,* 358–369.

Saglio, C. (1979). Tourism for discovery: A project in lower Casamance, Senegal. In E. de Kadt (Ed.), *Tourism—Passport to development? Perspectives on the social and cultural effects of tourism in developing countries.* New York, NY: Oxford University Press.

Saglio, C. (1985). Senegal: Tourisme integre rural en Basse Casamance. *Espaces, 76,* 29–32.

Sanghera, J. (1986). *Creating international brothels: Sex tourism and social change in some Asian countries.* Berkeley, CA: University of California.

Schuchat, M. (1983). Comforts of group tours. *Annals of Tourism Research, 10,* 465–477.

Seaton, A. V., and Palmer, C. (1997). Understanding VFR tourism behavior: The first five years of the United Kingdom tourism survey. *Tourism Management, 18,* 345–355.

Selwyn, T. (Ed.). (1996). *The tourist image: Myths and myth making in tourism.* Chichester, UK: John Wiley and Sons.

Sharpley, R. (1994). *Tourism, tourists and society.* Kings Ripton, UK: Elm Publications.

Sheldon, P. J. (1997). *Tourism information technology.* Wallingford, UK: CAB International.

Shivji, I. (1973). *Tourism and socialist development.* Dar es Salaam, Tanzania: Tanzania Publishing House.

Sindiga, I. (1995). Wildlife-based tourism in Kenya: Land-use conflicts and government compensation policies over protected areas. *Journal of Tourism Studies, 6,* 45–55.

Sindiga, I. (1996). International tourism in Kenya and the marginalization of the Waswahili. *Tourism Management, 17,* 425–432.

Smith, G., and Pizam, A. (1998). NAFTA and tourism development policy in North America. In E. Laws, B. Faulkner, and G. Moscardo (Eds.), *Embracing and managing change in tourism.* London, UK: Routledge.

Smith, S. L. J. (1988). Defining tourism: A supply-side perspective. *Annals of Tourism Research, 15,* 179–190.

Smith, V. L. (Ed.). (1989). *Hosts and guests: The anthropology of tourism* (2nd ed.). Philadelphia, PA: University of Pennsylvania Press.

Smith, V. L. (1992). Boracay, Phillipines: A case study in alternative tourism. In V. L. Smith and W. R. Eadington (Eds.), *Tourism alternatives.* Philadelphia, PA: University of Pennsylvania Press.

Smith, V. L., and Eadington, W. R. (Eds.). (1992). *Tourism alternatives.* Philadelphia, PA: University of Pennsylvania Press.

Spalding, S. (1991). Lanai's plantation past fades with opening of hotel. *The Maui News,* April 14.

Stott, M. (1996). Tourism development and the need for community action in Mykonos, Greece. In L. Briguglio, R. Butler, D. Harrison, and W. L. Filho (Eds.), *Sustainable tourism in islands and small states: Case studies.* London, UK: Pinter.

Swarbrooke, J., and Horner, S. (1999). *Consumer behaviour in tourism*. Oxford, UK: Butterworth-Heinemann.

Taylor, G. (1995). The community approach: Does it work? *Tourism Management, 16,* 487–489.

Teye, V. B. (1988). Coup d'etat and African tourism: A case study of Ghana. *Annals of Tourism Research, 15,* 329–356.

Theobald, W. F. (Ed.). (1998). *Global tourism* (2nd ed.). Boston, MA: Butterworth-Heinemann.

Theroux, P. (1979). *The old Patagonian express*. Boston, MA: Houghton Mifflin.

Thompson, C., O'Hare, G., and Evans, K. (1995). Tourism in the Gambia: Problems and proposals. *Tourism Management, 16,* 571–581.

Townley, J. (1985). The grand tour: A key phase in the history of tourism. *Annals of Tourism Research, 12,* 297–333.

Tribe, J. (1997). The indiscipline of tourism. *Annals of Tourism Research, 24,* 638–657.

Trousdale, W. J. (1999). Governance in context: Boracay island, Philippines. *Annals of Tourism Research, 26,* 840–867.

Truong, T. D. (1983). The dynamics of sex tourism: The case of Southeast Asia. *Development and Change, 14,* 533–553.

Turner, L., and Ash, J. (1975). *The golden hordes: International tourism and the pleasure periphery*. London, UK: Constable.

Turner, V. (1973). The center out there: The pilgrim's goal. *History of Religion, 12,* 191–230.

UNESCO. (1976). The effects of tourism on sociocultural values. *Annals of Tourism Research, 4,* 74–105.

Urry, J. (1990). *The tourist gaze: Leisure and travel in contemporary societies*. New York, NY: Sage.

Var, T., and Ap, J. (1998). Tourism and world peace. In W. F. Theobald (Ed.), *Global tourism* (2nd ed.). Boston, MA: Butterworth-Heinemann.

Wagner, U. (1981). Tourism in the Gambia: Development or dependency? *Ethnos, 46,* 190–206.

Wagner, U., and Yamba, B. (1986). Going north and getting attached: The case of the Gambians. *Ethnos, 51,* 199–222.

Wall, G. (1996). Terrorism and tourism: An overview and an Irish example. In A. Pizam and Y. Mansfield (Eds.), *Tourism, crime and international security issues*. Chichester, UK: John Wiley and Sons.

Weaver, D. B. (1998). *Ecotourism in the less developed world*. Wallingford, UK: CAB International.

Weber, M. (1947). *The theory of economic and social organization* (edited by T. Parsons). New York, NY: Oxford University Press.

Wood, R. E. (1984). Ethnic tourism, the state, and cultural change in Southeast Asia. *Annals of Tourism Research, 11,* 353–374.

World Tourism Organization. (1983). *Domestic and international tourism's contribution to state revenue.* Madrid, Spain: Author.

Witt, S. F. (1998). Opening of the former communist countries of Europe to inbound tourism. In W. F. Theobald (Ed.), *Global tourism* (2nd ed.). Boston, MA: Butterworth-Heinemann.

Wyllie, R. W. (1968). Ritual and social change: A Ghanaian example. *American Anthropologist, 70,* 21–33.

Wyllie, R. W. (Ed.). (1990). *Ghana tourism: Prospects and possibilities.* Accra, Ghana: Akan-Torede.

Wyllie, R. W. (1993). Domestic tourism revisited. *Annals of Tourism Research, 20,* 216–218.

Wyllie, R. W. (1994a). Gods, locals and strangers: The Effutu Aboakyer as visitor attraction. *Cultural Anthropology, 35,* 78–81.

Wyllie, R. W. (1994b). The future role of domestic tourism in Ghana. *Journal of Developing Societies, 10,* 243–252.

Wyllie, R. W. (1998a). Hana revisited: Development and controversy in a Hawaiian tourism community. *Tourism Management, 19,* 171–178.

Wyllie, R. W. (1998b). Not in our backyard: Opposition to development in a Hawaiian tourism community. *Tourism Recreation Research, 23,* 55–64.

Index

Index of Places

Other Books From Venture Publishing, Inc.

❋   ✦   ✳   ╬   ❋

The A•B•Cs of Behavior Change: Skills for Working With Behavior Problems in Nursing Homes
    by Margaret D. Cohn, Michael A. Smyer, and Ann L. Horgas

Activity Experiences and Programming Within Long-Term Care
    by Ted Tedrick and Elaine R. Green

The Activity Gourmet
    by Peggy Powers

Advanced Concepts for Geriatric Nursing Assistants
    by Carolyn A. McDonald

Adventure Programming
    edited by John C. Miles and Simon Priest

Aerobics of the Mind: Keeping the Mind Active in Aging—A New Perspective on Programming for Older Adults
    by Marge Engelman

Assessment: The Cornerstone of Activity Programs
    by Ruth Perschbacher

Behavior Modification in Therapeutic Recreation: An Introductory Manual
    by John Datillo and William D. Murphy

Benefits of Leisure
    edited by B. L. Driver, Perry J. Brown, and George L. Peterson

Benefits of Recreation Research Update
    by Judy M. Sefton and W. Kerry Mummery

Beyond Bingo: Innovative Programs for the New Senior
    by Sal Arrigo, Jr., Ann Lewis, and Hank Mattimore

Beyond Bingo 2: More Innovative Programs for the New Senior
    by Sal Arrigo, Jr.

Both Gains and Gaps: Feminist Perspectives on Women's Leisure
    by Karla Henderson, M. Deborah Bialeschki, Susan M. Shaw, and Valeria J. Freysinger

Dimensions of Choice: A Qualitative Approach to Recreation, Parks, and Leisure Research
by Karla A. Henderson

Effective Management in Therapeutic Recreation Service
by Gerald S. O'Morrow and Marcia Jean Carter

Evaluating Leisure Services: Making Enlightened Decisions
by Karla A. Henderson with M. Deborah Bialeschki

Everything From A to Y: The Zest Is up to You! Older Adult Activities for Every Day of the Year
by Nancy R. Cheshire and Martha L. Kenney

The Evolution of Leisure: Historical and Philosophical Perspectives (Second Printing)
by Thomas Goodale and Geoffrey Godbey

Experience Marketing: Strategies for the New Millennium
by Ellen L. O'Sullivan and Kathy J. Spangler

Facilitation Techniques in Therapeutic Recreation
by John Dattilo

File o' Fun: A Recreation Planner for Games & Activities—Third Edition
by Jane Harris Ericson and Diane Ruth Albright

The Game and Play Leader's Handbook: Facilitating Fun and Positive Interaction
by Bill Michaelis and John M. O'Connell

The Game Finder—A Leader's Guide to Great Activities
by Annette C. Moore

Getting People Involved in Life and Activities: Effective Motivating Techniques
by Jeanne Adams

Great Special Events and Activities
by Annie Morton, Angie Prosser, and Sue Spangler

Group Games & Activity Leadership
by Kenneth J. Bulik

Hands on! Children's Activities for Fairs, Festivals, and Special Events
by Karen L. Ramey

Inclusive Leisure Services: Responding to the Rights of People With Disabilities
by John Dattilo

Internships in Recreation and Leisure Services: A Practical Guide for Students (Second Edition)
by Edward E. Seagle, Jr., Ralph W. Smith, and Lola M. Dalton

Interpretation of Cultural and Natural Resources
by Douglas M. Knudson, Ted T. Cable, and Larry Beck

Intervention Activities for At-Risk Youth
by Norma J. Stumbo

Introduction to Leisure Services—7th Edition
by H. Douglas Sessoms and Karla A. Henderson

Introduction to Writing Goals and Objectives: A Manual for Recreation Therapy Students and Entry-Level Professionals
by Suzanne Melcher

Leadership and Administration of Outdoor Pursuits, Second Edition
by Phyllis Ford and James Blanchard

Leadership in Leisure Services: Making a Difference
by Debra J. Jordan

Leisure and Leisure Services in the 21st Century
by Geoffrey Godbey

The Leisure Diagnostic Battery: Users Manual and Sample Forms
by Peter A. Witt and Gary Ellis

Leisure Education: A Manual of Activities and Resources
by Norma J. Stumbo and Steven R. Thompson

Leisure Education II: More Activities and Resources
by Norma J. Stumbo

Leisure Education III: More Goal-Oriented Activities
by Norma J. Stumbo

Leisure Education IV: Activities for Individuals With Substance Addictions
by Norma J. Stumbo

Leisure Education Program Planning: A Systematic Approach—Second Edition
by John Dattilo

Leisure in Your Life: An Exploration—Fifth Edition
by Geoffrey Godbey

Leisure Services in Canada: An Introduction—Second Edition
by Mark S. Searle and Russell E. Brayley

Leisure Studies: Prospects for the Twenty-First Century
edited by Edgar L. Jackson and Thomas L. Burton

The Lifestory Re-Play Circle: A Manual of Activities and Techniques
by Rosilyn Wilder

Marketing for Parks, Recreation, and Leisure
by Ellen L. O'Sullivan

Models of Change in Municipal Parks and Recreation: A Book of Innovative Case Studies
edited by Mark E. Havitz

More Than a Game: A New Focus on Senior Activity Services
by Brenda Corbett

Nature and the Human Spirit: Toward an Expanded Land Management Ethic
   edited by B. L. Driver, Daniel Dustin, Tony Baltic, Gary Elsner, and George
   Peterson

Outdoor Recreation Management: Theory and Application, Third Edition
   by Alan Jubenville and Ben Twight

Planning Parks for People, Second Edition
   by John Hultsman, Richard L. Cottrell, and Wendy Z. Hultsman

The Process of Recreation Programming Theory and Technique, Third Edition
   by Patricia Farrell and Herberta M. Lundegren

Programming for Parks, Recreation, and Leisure Services: A Servant Leadership Approach
   by Donald G. DeGraaf, Debra J. Jordan, and Kathy H. DeGraaf

Protocols for Recreation Therapy Programs
   edited by Jill Kelland, along with the Recreation Therapy Staff at Alberta
   Hospital Edmonton

Quality Management: Applications for Therapeutic Recreation
   edited by Bob Riley

A Recovery Workbook: The Road Back From Substance Abuse
   by April K. Neal and Michael J. Taleff

Recreation and Leisure: Issues in an Era of Change, Third Edition
   edited by Thomas Goodale and Peter A. Witt

Recreation Economic Decisions: Comparing Benefits and Costs (Second Edition)
   by John B. Loomis and Richard G. Walsh

Recreation for Older Adults: Individual and Group Activities
   by Judith A. Elliott and Jerold E. Elliott

Recreation Programming and Activities for Older Adults
   by Jerold E. Elliott and Judith A. Sorg-Elliott

Recreation Programs That Work for At-Risk Youth: The Challenge of Shaping the Future
   by Peter A. Witt and John L. Crompton

Reference Manual for Writing Rehabilitation Therapy Treatment Plans
   by Penny Hogberg and Mary Johnson

Research in Therapeutic Recreation: Concepts and Methods
   edited by Marjorie J. Malkin and Christine Z. Howe

Simple Expressions: Creative and Therapeutic Arts for the Elderly in Long-Term Care Facilities
   by Vicki Parsons

A Social History of Leisure Since 1600
   by Gary Cross

A Social Psychology of Leisure
  by Roger C. Mannell and Douglas A. Kleiber

Steps to Successful Programming: A Student Handbook to Accompany Programming for Parks, Recreation, and Leisure Services
  by Donald G. DeGraaf, Debra J. Jordan, and Kathy H. DeGraaf

Therapeutic Activity Intervention With the Elderly: Foundations & Practices
  by Barbara A. Hawkins, Marti E. May, and Nancy Brattain Rogers

Therapeutic Recreation: Cases and Exercises
  by Barbara C. Wilhite and M. Jean Keller

Therapeutic Recreation in the Nursing Home
  by Linda Buettner and Shelley L. Martin

Therapeutic Recreation Protocol for Treatment of Substance Addictions
  by Rozanne W. Faulkner

A Training Manual for Americans With Disabilities Act Compliance in Parks and Recreation Settings
  by Carol Stensrud

❀   ╬   ✳   ✦   ❀

 Venture Publishing, Inc.
1999 Cato Avenue
State College, PA 16801

Phone: (814) 234-4561; Fax: (814) 234-1651